From Care to Accommodation

This title is the first book in a new series entitled
'Studies in Evaluating the Children Act 1989'

Series Editor: Professor Jane Aldgate

STUDIES IN EVALUATING THE CHILDREN ACT 1989

From Care to Accommodation

Support, Protection and Control in Child Care Services

Jean Packman
Christopher Hall

Dartington Social Research Unit

London: The Stationery Office

First published 1998

ISBN 0 11 321869 9

Published by The Stationery Office and available from:

The Publications Centre
(mail, telephone and fax orders only)
PO Box 276, London SW8 5DT
General enquiries 0171 873 0011
Telephone orders 0171 873 9090
Fax orders 0171 873 8200

The Stationery Office Bookshops
123 Kingsway, London WC2B 6PQ
0171 242 6393 Fax 0171 242 6394
68-69 Bull Street, Birmingham B4 6AD
0121 236 9696 Fax 0121 236 9699
33 Wine Street, Bristol BS1 2BQ
0117 926 4306 Fax 0117 929 4515
9-21 Princess Street, Manchester M60 8AS
0161 834 7201 Fax 0161 833 0634
16 Arthur Street, Belfast BT1 4GD
01232 238451 Fax 01232 235401
The Stationery Office Oriel Bookshop
The Friary, Cardiff CF1 4AA
01222 395548 Fax 01222 384347
71 Lothian Road, Edinburgh EH3 9AZ
0131 228 4181 Fax 0131 622 7017

The Stationery Office's Accredited Agents
(see Yellow Pages)

and through good booksellers

Printed in the United Kingdom for The Stationery Office
J44018 7/98 C10 10170

Contents

Tables

Foreword

The Children Act 1989 was implemented on 14 October 1991. At its launch the then Lord Chancellor, Lord MacKay, described the Act as 'the most radical legislative reform to children's services this century'. Shortly after the launch the Department of Health put together a strategy to monitor and evaluate the initial impact of the Act. Taking a tripartite approach, this drew on evidence from statistical returns, inspections and research to develop a rounded appreciation of early implementation. The subsequent strategy plan was published and circulated to relevant bodies, including social services and the major voluntary agencies, in 1993. This plan formed the backcloth for a programme of research studies commissioned by the Department of Health to explore early evaluation in more depth. It is these studies, some 20 in all, which form this new series.

The programme studies investigate the implementation of key changes introduced by the Act and evaluate the facilitators and inhibitors to the meeting of key objectives. A longer-term goal of the programme is to review the aims of the Act in the light of implementation with a view to reconsideration or amendment should this be felt necessary. Finally, a more general and important scientific aim is to consider how far change could be achieved successfully by changing the law.

There are several principles underlying the Children Act 1989 that permeate the research studies. An important strand of the Act is to bring together private and public law so that the needs of all children whose welfare is at risk might be approached in the same way. This philosophy is underpinned by the principle of promoting children's welfare. There should be recognition of children's time-scales and, in court cases, children's welfare should be paramount. To aid this paramountcy principle there should be a welfare checklist and delays in court hearings should be avoided.

The promotion of children's welfare takes a child development focus, urging local authorities to take a holistic and corporate approach to providing services. Departments such as health, education, housing, police, social services and recreation should work together to respond to children's needs. Children, the Act argues, are best looked after within their families wherever possible and, where not, the continuing support of parents and wider kin should be facilitated by avoiding compulsory proceedings whenever possible. Parents should be partners in any intervention process, and children's views should be sought and listened to in any decision-making affecting their lives. To promote continuity for children looked after, contact with families should be encouraged and children's religion, culture ethnicity and language should be preserved.

Local authorities have a duty to move from services to prevent care to a broader remit of providing family support, which could include planned periods away from home. However, family support services should not be universal but target those most in need. The introduction of Children's Services Plans in 1996 has made the idea of corporate responsibility a more tangible reality and seeks to help local authorities look at how they may use scarce resources cost effectively.

The themes of the Children Act have relevance for the millennium. The concern with combating social exclusion is echoed through several of the studies, especially those on family support and young people looked after by local authorities. The value of early intervention is also a theme in the studies on family centres, day care and services for children defined as 'in need' under the Act. Further, the research on the implementation of the Looking After Children Schedules emphasises the importance to children in foster and residential care of attaining good outcomes in education. Lastly, attending to the health of parents and their children is another strand in both the family support and 'children looked after' studies.

To accompany the 20 individual studies in the research programme the Department of Health has commissioned an overview of the findings, to be published by The Stationery Office in the style of similar previous publications from HMSO: *Social Work Decisions in Child Care 1985*; *Pattern and Outcomes in Child Care 1991*; *Child Protection: Messages from Research 1996*; and *Focus on Teenagers 1997*.

The editors would like to express their appreciation to the members of the research community, professionals from different disciplines, and service users, among others, who have contributed so willingly and generously to the successful completion of the research studies and to the construction of the overview. Without their help, none of the research would have been written or disseminated.

Jane Aldgate
Carolyn Davies

Leicester, Summer 1998

Part

1 Background

1 Introduction

The Children Act 1989

Under Section 20(1) of the Children Act 1989, children who are lost or abandoned or for whom no person has parental responsibility (yesterday's 'orphans') and those whose carers are prevented, 'whether or not permanently and for whatever reason', from providing 'suitable accommodation or care' must be offered accommodation by the local authority. Section 20 has been described as 'one of the most important changes of philosophy in the Act' (White et al. 1990, p.62). It replaces the old so-called 'voluntary' route into care, first formulated in Section 1 of the Children Act 1948, and despite evident continuities with the older legislation, it breaks new ground and exemplifies some of the major principles of the Act as whole.

Links with previous legislation lie in the circumstances in which the need for accommodation might arise, the open-endedness of the reasons for its use, and the time-scales involved, which are also familiar, though couched in modern phraseology.

Under both the 1948 and 1989 Acts there must be consideration of the children's 'welfare' (1948) or 'needs' (1989), and once they have entered accommodation, the local authority is obliged to 'look after' them and to review their progress, whatever the reason for admission (Children Act 1989, Sections 22 and 23). Despite such continuities, however, the 1989 Act brings about significant changes, which its accompanying volumes of Guidance and Regulations elaborate upon and seek to emphasise.

A positive role for accommodation

Accommodation is recast in more positive terms. Most crucially, Section 20 appears under the umbrella heading of 'local authority support for children and families', which constitutes Part III of the Act. 'The accommodation of a child by a local authority is now to be viewed as a service providing positive support to a child and his family' (DoH 1991a). In effect, voluntary care in its new guise stands alongside what were previously thought of as 'preventive' services – day care, family aides, material help, and so forth – and is no longer to be seen as an unfortunate outcome which such services are specifically designed to prevent.

This positive status is further enhanced by the 'no order principle' (Section 1(5)), which seeks to limit the use of compulsory powers (including Care Orders) in favour of voluntarily agreed solutions wherever this is in the interests of the child's welfare. Where a child needs to be cared for away from home, accommodation is therefore the preferred option in some cases. The corollary, which the White Paper that introduced the new legislation indicated, is that local authorities 'will no longer be under an obligation to *diminish* the need to receive children into care' (DHSS et al. 1987).

This does not mean that accommodation is now a service available to any family on demand. As we have indicated, under Section 20 the local authority must first establish that the child is 'in need': that s/he is 'unlikely to achieve or maintain . . . a reasonable standard of health or development', or that 'his health or development is likely to be significantly impaired' without the provision of such a service. Disabled children are for the first time included in the definition of 'in need'. The Guidance also implies that accommodation lies at one extreme of a continuum of support services. The *Introduction to the Children Act* states: 'The Act rests on the belief that children are generally best looked after within the family,' and heralds 'a new duty to promote the upbringing of children in need by their families' (DoH 1989, para.1.7).

So the messages are subtle and complex: accommodation is to be viewed much more positively, as a genuinely supportive option that can help families and their children in both the short and long term; but home-based services, involving minimal disruption for the child, will nevertheless be preferred wherever possible.

Voluntariness and parental responsibility

A second crucial cluster of changes concerns the enhanced 'voluntariness' of accommodation, which in turn relates to the recasting of the concept of parental responsibility. 'Parental responsibility' replaces the older notion of 'parental rights', and endures in every circumstance apart from a child's adoption or the death of a parent. In terms of accommodation, the local authority's power to require 28 days' notice of a parent's intention to remove a child who has been in voluntary care for at least six months (Child Care Act 1980, Section 13(2)) no longer exists, so if a local authority wishes to delay a child's return home, it must do so by persuasion and with the agreement of the parents. The much older local authority power to assume parental rights over children in voluntary care on grounds of parental unfitness or length of time in care has also been abolished, more than forty years after the Curtis Committee condemned it as an unjust anachronism (Home Department et al. 1946). The distinction between the status of children 'in care' on a court order and children who are voluntarily accommodated is sharpened as a result.

The role of parents in initiating and remaining involved in accommodation arrangements is also emphasised. Volume 3 of the Guidance to the Act states that parents may 'suggest' or 'specifically request' such a service, or will otherwise 'accept proposals' made by the social services department (DoH 1991b). They are also encouraged to remain in touch with their accommodated children, to participate in the planning and decision-making before and during their stay, and, where appropriate, to continue to play an active part in their care. In the absence of sanctions, and with the emphasis on participation and partnership, the voluntary nature of the service is underlined.

The child's perspective and rights

A third significant group of changes relates to the child's role in negotiations regarding accommodation. For the first time in law, a child's wishes and feelings must be taken into account *before* s/he enters care or accommodation, and not, as previously, only once the admission has occurred (Section 20(6)). However, the extent to which such wishes and feelings will be acted upon remains, as before, related to 'age and understanding'. Nevertheless, young people of 16 and over are now able to choose for themselves whether to enter or stay in local authority-provided accommodation, whatever the wishes of their parents (Section 20(11)). Further, children of any age who are being looked after may make (or ask others to make) 'representations' or complaints about the care they are receiving or the plans that are being made about them – a shift in emphasis from the child as an object of concern (DoH 1988) to a person who is an active participant in negotiations about his/her welfare.

Thus at least four of the major principles on which the Children Act 1989 is based – the concept of enduring parental responsibility, the emphasis on working in partnership with families, the shift in 'prevention' from the gateway to the care system to the door of the courtroom, and an increased attention to the voice of the child – are all firmly encapsulated in the provision of accommodation. Research on the Act's implementation can therefore provide useful insights into how far such good intentions are being put into practice, and what, if any, the barriers to this might be.

The influence of earlier research

The role of research in helping to shape the new child care legislation has been rehearsed elsewhere (Parton 1991; Packman and Jordan 1991), and this will be discussed only in terms of its influence on the design of the present study.

Between 1980 and 1984, the DHSS funded a number of linked child care studies. One examined decision-making about the admission of children to local authority care, whether by means of a court order or 'voluntarily' under Section 2 of the Child Care Act 1980, in two matched local authorities in the South of England, and the report was entitled *Who Needs Care?* (Packman et al. 1986). Parental perspectives were included, as well as those of social workers, and families whose children had been admitted to care on a voluntary basis seemed the least dissatisfied group compared to those whose children had been removed on a court order and even those whose children had not been admitted to care at all. Yet voluntary admission to care had been shrinking steadily as a proportion of all admissions, whereas removal by court order – especially emergency Place of Safety Orders – had escalated since the early 1970s.

Voluntary care for children was *valued* as a service by many families in difficulties, rather than being seen as an awful fate that some social workers and their departments were anxious to prevent. The importance to parents of working in collaboration with social workers, of being listened to, understood, taken seriously, and participating in decisions about their children was evident in this and many other studies during the early 1980s, and this contributed to the shift in emphasis in the new Children Act. The preference for access to local authority accommodation by negotiation rather than being imposed by court orders, the stress on working in partnership with families, and the assertion that accommodation should be offered as a positive support to families and children in need all owe something to the research evidence that accumulated during this period.

The research material gathered during the early 1980s allows us to compare policies and practice before and after the Children Act, and has advantages over data gathered at a later date. After all, the Act was a long time coming, and the ideas within it were widely discussed for several years before implementation. Even before all the studies had been completed, fresh legislation (Health and Social Security and Social Services (Amendment) Act 1983) was passed, which was influenced by the Dartington Social Research Unit study on maintaining links between children in care and their families (Millham et al. 1986), and it attempted to improve practice in this regard. A year later, the Short Report was published (House of Commons Social Services Committee 1984), and it also drew heavily on the research that was coming to its conclusions at that time.

The Social Services Committee, in turn, called for a thorough overhaul of child care law, which was immediately set in train. Meanwhile, the influential DHSS review of the completed programme of child care research was published (DHSS 1985) and was widely disseminated. By 1986, discussion documents on all aspects of proposed changes in the law were being circulated for comment, and a year later the White Paper on the new proposals was published (DHSS et al. 1987). The Children Act itself followed in 1989, but was not implemented until October 1991, so for at least seven years changes in the law and the direction they might take had been under discussion, and this might have had a gradual influence on practice well before the legislation came into force. Using a data set from the early 1980s, before these influences were at work, therefore seemed a logical strategy in order to highlight changes.

The focus and design of this study

In the present study we returned to the same two local authorities which had been the subject of the *Who Needs Care?* research on decision-making in child care between 1980 and 1984 (Packman et al. 1986) in order to capitalise on the earlier data. Each is a large county containing more than one previously independent borough, and the bulk of our research concentrates on the two cities which were the focus of the previous study. We call them Clayport, which is administered by County, and Shiptown, administered by Shire.

Our inquiry aimed to explore the implementation of Section 20 of the Children Act 1989 on a number of dimensions:

1   Who were the families and children who were now being offered accommodation, and how did they compare with those who received voluntary care in the past? Were the 'no order principle' and the positive reframing of accommodation leading to more admissions than in the past, and/or to a more heterogeneous group of children with a wider range of problems than would once have been the case? In other words: would those who would have been candidates for Emergency and Care Orders before the Act now be found among the accommodated children?

2   How far were the aims of participation and partnership being realised? Were parents and young people actively involved in the planning process, and in what ways was this achieved? To what extent was 'voluntarism' a reality, or might the contentiousness and severity of some family problems undermine accommodation's voluntary status?

3   Was the desired attention to the importance of continuity and family integrity evident in practice? Were siblings kept together? Was continuing contact with family members and with schools achieved? Did parents continue to share in the decisions about and care of their accommodated children?

4   How far were the ideals of careful planning, which form the backbone of all the Guidance to the Act, being met in practice? To what extent were the elements of investigation, consultation, multidisciplinary co-ordination, assessment and the making of child care plans for every individual discernible in the negotiations concerning accommodation? Had the predominantly reactive and somewhat hectic practice that had been evident a decade earlier been improved?

5   Were there any indications that the ways social services departments were organised and the extent to which local child care policies were espoused affected the manner in which accommodation was arranged and the extent of its use? One feature of the *Who*

Needs Care? study was the much greater use of compulsory measures in Shiptown. Would this still be the case, or would the Act and its comprehensive messages have identical effects in the two sample authorities?

The project was divided into two phases. The first year, October 1991–October 1992, was concerned with re-examining and reworking the old data and updating our knowledge of the two authorities. Ten years is a long time in the history of any social services department, and it was important to chart and compare the patterns of their child care statistics over the decade, to understand the implementation and reasons behind the organisational upheavals that had taken place in both authorities, and to compare the development and dissemination of policies that affected services for children and families. How far had the two authorities travelled since the *Who Needs Care?* study, and had the old similarities and differences changed? It also allowed the social services departments a year to settle into implementing the new legislation, and we hoped this would help to avoid some of the inevitable confusion and inconsistencies that could be expected to follow such a major statute.

The second phase of the research, from October 1992, was concentrated on the two cities, Clayport and Shiptown. It was not possible to replicate precisely the areas of study that had been targeted ten years before, because of boundary changes in the intervening period and current organisational upheavals. In the event, we included the northern half of Clayport city, together with a large, adjoining rural area that had been part of the previous study, and compared this with the city of Shiptown (the smaller of the two) in its entirety. The sample area in County was made up of five administrative 'Areas'; Shire's amounted to three, but the relevant population size, around 35,000 children and young people under the age of 18 years, was similar in each authority.

For the first phase of the study, during which the recent history of both social services departments was assembled, we drew on departmental child care statistics and the Department of Health's own publications, collated from local authority statistical returns. In charting changes in organisation structures and child care policies, we examined numerous plans and policy documents spanning the period since the *Who Needs Care?* study, and interviewed staff at several levels of each hierarchy to elicit accounts of why and how such changes had come about.

In the second phase we were concerned to monitor implementation of Section 20, and here we departed from the design of the *Who Needs Care?* study. In the early 1980s Packman et al. had focused on how and why social services departments decided whether or not to admit children to care, and what legal routes were involved. Their starting point was *before* any admission took place, but when it was being seriously considered as an option. The resulting sample consisted of three groups of cases:

- those who were admitted voluntarily
- those who came into care via the courts or on emergency orders
- those who were not admitted to care at all.

Replicating this model for the present study would have offered some obvious advantages, not least in emphasising what choices of service were being made. But amassing a large enough group of new Section 20 cases for meaningful analysis would have meant sifting through unwieldy numbers of other cases. On balance, a detailed scrutiny of accommodation admissions, rather than a broad survey of children receiving all kinds of care or any of the full range of Part III services, seemed the preferable option. Therefore all 177 admissions to accommodation in the sample areas during a period of eight months from October 1992 to May 1993 were examined by means of file search and structured interviews with social workers. Using the same two sources of information, each case was then followed up twice: first approximately six months after admission, and then around two years after the original admission to accommodation. This provides the basis for the extensive aspects of the study.

The complementary intensive dimension of the study was achieved using two main methods. Although it was not part of our original design, the opportunity arose to attend some of the planning meetings at which accommodation was being considered. It was evident that such meetings were an integral part of the planning and decision-making process in both authorities, and that the presence of family members, social services staff and other professionals meant they were also an arena in which the Act's intentions concerning participation, partnership and interdisciplinary co-operation would be played out. Attendance depended on the willingness of all parties to include us as non-participant observers, and on the feasibility of time and place. We were present at 29 meetings – the majority of them in the Shiptown area. (This was not because of reluctance on the part of Clayport personnel, nor because of a significant difference in the number of meetings held in that authority, but was dictated by the logistics of covering five separate sites and the difficulties of ensuring the researcher was in the right place at the right time.) The experience of witnessing the negotiations between professionals, parents and sometimes children when needs were being assessed and accommodation was on the agenda added a valuable dimension to our study.

In addition, as part of our original remit, through social workers we approached a small proportion of the parents, children and carers within our sample, asking whether they would be prepared to talk to us. If they agreed, we met them on home territory, and by means of tape-recorded, semi-structured interviews invited them to share their perceptions of why and how accommodation had been arranged and their experiences of the service. We aimed to include a cross-section of examples from the range of uses of accommodation that were emerging in our analysis of the 177 admissions of 153 children studied, covering:

- adolescents admitted because of their disruptive behaviour
- children who were thought to be at risk of harm
- short-term admissions of children whose parents were hospitalised or absent for other reasons
- cases where respite care had been arranged for disabled or non-disabled children.

By no means were all parties seen in every case, and whilst the older youngsters were interviewed separately, younger children were seen in the company of their parents or carers. In all, 59 people were interviewed concerning the accommodation of 27 (18%) of the 153 children in the cohort. They comprised 18 mothers, 5 fathers, 18 children and 18 carers (both male and female). Such a small sample cannot be regarded as representative of the cohort as a whole, but it did raise many important issues which had more general relevance.

Finally, we also interviewed staff in related statutory and voluntary services whose responsibilities complemented or overlapped with the social services department's duties to accommodate, in order to appreciate the wider context in which decisions under the Children Act were being made.

Summary

Our present study of the implementation of Section 20 uses the *Who Needs Care?* data to help evaluate the extent and direction of changes in practice, but its primary focus is on the family problems presented since the Act came into force, the interaction and processes of negotiation between parents, children and the social services departments, and the decision-making that ensues. Some important consequences of those decisions are assessed in the immediate aftermath of admission, and twice more, after six months and then two years had elapsed. In the process, the impact of some of the major principles of the Act and its accompanying Guidance is examined.

For the reasons already outlined, this study does not attempt an inclusive survey of *all* children admitted to the care system by other legal routes, though it does shed some light on the shift from accommodation to subsequent court proceedings in a minority of cases. In this sense it complements other DoH-sponsored research (Hunt et al. forthcoming). Nor have we attempted to map out a comprehensive picture of 'support for families' by including all those who received services other than accommodation, but again, the overlap is demonstrated by the degree to which other forms of support precede, accompany and follow on from periods of accommodation.

Finally, although we have not pursued a detailed evaluation of the development and well-being of the children concerned, we are able to offer some key indicators of the positive and negative features of the accommodation experience, and its immediate and longer-term aftermath.

2
Organisational changes in Shire and County

In common with most other social services departments (see Challis 1990), the two sample authorities, Shire and County, underwent a series of organisational upheavals throughout the 1980s. These changes affected all public services, including education, the NHS, police and probation, and were in part driven by central government policies to promote 'efficiency and effectiveness' and 'value for money'. James offered an even wider perspective, suggesting: 'the obsession with the restructuring of large care service bureaucracies in the 1980s can be seen as a mirror image of changes that are taking place in the disintegration and reconstruction of firms in the market place' (James 1994, p.27).

Analysis of such upheavals in the public sector and beyond has been extensive (for example, Challis 1990; Flynn 1990; Jones and May 1992; Clarke et al. 1994; James 1994; Jones and Bilton 1994), and it is not the intention of this study to challenge or expand on theories of organisational change. More pragmatically, we needed to understand the prevailing (but still fluid) context in which the Children Act 1989 was being implemented, how and why it had changed compared to ten years earlier, and how, if at all, it was affecting current child care decision-making.

The organisational changes did not come to a convenient halt once we began to study implementation of Section 20 of the Children Act: both social services departments remained in a state of flux throughout the research project, as they grappled first with the implications of Community Care legislation and then with anticipated local government reform. In this chapter we therefore concentrate on the changes that had taken place since the *Who Needs Care?* study (Packman et al. 1986), and until our arrival on the scene in late 1991, based on the authorities' own documentation and our interviews with key personnel. In Chapter 4 we will extend the analysis of the authorities' organisational and policy developments to encompass the duration of the research project, from 1991 to 1994.

The *Who Needs Care?* research was conducted between 1980 and 1983, when the structures of the two social services departments of County and Shire had much in common. No doubt because they were large county authorities which had absorbed several previously independent county boroughs, they had both opted for a three-tier structure that took into account both geographical diversity and historical tradition:

1   Headquarters
2   Divisions
3   Areas.

The local authorities' Headquarters – Shire Hall and County Hall – were located in their respective county towns, but each authority was divided into large administrative units that we will call 'Divisions', each with their own committee, director and staff, reflecting the hierarchical pyramid at the centre. Shiptown in Shire and Clayport in County, the large cities that were the focus of our monitoring exercise, were each at the centre of a Division. Management roles at Headquarters were divided on functional lines – finance, administration, professional services, and so on – and the pattern was repeated at Divisional level, with additional roles for residential and day care management. There was then a third tier of management, which we will call 'Areas'. These, too, had their own directors and support staff, and were responsible for the fieldwork activities of a cluster of social work teams, each with its own team leader.

Specialisation by client group was not reflected in the management chain of either authority, but was located in developmental and advisory posts, both at Headquarters and at Divisional level. Both authorities recognised child care as a crucial specialism within these roles, but both were also firmly 'generic' in their management and in the scope of their fieldwork teams. Differences between the two authorities were slight, mainly evident in the detailed division of tasks, and the terminology used to describe the structure.

A significant point of similarity between the two authorities was the degree of power and influence that was perceived to exist in the second tier of management – Divisional level – and the part this played in subsequent reorganisations. In both social services departments, Divisions were regarded as mini-empires, or 'fiefdoms' in Challis's (1990) terms, with their own distinctive way of doing things and their own brand of child care policy. In County, the West Division had conducted its own review of child care establishments, set in train important changes with little reference to County as a whole, and fashioned its own Child Care Strategy before an authority-wide equivalent had been constructed. It reorganised its Area structure and redrew team boundaries independently of the wishes of County Hall.

In Shire, the Divisional Director whose territory encompassed Shiptown, where we were monitoring child care decision-making, was reputed to have 'a high tariff view of care': 'You only get into care on a statutory order' – a pattern that certainly seemed to be reflected in the research data for the *Who Needs Care?* study.

But these organisational features were not to last long. Indeed, Shire's structure had already undergone revision before the *Who Needs Care?* study had been completed, and the repercussions of West Division's unilateral upheaval in County had wider implications soon after the researchers withdrew.

Reorganisation in the early 1980s

Shire

Shire's first reorganisation during the 1980s was being planned from the beginning of the decade, and was effected in 1982/3, when the *Who Needs Care?* research project was drawing to a close. The overt spur in Shire was economy, and the prime actors were the politicians. There had been a significant overspend, and the council was seeking ways of reducing costs in future. Pruning its rather elaborate organisational structure seemed the answer. A related argument was the perceived need for 'reasonably consistent county-wide policies' – something that seemed difficult to achieve when the middle tier of management was so strong and idiosyncratic. Indeed, reducing the power of the previously independent boroughs was the other side of the 'consistency' coin, and a strong subtext to the economic arguments. Not surprisingly, reorganisation was wholeheartedly endorsed by the leader of Shire County Council. The chosen remedy was simple abolition: the Divisions had to go.

In the new structure, Shire Headquarters was able to build up a large, central management team (temporarily augmented by the soon-to-retire former Divisional Directors), with more explicit 'programme development' functions and a large team of specialist Advisers focused on different client groups. A small number of new responsibilities were delegated to the operational Areas (Section 1 budgets for immediate financial aid to families and some grants to voluntary child care organisations, for example), and some key Headquarters staff (residential and day care managers, for instance) were 'out-posted' to that level as well. There were a limited number of changes at Area level, and a small reduction in the number of Areas.

County

Whereas by the time the *Who Needs Care?* research was complete the organisational map of Shire had changed significantly, in County the process took longer, coming to fruition in 1987, and although it shared some similar themes, the emphasis and outcomes were rather different. The unilateral reorganisation within West Division in 1983 had focused attention on both the third tier of management – the Areas – and on the social work teams for which they were responsible. Area boundaries were redrawn to relate more closely to the reality of Clayport city at the heart of the Division, and team boundaries were adjusted to encompass what were seen as distinct 'communities'. The management of domiciliary services (home helps and occupational therapists) was devolved to the Areas, with the aim of improving integration of related tasks.

This emphasis on the operational level of the organisation, and notions of 'going local' (Barclay 1982) appealed to County's new Director of Social Services, who was appointed at this time. He toured West Division, seeking a wide range of opinions on the new structure, and by summer 1984 proposed an organisational review. His analysis of the problems to be tackled in County echoes some of the shortcomings identified in Shire:

- too many levels of management, with consequent confusion and wide variability of practice across Divisions and Areas
- too few specialists offering advice and support to operational staff
- a service in which 'well established policies or practices are not known or understood by staff or are not working'.

Unlike Shire, however, the drive to reorganise was not directly fuelled by financial crisis and cost-cutting (that came later, and precipitated County's second reorganisation): the process was instigated from within the social services department, and hence was 'self-inflicted' (see Challis 1990), not imposed by County's politicans.

The review process took two years and was documented in weighty reports which, between them, covered over 150 pages, plus as many again in appendices. The genuinely democratic and devolutionary ideals of the Director of Social Services were reflected in the composition of the first working group, which consisted of a range of staff from team leader to principal officer, but included no senior managers from Headquarters. Perhaps predictably, the group's formula for change proved somewhat too radical to be acceptable, but it was only slightly modified by a second working party of County Hall elite.

The organisational solution to the problems posed was not to abolish the middle tier of management, as in Shire, but to reorganise the third tier, which had been directly responsible for the operational teams of fieldworkers. In County, Areas were to be increased in number, and would therefore have a smaller span of geographical control but enhanced managerial responsibilities. They would have their own managers, who would be responsible for a small handful of 'patch' teams, each with its own team leader. The size of County – twice the area of an average county authority – meant that some 'patches' were still very large, and nothing like the models invoked by researchers such as Hadley and McGrath (1981).) Management of day and residential resources was devolved to the Area, and Area Managers were to be responsible for their own budgets and their own Area Plans. In effect, they were to be, as internal documents stated, 'the key unit upon which the new organisation is based . . . delivering virtually all departmental services to the local community'.

The second-tier Divisions were to remain, but no longer as managers of the Areas. Rather, they were to engage in joint planning with other agencies, and to co-ordinate, advise, monitor and evaluate the work of the operational units, as well as acting as a channel between them and Headquarters. The wider geographical view that the old Divisional structure had promoted was to be achieved by corporate management, through an Area Manager's Group, chaired by the Divisional Director.

The role of Headquarters was to be more clearly focused on setting broad policy goals, providing centralised information, and monitoring and evaluating the outcomes of policy. It would be concerned with the 'what' of policy – establishing a sense of direction and setting out the social services department's aims for all client groups. To improve its policy-making and dissemination, an expanded Advisory Service, specialising by client group (and therefore including a strong 'child care' contingent) was to be located at County Hall and in the four Divisions. It would then be up to each Area to work out the 'how' of policy implementation to suit its own communities and the resources at its disposal.

Thus, in the two sample authorities there were some similarities in the problems which the first reorganisation of the 1980s was supposed to address. In both there was a strong sense that sufficiently clear, authority-wide policies were not being generated, disseminated or owned by the social services department as a whole – a sense which was reinforced by the findings of the *Who Needs Care?* research. In both, the powers of the middle tier of management – the Divisions – were under suspicion, and were blamed in part for the lack of consistency in the nature and standards of the service provided.

In other respects the catalysts for change and the form they took diverged dramatically in the two local authorities. In Shire, reorganisation was clearly politically led and driven by considerations of economy and power. A model was chosen which dismantled a whole tier of management and concentrated power in the centre. The periphery gained a little, but most roles of responsiblility moved upwards to Shire Hall, the management of day and residential care being a prime example. Some staff might be 'out-posted' to the Areas, but their reference group and authority were still centrally based.

In County, by contrast, changes were professionally inspired, and the periphery played a major part in determining the new structure, under which it made significant gains. So, in contrast to Shire, the Divisional tier was preserved in a somewhat emasculated form, but the management of day and residential care moved down to the new, small Areas, together with budgets and the responsibilities that went with them. The number of these operational units emphasises the contrast between the two authorities: in County, 34 Areas were created; in Shire there were only 16. County had taken a much greater stride towards 'devolution' and the ideals of 'community-based' services.

Nevertheless, the disruption and stress that reorganisation imposed on staff was probably no less in County than in Shire, where protest had been vigorous. A report pleaded for a widespread programme of personal counselling and staff support to pick up the pieces after the anxiety (and sometimes humiliation) of reapplying for jobs that had once seemed secure. Perhaps such a large-scale, internally generated upheaval is harder for some than a change imposed by an easily identifiable 'enemy without'.

Changes in the late 1980s

Neither of the new structures that had been devised in the two authorities was set in concrete, and further adjustments were made as staff left or fresh problems emerged. In Shire, for example, reorganisation had not at first altered the 'generic' core of the enlarged senior management team at Headquarters. Assistant Directors of Social Services continued to work to a functional or territorial brief, the latter reflecting the old Divisional structure. But as the previous Divisional staff retired, they were replaced by assistant directors who were responsible for specific client groups, and for the first time there was an Assistant Director for Children and Families.

The structure that 'broke the power of the Division' and enabled the development of more coherent Shire policies also began to reveal weaknesses. A need for more local provision and management of child care resources in particular was expressed, and by 1987 there was thought to be a 'lack of co-ordination of planning . . . between centrally managed residential and day-care and field workers'. A plan to split residential and day care into six regions was discussed (though never implemented), with the aim of reducing 'top-heavy decision-making' and in the hope of achieving both 'firm central direction' and 'maximum regional autonomy'. The problem of balancing central control and consistency with appropriate flexibility and diversity was evident.

In County, modifications to the major reorganisation of 1987 had more traumatic origins. In fact, the structure ran into trouble almost immediately. At its birth it faced a serious social services department overspend (like Shire at the beginning of the 1980s) which provoked a political storm. Some elected members blamed the costs of reorganisation itself, and there were also suspicions that the degree of devolution the reorganisation entailed would lead to weak management and waste. For two years the social services department battled to balance its budget and answer its critics, but in 1989 the Chief Executive was asked by members 'to carry out a review . . . and to take stock following its restructuring'. The exercise was brief and there was no published report, but two features of the organisation were targeted for abolition: the middle-tier Divisional structure (to allow a more direct line of accountability from the Areas to Headquarters), and the specialist Advisory Service at both Headquarters and Divisional level – presumably because it was seen as a luxury that the authority could not afford.

With the coming of another new Director of Social Services in 1990, the broad outlines of the proposed changes were implemented. The four Divisions were reduced to three, and the staff who remained at that level were now regarded as being 'out-posted' from Headquarters to tighten the link with the centre.

In place of the Advisory Service at County Hall, an Assistant Director of Policy Development and Evaluation was appointed. In effect, some of the functions that had been undertaken and developed by the Advisers were relocated, 'sharpened up' and given a new and less ambiguous label. At the Divisional level, Advisers were replaced by Development Officers with a specialist brief – a proportion of them in the fields of child care and child protection. Some posts disappeared in the process, but a shadow of the old Advisory Service remained, under a new name.

Shire also had a new Director of Social Services, and at the end of 1988 he requested a consultant's review of the departmental structure, in preparation for the new style of management that would follow implementation of Community Care legislation. The main aims of the proposed changes were strongly reminiscent of those espoused in County two years earlier: integrated management and devolution. The former was deemed necessary to enable flexibility and the capacity to deliver 'packages of care'; the latter meant that power and responsibility should be devolved 'as near to service delivery as possible' in order to respond to client need.

Revival of Divisions on the old model was considered, but was rejected as an 'unnecessary link' in the management chain. Nevertheless, the need for some strategic planning and co-ordination at a level intermediate between Headquarters and the Areas was recognised, and four new-style Divisions emerged, coterminous with Health Districts, to facilitate Community Care planning – a role County's Divisions were also undertaking.

Greater devolution meant more power and responsibility for the Areas. Shire's Area Managers were upgraded and declared 'the building block of the management structure', accountable for all the major elements of service in their Area. Like County's Area Managers, they were given more explicit responsibility for strategy, inter-agency liaison and policy development within their Area, and management control over the whole span of resources – fieldwork, day and residential care, and (by April 1992) their own budgets.

The role of Shire Hall was also framed in terms similar to those used in County: the formulation of clear policies and promotion of consistent standards, overall budgetary control and resource management, and support for professionals through research, disseminating information, planning and personnel training. Four assistant directors for specific client groups (one of them for Children and Families) were retained, but given additional responsibility for one of the newly designated Divisions – a conjunction of responsibilities not replicated in County. The Advisory Service at Shire Hall was also retained, and was divided into client-based specialisms including Children and Families, though it had less contact with the problems of individual cases and specific situations than before.

Summary

Our review of the recent history of organisational change in the two authorities therefore revealed some common themes, as well as some significant differences.

Both County and Shire are large authorities, containing areas of great contrast, with sparsely populated rural tracts, small and sizeable market towns, and large cities like Shiptown and Clayport, with their share of inner- and outer-city decay and deprivation. The distances involved and the diverse communities that had to be managed and served created problems of communication and control, and the challenge of achieving an appropriate balance between variety and consistency of policy and provision. Attempts to achieve this balance had been evident throughout the years in both authorities, as responsibility and power shifted to and fro between the centre and the periphery, and as they grappled with the awkward role of their Divisional tiers.

The search for effective and apparently logical ways of dividing up the work of the social services department whilst also enabling the necessary co-ordination between the parts was another theme common to both authorities. In the past, both had seen residential, day and domiciliary care and fieldwork as distinct domains, with their own separate management structures. In the earlier organisational models the functional divide between them began at a high level, but was gradually pushed down the hierarchy, until they were united under the managers of the multi-purpose operational 'Areas'. Their shared aim was to achieve flexibility of service that would better meet individual needs. The significance of resources – or the lack of them – in forcing organisational change was another feature that the two authorities had in common. Overshooting budgets (or mismanaging them, in the eyes of politicians) led to hard questions being asked, and shortening and tightening lines of accountability was a common response.

But despite these similarities, two major differences stand out that are of potential relevance to the present study: the role of specialism by client group, and the degree and depth of devolution that is tolerated.

In the early 1980s, at the time of the *Who Needs Care?* research, neither social services department had any senior managers at Headquarters or Divisional level with responsibility for particular groups of clients. Assistant directors specialised by function, not by client group. Focusing on children was the province of Advisers, who were supporters but not managers of operational staff, and had no place in senior management teams with their direct access to the councils' elected members. Their roles were influential, but ambiguous in relation to the staff at lower levels in the hierarchy. At the fieldwork level, many teams remained generic, and any specialism tended to be informal. Only day and residential care units specialised according to their user groups.

During the 1980s that pattern changed dramatically in Shire, which appointed assistant directors with a specialist brief, so issues concerning children and families were represented at the highest level, a large, client-specific Advisory Service remained, and earmarked budgets were devolved to the Areas, where there were specialist child care teams – some were even further subdivided into those specialising in child protection or children under 8 years of age.

By contrast, in County there had never been a manager at Headquarters (or indeed at any level) with specific responsibility for child care. Even the client-focused Advisers were disbanded or relabelled in the last reorganisation. The social services department's generic philosophy was expressed at the top, in the Policy Development Unit that superseded the Advisory Service and avoided specialist titles for its personnel. Genericism was also apparent in mission statements and policy documents that incorporated 'Children and Families' under the broad umbrella of 'Community Care'. At the periphery, generic teams serving relatively small communities still survived, though creeping specialisation accompanied County's move towards greater devolution.

Devolution – or rather the *degree* of devolution – is the second major feature which distinguished the two authorities. Both had moved in that direction, and the key level of operational management – the Area – had enhanced powers and responsibilities compared with the situation in the early 1980s. But at the time the present study was being undertaken, County's Areas were much smaller and more numerous, and therefore potentially in closer touch with the communities they served. Devolution of budgets had also occurred much earlier, and was well established compared with Shire, where the move was made after the present research project was launched. It was therefore our impression that County's devolved Areas had put down stronger roots than those in Shire – a hypothesis the research might be expected to test.

Our argument for trying to unravel the recent history of organisational changes in Shire and County is fourfold:

1   The two authorities were chosen for the *Who Needs Care?* research in the early 1980s partly because there were strong similarities in their character and structure. We needed to know how far that was still the case.

2   We also needed to grasp the features and the logic behind the authorities' contemporary organisational framework in order to design a feasible monitoring exercise.

3   More importantly, we wanted to move beyond an assimilation of contemporary charts and job descriptions (which in any case proved to be tantalisingly ephemeral) to a better understanding of the history of the changes, and the processes by which they had come about.

4   We hoped to discover whether there was any discernible association between the number and nature of decisions concerning the accommodation of children and the organisational structures in which they were made.

3 Child care policy in Shire and County

In this chapter we outline and compare some major features of social services' child care policy as they had developed in the two authorities since the *Who Needs Care?* study (Packman et al. 1986).

The absence of a comprehensive and coherent child care policy that applied throughout each authority and was recognised and 'owned' by practitioners was a feature of both social services departments at the time of the *Who Needs Care?* study. The picture then was of discrete pieces of policy, dating from different periods and deriving from different parts of the organisation, of which only some of the staff were aware. Even when social workers and their managers knew of such policies, their wisdom and authority was sometimes disputed, so there was little sense that they were accepted by the social services department as a whole. In this, the sample authorities were far from unique, as the accumulated research findings of the DHSS's review demonstrated (DHSS 1985).

Policy and the organisational context within which it is conceived are obviously linked, and in tracing a decade's developments in the two authorities, the interplay between them is very evident. For example, the old structures, with their strong middle tier of Divisions, certainly contributed to and reinforced the fragmentary picture of the early 1980s. As we saw in Chapter 2, by 1983 the West Area of County had set in train its own independent residential child care review and produced its own targets for a reduction in numbers in care. In Shiptown, the Divisional Director was reputed to take a tough line on admitting children to care, favouring court orders over voluntary agreements, and thus contributing to the distinctive profile of admissions which was demonstrated in the earlier *Who Needs Care?* research but which was not typical of the rest of Shire.

Perhaps the most striking impression on comparing the situation in the two authorities in 1991 with that of the early 1980s was how dramatically the picture had changed. The formulation of authority-wide policies had become a much more self-conscious and high-profile task for

Headquarters staff – indeed, it had been one of the major goals of the organisational upheavals that had taken place. Developing mechanisms for involving a wide range of staff in shaping and disseminating policy – in the hope they would thereby 'own' it – was another strong theme.

In this chapter we compare these policy-making developments in County and Shire: the pressures that have propelled them forwards, their content and some of the processes involved.

Child care strategies and the role of accommodation

Both Shire and County set out their first major Child Care Strategy in the same year, 1984. This was a year after completion of the *Who Needs Care?* research, but whether or not this was coincidental is hard to judge. The factors which triggered the production of these documents appear very similar, though the processes by which they came about were rather different.

In both authorities (and in England as a whole), numbers of children in care had been declining since 1980, from nearly 3,000 to less than 2,500 by 1984 in Shire, and from over 1,700 to 1,400 in County. Although this was in part a reflection of a shrinking child population, there was also a decline in the rate of children in care, both locally and nationally. Between 1980 and 1984, County's under-18 rate had fallen from 7.7 per 1,000 to 6.4, and Shire's from 7.4 to 6.5 per 1,000. In England, the rate had fallen in similar fashion from 7.8 to 6.5 per 1,000.

Falling numbers meant less pressure on accommodation for children in care, and in both authorities this was affecting the residential homes the most. Shire, which had a large stock of its own homes (51, compared with 20 in County) as well as voluntary establishments that it could use, accommodated over 900 children in residential care in 1980 – 2 in 5 of all its children in care. By 1984, both the number and the proportion had dropped dramatically, to over 600, or 1 in 3 of the 'in care' population. In County, numbers in residential care had also fallen (from 400 to less than 300), but there was a less striking decline in the proportion from 28% to 25%. In both authorities, therefore, a breathing-space was offered after what must have seemed the inexorable climb in the numbers of children in care throughout the 1970s. In the words of the original Shire document, there was 'opportunity for a redistribution of resources'.

A further spur to the review of residential care was its high cost – a cost that paradoxically rose even more once the numbers of children in residence began to fall. Under-occupancy of residential homes inevitably meant that costs per child rose and were then compared even more unfavourably with the misleadingly modest costs of children who were placed in foster homes (Knapp 1987). Both authorities were therefore concerned to tip the balance further in favour of family placements – the 'better and cheaper way' of caring for children. In County there was also concern that improvements and alterations to existing residential stock were in the pipeline, to the tune of over £1 million, and that this might be money wasted if the numbers of children in care continued to fall and if diversion into family placements could be increased. So economic and professional arguments coincided with declining numbers of children in care.

In Shire, the framing of a new child care policy was given extra impetus by the reorganisation that had recently taken place. A major aim had been to break the power of the Divisions, and in the wake of their demise the opportunity to develop a truly departmental policy was seized upon. A working party, led by a senior child care adviser and guided by briefing papers that were informed by recent child care research, met for some months to hammer out a new strategy.

In County, the process was rather different. The origins of County's 1984 Child Care Strategy are somewhat obscure: to one child care development officer, it simply 'came careering out of County Hall'. Early versions are unattributed, but County's Principal (Advisory) Officer (Child Care) and her staff were not involved. Rather, it seems to have stemmed from the Research and Intelligence Section at Headquarters, influenced perhaps by the earlier strategy document for the West Area of County, whose director was on the senior management team. The genesis of both authorities' strategy documents therefore seems to reflect their organisational structure and character at that particular time: Shire with its newly restructured social services department, and County still operating under the old regime.

There are several similarities in the content of the two child care strategies, but also some significant differences. Both were concerned to reduce the numbers of children in care still further, and the County document sets three-year targets for this: reduce the 'in care' figure by 15%, reduce admissions by a third, and increase discharges so that 'no child stays longer than absolutely necessary'. Shire's document approaches the issue in rather more positive vein: 'community-based provision' must be developed so that fewer children need to leave home.

Both local authorities were also keen to reduce the use of residential care and to increase family placements. Fewer residential establishments would cater for fewer children, whose stay in residence would be time-limited. Individual homes would focus more sharply on the particular needs of certain groups: teenagers, children in need of therapy, group work or respite, and so on. On the other hand, foster homes must be developed for a wider range of children and for different purposes. Targets were set in the two authorities for both of these goals. County wanted 100 fewer residential places within three years, matched by 100 new special foster homes. Shire, starting from its much higher residential base, aimed at 250 fewer residential places by the end of the 1980s.

The main differences between the two child care strategies lie in their emphasis and in the detailed means of achieving rather similar ends.

County's strategy is starkly expressed, in somewhat negative terms. The route to lower numbers in care and fewer children in residence is to reduce admissions and speed up discharges; call a halt to adaptations and improvements to existing residential stock and close down more homes; aim at time-limits for children in residential care, and use residential places as a resource for children over 10 only. Alternatives are touched on in similarly terse form: 'complementary day care' should be developed, and fostering and adoption placements should be increased.

Presumably because the child care specialists had played no part in drawing up County's Child Care Strategy, justification in terms of 'good practice' are not spelled out or debated. Such professional concerns had to await the arrival of the Child Care Policy a year later, produced by the child care team that hadn't been involved in drawing up the Child Care Strategy. In spite of its enthusiasm for the fine distinctions between concepts like 'mission statements', 'policies' and 'strategies' at that time, County had put the cart before the horse in this instance. The policy had a more positive tone, and fleshed out the strategy's skeleton with a philosophy – 'help families in difficulties', 'respect, preserve, enhance the dignity and integrity of individual and family', 'the welfare of the child is paramount' – and a more proactive role for the department in meeting needs.

But despite the strategy's shortcomings (the figures on which it based its original targets proved to be 'grossly inaccurate') it had a lasting impact, providing a crude basis for measuring 'progress' for at least five years, and putting those responsible for its implementation on the defensive. In this it seems to have acted as a goad rather than an inspiration – something to be argued with or redefined by those with child care expertise, rather than a banner to be followed with enthusiasm.

In contrast, Shire involved its child care experts from the beginning, and spelled out in greater detail how its aims should be met. It had much more to say about support services for families, and was self-critical of the 'present pattern of service [which] gives greater emphasis to assuming care when families break down, and not supporting those at risk'.

'Support' was envisaged as comprising many elements, including respite care, befrienders, family support workers, day care, group work, advice, counselling, material help and lodgings. A key focus for many of these services would be new family resource centres, and other local authorities with somewhat similar establishments were visited in search of possible models. It was suggested that both 'in-house' services (such as group work and day care) and 'outreach' functions (such as finding and managing respite, befriending and child-minding facilities) might be offered through such centres. A more extensive form of 'outreach' in the guise of 'community development' which would go beyond the client emphasis of other services was also envisaged.

The Shire Child Care Strategy therefore offered a range of ideas regarding how the proposed reductions in admissions and numbers in residential care might be achieved, and introduced a new model establishment to replace some of the children's homes it intended to close. Like County, increases in family placements were also planned, but unlike County, they were to be part of a wider range of options on offer through its new family resource centres.

Nevertheless, Shire's strategy, like County's did not receive universal approval. The council's elected members expressed reluctance to see so many children's homes close, perhaps because they were among the most tangible demonstrations of service provision. Field social workers were inclined to be suspicious of the proposed family resource centres, seeing them as taking over many tasks that were traditionally theirs, and no doubt feeling undermined and undervalued in consequence.

Producing departmental policy documents did not guarantee universal enthusiasm or acceptance in either authority.

Developments in the late 1980s

By the mid-1980s, therefore, in common with many others, the two sample authorities had produced written child care policies and/or strategies, giving a departmental sense of direction, setting some precise targets, and outlining various means of achieving them. We can now follow the development of the different strands within those policies into the 1990s, and since it was such an important factor in both County and Shire, we will begin with numbers of children in care.

As we have seen, at the time their child care strategies were launched in 1984, numbers of children in care in both authorities had been falling for several years, and both were keen to see this continue: in County, according to the published statistics at that time, they stood at 1,400, and in Shire there were 2,400. Rates per 1,000 were similar (6.4 and 6.5 respectively), both close to the figure for England as a whole (6.5).

The continued downward trend of County's figures then becomes difficult to gauge precisely, because for at least three years internal statistics were in disarray, a new computing system was giving trouble, and they more than once failed to make the usual annual returns to the Department of Health (questions were even asked in Parliament). Reflecting this confusion, the rough-hewn 1984 Child Care Strategy set a three-year target which, it emerged, had already been reached, so 'success' was instant. Although the pace of change is therefore impossible to assess, by 1988 County's figures appear to have reached a plateau of just over 1,000 children in care at any one time. On the other hand, the rate of children in care had increased from a low point of 4.6 per 1,000 in 1989 to a figure of 4.8 per 1,000 in 1991, but well below the English average of 5.5 per 1,000.

Developments in Shire are easier to follow, and have been even more dramatic. Decline was fairly slow in the first three years after the Child Care Strategy of 1984, but after that it accelerated, so the figures for 1991 show fewer than 1,500 children in care (1,000 fewer than in 1984) and a rate of 4.2 per 1,000, well below that in County, or in England as a whole.

Table 3.1 outlines the pattern of declining numbers in care in the two sample authorities and in England as a whole, before implementation of the Children Act 1989.

Table 3.1   *Numbers and rates per 1,000 of those under 18 in care, 1980–91*

	Shire		County		England	
	No.	Rate	No.	Rate	No.	Rate
31 March 1980	3,016	7.4	1,775	7.7	95,298	7.8
31 March 1984	2,446	6.5	1,417	6.4	74,845	6.5
31 March 1988	2,134	5.9	1,061	4.8	64,352	5.8
31 March 1991	1,487	4.2	1,040	4.8	59,834	5.5

Source: DoH Personal Social Services, Local Authority Statistics, *Children in Care of Local Authorities* (1980, 1984, 1988, 1991), England. Prepared by the Government Statistical Service.

The reasons for such a decline in numbers are not easy to determine, and must depend upon a whole host of interacting factors – some of them (like fluctuating referral rates) outside the direct control of the social services departments themselves. However, both authorities adopted 'gatekeeping' mechanisms which may have contributed to the fall in numbers.

Gatekeeping

County

County's child care policy in 1985 gave prominence to two such measures: child care planning meetings that had to be held whenever admission to care was being considered, and children's resources panels, designed 'to consider placements for all children and young people admitted to residential care'. The child care planning meetings were to be held whenever separation from their family had been identified as a possibility for a child, and were to involve 'the department, members of the family where appropriate and other relevant parties'. Essentially, they were intended to explore all alternatives to admission, but where care was considered appropriate, they would determine the purpose, length of stay and legal status of the admission, encapsulating this in written agreements and having regard to proper preparation of the child and family and the maintenance of family links. These meetings took place, case by case, at the operational level of the Area teams, and they required corporate and disciplined decision-making by grassroots staff and their immediate managers. There was no involvement of higher management, and the policy document (unlike its predecessor, the strategy) lays no stress on reducing admissions *per se*.

Children's resources panels were gatekeepers, not to the child care system as a whole but to precious and expensive residential placements, although they had a potential indirect influence on admission decisions. A prototype panel had been running in the West Area of County for some years, and was of significance in the *Who Needs Care?* study (Packman et al. 1986). It consisted of a group of Area Managers and Advisers, meeting frequently and regularly, to whom social workers had to make a case for any residential placement they required. It was intended to bring better order into the matching of children to residential resources (an outspoken Adviser put its purpose more baldly: 'exercising adequate and positive gatekeeping [to check] the fads and fancies of individual social workers seeking expensive out-county resources'). In the process, alternatives to admission might be explored.

County's policy in 1985 was to build up a network of such panels and to move towards the goal of fewer and more appropriate residential placements for those for whom residential care was 'the preferred option'. Progress was fairly slow, and by 1988 one Area was still without a children's resources panel, whereas another had extended its range and incorporated family placements in its remit. We can only speculate that the increased emphasis on formal consultation and deliberation at the gateways to the child care system and its most expensive resources may have had a restraining effect on admissions in the mid-1980s, and therefore on the falling numbers in care.

Shire

In Shire, explicit gatekeeping was introduced later than in County, but with a more comprehensive set of objectives. Resources groups were launched by means of pilot schemes in the summer of 1988, and were then extended throughout Shire. They remained in existence for three years. Their brief was: 'to support the implementation of departmental policies about offering alternatives to care, improving planning to care, reducing legal interventions, defining the aims of residential care, increasing support to family placements and generally ensuring a widely-based decision-making process'.

In effect, the resource groups embraced the functions of both County's children's resources panels and child care planning meetings, but went wider still, and unlike County, were firmly linked to the centre. A Headquarters manager usually chaired the meetings, and case social workers, residential, day and family placement managers and the Area

Office Managers all attended. All cases where care was being requested or considered were to be presented to the groups, and emergency admissions had to be scrutinised soon after the event.

Consistency of practice was to be achieved by means of having a specific chairperson for each resources group and by holding regular meetings between the chairpersons of all the groups. The twin purposes of planning and resource allocation were clearly an intervention into the decision-making powers that had previously rested within the Areas and the resource unit, and they raised some problems that were also evident in County. Were social workers guilty of subversion, through by-passing the system and admitting and placing children in local foster homes? Were the resources groups empowered to recommend or to decide?

Ambiguities seem to have remained, but nevertheless, to the policy-makers at Headquarters, the resource groups were regarded as highly successful in advancing the aims of Shire's original Child Care Strategy, and in particular in reducing the numbers in care by 'supporting the social worker in sharing the risks involved when not admitting to care'. The published figures appear to support their claims. The prevailing downward trend in numbers of children in care more than doubled in the three years of their existence (1988–91). There were 647 fewer children in care in 1991 than there had been in 1988 and the rate per 1,000 dropped from 5.9 to 4.1. By 1991, however, Shire's latest restructuring had taken place and power had been devolved to the Areas, so although they lingered for a time, resources groups in their old, centrally directed form finally disappeared.

Preventive services

Shire

Gatekeeping was not the only means of reducing the numbers of children in care. Both authorities were committed to supporting families so that admissions could be avoided, but as we have already outlined, Shire placed the greater emphasis on this aspect of policy through its family resource centres, which were to be at the hub of family support. The initial long-term strategy was to develop eight family resource centres (some of them on the premises of children's homes and 'community homes with education' (CHEs) marked down for closure), and the first pilot establishment was opened in 1986, offering a variety of styles of group work with children and families with different levels of need, and short periods of respite with local families, without formal admission to care. A second family resource centre in the same town adopted a different emphasis and was not wholly concerned with 'prevention', but concentrated on offering local families respite, assessment, and long- and short-term placements for children, whether in or out of care.

After a slow start, targets for opening family resource centres were raised, and there were 13 of them by 1991, when our research began. The range of their activities was wide, but varied between one establishment and another, with some targeting families at high risk of losing their children and teenagers to the care system, and others more concerned with community initiatives which reached out to a broader spectrum of families. Their efforts in both directions are believed to have contributed to the reduction in numbers in care, and they have clearly given 'prevention' a high profile within Shire's social services department. Managers of family resource centres are potentially influential people, with ready access to Headquarters and the Child Care Advisers. Clarification of their role and function in the newly organised department, with its more powerful Area structure and with its future role as 'purchaser' of the services the centres provide, was in progress during the present study.

Alongside the family resource centres, Shire has also developed a network of family centres which also have a clear, and even overlapping, preventive role to play: these are former day nurseries for under-fives which were developed at the same time as the family resource centres and whose precise role was also under review during the period of this study.

Thus, much of Shire's support for families since the mid-1980s focused on multi-purpose establishments which replaced or revamped previous day and residential facilities, and which – at least so far as family resource centres are concerned – took on some roles that would once have belonged to fieldwork teams. Their impact is thought to have been considerable in changing the direction and emphasis of child care in Shire.

County

In County, policies of support for families were more diffuse and less firmly directed from County Hall. The Child Care Policy document of 1985 picks up where the Child Care Strategy of the year before left off: promoting preventive services and suggesting a two-tier model. Primary preventive services should be provided in conjunction with other agencies, and were characterised as 'positive in intent and non-specific in application'. In other words, they were the community initiatives with which some, but not all, of Shire's family resource centres engaged. Secondary preventive services are targeted at particular individuals or families causing concern, and the main criterion for such interventions 'should be the developmental needs of the child or young person', but no particular forms of service are suggested for this purpose in the policy document.

In practice, the major means of offering help of this kind in County have been threefold – Section 1 monies, family aides and family centres. Development of family centres was under way in the 1980s, but uneven. In West County, for example, contrasting models of family centres were in existence at the time of the *Who Needs Care?* study. There was a social services unit for intensive work with families of children at risk of abuse – the 'client-focused' model of Holman's classification (Holman 1988) – and an open-door centre in a deprived area on the 'neighbourhood' model, run by a voluntary organisation. A third centre, offering residential care for whole family units (again 'client-focused') was developed in an old children's home following the review of residential care that was conducted in West County in the early 1980s.

A similar range of establishments grew up throughout County during the 1980s, both within and outside the social services department, but their development was *ad hoc* and seemingly arose from local initiatives, encouraged by the department's devolved structure. Like Shire, some were adapted versions of old day nurseries, and others catered for a wider age range of children, although there was less emphasis on offering services to adolescents. By 1989 they were unequivocally seen as Area enterprises, offering 'flexible service' to meet 'local needs', and many had multi-agency funding and considerable community involvement in their establishment and running.

The development of family aides to support families in their own homes seems to have been similarly uneven, and a report in 1986 notes that their use is very variable and that there is resistance to their employment in some parts of County. Section 1 monies were also used to differing degrees, and both of these preventive strategies were not helped by the large overspend into which County's social services department was sliding in 1987. Both were significant contributors to the deficit (unlike family centres, which because of slower than anticipated development had underspent their budget), and a contemporary report puts staff in a double bind by urging them to 'keep a tight hold over Section 1 payments and expenditure on family aides' whilst at the same time it acknowledges their preventive value. From that point on, complaints of serious underfunding and bids to increase budgets jostled with arguments for strict economy, and the climate was clearly not favourable for expansion, but reinvestment in family aides and Section 1 monies was still on the agenda of Child Care Advisers in 1990.

Summary

We have already seen that the role and scale of residential care for children was a major concern of the child care strategies of 1984 in both the sample authorities. The directions in which Shire and County intended to go and the arguments in support of their intentions are remarkably similar, but their starting points contrast sharply.

From the beginning of the 1980s, and even as far back as its Children's Department days in the 1950s and 1960s, County had always placed a lower than average number of children in care in residential establishments; family placements in foster and adoptive homes had always been the preferred option. In contrast, Shire had been a relatively heavy user of children's homes – a feature that was probably reinforced by the large numbers of adolescents who were being committed to care in the early 1980s. By 1984, however, both authorities had witnessed – and encouraged – a decline in numbers and, to a lesser extent, the proportion accommodated in this way. Both were also faced with under-occupied homes and rising costs. In Shire, for example, residential costs were said to account for 75% of the child care budget, and in County the apparently high cost of keeping a child in a children's home compared with a family placement was frequently debated.

The residential situation was therefore ripe for review. Both authorities determined to set targets for reducing the numbers of children in care still further. As we have seen, County aimed to have 'at least 100' fewer residential places within three years, and Shire wanted to cut its figure by 250 by the end of the 1980s. Reduction in the use made of extra-departmental establishments – especially those outside County, which were especially expensive – was another aspect of County's plan, and further closures of unwanted establishments within its boundaries, both its own and those of voluntary and private bodies, were also anticipated. Given its extensive stock, Shire was even more ambitious to close and sell off, or reuse, some of its homes for other purposes, and in its original Child Care Strategy no fewer than 20 homes (or 40% of its residential establishments) were destined for closure.

Policies to reduce numbers and close homes were by no means purely negative. Both were to be matched by expansion of preferred alternatives: family placements in both authorities, and family resource centres as an additional facility in Shire. Both authorities were similarly concerned to fashion their remaining residential homes in ways that would better meet children's needs. County proposed that children under the age of 10 should only be accommodated in exceptional circumstances, and aimed at time-limited periods of residence. Both authorities decreed that the tasks and purposes of establishments should be differentiated and clarified; so, according to County policy, each home should have its own clear objectives and should develop a 'prospectus' (an interesting forerunner of the 'business plans' demanded by Community Care legislation). Stabilising the child, preparations for fostering or adoption, care and control for behavioural problems, preparations for independent living and remand were some of the tasks envisaged in County's policy. Shire's preference was for small units, serving a distinct locality, with time-limited care, and preparation for moving on. The model was developed by the pilot family resource centres, which worked closely with a cluster of small, local children's homes and introduced weekly planning meetings to oversee admissions. Admission rates dropped slightly, but more significantly the length of stay in care was considerably reduced. Reception, respite, treatment and therapeutic work with whole families were also on Shire's agenda. Both authorities also ran secure units, as alternatives to custody.

In the end, both authorities were highly successful in reaching their targets, though not without some problems on the way. By 1988, County had overshot its target for numbers in residential care by 50% – 150 fewer children in homes, with the proportion reduced to 15%. Three years later, numbers had fallen lower still, to a little over 100, or 12% of the total in care. Shire was similarly successful. By its target year of 1989, numbers had fallen by 300, and the proportion was no longer above the English average. Again, like County, the decline continued into the 1990s, and in 1991, the year we began our research, it stood at 220 – a little over a third of the figure eight years earlier, and below the proportion for England. It had also closed 17 residential homes in five years. Shire, in particular, had achieved a massive turnaround in policy and resources.

Problems on the way to these achievements were various. Closing homes was not always straightforward. Shire experienced considerable resistance from its elected members, and the proposals it put forward were sometimes severely amended, so the social services department planned to close ten homes at the end of the 1980s, but the committee would only sanction three closures. Both departments experienced frustration and a time lag in developing alternatives to residential care. Recruitment of foster families to match the decline in residential places was slower than anticipated. It took time to appoint the extra staff required, and the tasks demanded of family placements became harder as the residential sector was squeezed and restricted.

Alternatives to residential care also proved expensive. This was most clearly demonstrated in County's fateful overspend in 1987/8. The sins of placing children in non-County council homes were revealed by their £160,000 contribution to the deficit, and staff were urged to try harder to avoid such placements. Exaggerated estimates of 'out-county' placements were used by elected members to belabour the department. 'Under-occupancy' was another recurrent theme in the minutes of the period, with a good deal of misunderstanding about 'unit costs' and the apparent extravagance of the whole residential child care system.

Yet alternatives to residential care were responsible for an even greater share of the imbalance. Fostering and Adoption Allowances, family aides, Section 1 monies and family placements arranged by British Agencies for Adoption and Fostering together accounted for £500,000 of the overspend. The financial benefits of the policy were not so straightforward or self-evident as had been hoped or believed.

Finally, some of the human costs of pursuing the streamlining of residential care so vigorously can be glimpsed in the interchanges between staff within the social services departments. In the late 1980s a County Area Manager wrote to Headquarters about the plight of nine children considered for but denied residential care by the Children's Panel on one day: 'They need specialised residential care ... We may save money now by reducing residential provision, but in the long term the repercussions of such decisions will be even more costly.' A month later another Area Manager informed the Divisional Director that a small voluntary home for eight children now had 13 residents, and a substantial waiting list of County children: 'Please don't ignore these *facts* when deliberating on *philosophy*!'

4 *Service delivery after the Children Act*

We began our present study by looking back to the 1980s and spending time trying to unravel the recent history of organisational change and policy development in Shire and County. We did this for three reasons: to update our previous knowledge of the social services departments, to understand the context in which the Children Act was being implemented, and to allow time for the Act to 'bed down' and become more familiar before attempting to study its implementation. Predictably, however, structural and policy changes did not come to a convenient halt during the lifetime of the research project, and we will now discuss how the two social services departments, and the policies they generated, continued to evolve and interact in the years between 1991 and 1994.

Three factors were uppermost in this period: the Children Act itself, Community Care legislation and the looming Local Government Review. In County, in terms of organisational change, the advent of Community Care was having the greatest impact.

The impact of new legislation in County

The Division was the natural locus for inter-agency planning of Community Care services for adults, and this was already well under way when we arrived. But County had also boldly grasped the nettle and decided to pursue the purchaser–provider split for all its services, including child care. Inevitably, this meant that the whole organisational chart was destined to be redrawn again. To the Divisional responsibility for inter-agency planning was added the task of co-ordinating the purchasing and commissioning of services on behalf of the Areas. Provision of services, on the other hand, was to be managed separately outside both the Area and Divisional structures. This meant that day and residential service management and the recruitment and support of foster homes were to be moved out of the Area, where they had taken root in earlier reorganisations, and into new, specialist structures operating on client-specific lines that distinguished between services for children and adults. This pattern was to have knock-on effects for the fieldwork 'purchasers' who were to remain at Area level. Since providers were to specialise in terms of client group, logic demanded that purchasers should do so too, and the last vestiges of genericism at the Area level looked set to wither away.

But specialist fieldwork teams, which had lost half their responsibilities and which also operated in relatively small geographical patches, were no longer seen to be viable, so the number of Areas was to be halved by means of mergers, with a return to the much larger operational units of the distant past. Although these changes were beginning to be made during our monitoring period, the process was incremental, and none of the operational Areas studied was directly affected at that time. Nevertheless, anxiety and anticipation of what was to come were palpable in all the Area offices we visited, which were grappling with the implications of putting the new child care legislation into practice.

The significance of the Division was also likely to be further enhanced by the Local Government Review. Clayport and Shiptown were regarded as prime candidates for unitary status, and staff in West Division claimed to be 'thinking Clayport' in anticipation of what was to come. Erosion of the middle tier of management in County had never reached the extremes of Shire, and West Division, with Clayport at its centre, had always been regarded as particularly strong. Nevertheless, there was a special irony in the fact that it might soon regain the independent status that had been removed twenty years before.

The fact that the advent of the Children Act coincided with organisational changes as a result of Community Care legislation meant that those with a special interest and investment in children's services believed they were somewhat neglected. Distinctive policies concerning the Children Act as a whole, and Section 20 in particular, were not spelled out in the first instance, and the legislation was allowed to speak for itself. This is hardly surprising given its comprehensiveness and the unprecedented weight of its ten volumes of Guidance and Regulations. The legal framework – itself a hefty skeleton – was fleshed out in every detail, in contrast to earlier Acts, which were generally accompanied by thin explanatory Circulars.

County responded by embracing the Act's principles and issuing large procedural manuals and forms to cover all aspects of the legislation. These faithfully adapted practice guidelines to the new legal requirements, but did not add any specific commentary on the place and role of 'accommodation' in the new scheme of things. This was left to the numerous seminars and training sessions that were conducted throughout County's social services department (though, interestingly, less comprehensively in West Division), which were used to spread the word. At local authority level there was early attention to constructing a definition of 'need' and to reviews of services for under-eights. Children Act monies of £2,500,000 were allocated in the first two years after implementation, and inevitably, priorities were set. At first, the bulk went to expanding the Guardian ad Litem service and setting up a Registration and Inspection Unit at Headquarters, matched by funding for more social workers at the Area level. In the second year, the major share of the monies went to the Areas, with special emphasis on accommodation, residential care and family centres.

Suggestions for clarification and development of policies also emerged from the grassroots. A year after implementation, and as our fieldwork was beginning, a series of Children Act Monitoring Groups were set up, involving a wide cross-section of staff, including carers. In the light of experience, there were, for example, requests for fresh policies to draw disabled children under the umbrella of Section 20, and for the provision of 'safe houses' for runaway adolescents. In contrast, there was also a sense among some participants that accommodation was now being provided too freely. Some residential workers thought that County allowances were too generous in comparison with what most families could afford and thus were encouraging youngsters into the system. Others thought 'too much parental empowerment' meant foster carers were 'being messed about'. Practical experience of implementation was posing problems that the policy-makers were being challenged to solve.

A year after implementation, a comprehensive review of progress was prepared for senior management which drew heavily on the feedback from the grassroots. Considerable unease was expressed at the effects that the Community Care reorganisation was likely to have on child care, which was 'not wholeheartedly supported by practitioners . . . ways of accommodating child care's different needs must be found if we are successfully to implement the Children Act'. Specific problems relating to accommodation were also aired. Services for the 16-plus age group were said to represent 'the biggest gap in implementation', and required a much greater degree of inter-agency collaboration. The resource problems created by a rise in numbers of children being accommodated were also highlighted. But again, reference was made to the intentions of the legislation: 'Providing accommodation is much more being seen as part of the range of Part III Services, as the Act intended.'

By 1994 a Child Care Strategy Review, conducted by top management, was able to take stock. It noted a dramatic increase in admissions to accommodation during the first year of implementation – a rise of over 50% which, whilst it had steadied, showed no signs of decline. It was apparent that senior management had not anticipated or 'planned' this, and there were urgent requests for explanations. Those with a child care brief within the policy unit (which by now had shed its apparent genericism insofar as individual responsibilities were concerned) responded by referring to the Act itself: 'The Children Act 1989 sought to open up accommodation as a service rather than a barrier to cross.'

Developments in Shire

In Shire there was much less organisational upheaval during the study period, and no attempt was made to combine children's and adults' services under the same umbrella. However, like County, there was an initial absence of any clear and distinctive policy statements about Section 20 or about the Act as a whole, beyond what the Act and Guidance said for themselves. Again, the Act's principles were warmly accepted, but there appeared to be a widely held assumption within Shire social services department that, in essence, 'We're doing this already.' A comprehensive policy document based on the Act did not appear until the autumn of 1993, after we had completed the first stage of our monitoring exercise.

Paradoxically, policy developments were beginning to emerge at the Divisional level during our research. As we have seen, the middle tier (Divisions) had been reduced to a somewhat ghostly presence in Shire, and no staff were employed at that level. Nevertheless, the Division had begun to be seen as an important focus of resource allocation and management, particularly with the distribution of extra monies to implement the Children Act, (the likely effects of boundary changes were also reinforcing this tendancy). The major part of the child care budget was allocated to the Areas to employ office-based social workers and residential, fostering and day care staff managed by the Areas. However, the extra Children Act monies were allocated to the Divisions as a whole, to develop new initiatives. The money was used to develop particular projects which were seen to supplement services offered by each Area and to address gaps in services that resulted from particular local problems, or Division-wide concerns. This initiative was bringing the Areas which made up each Division closer together in terms of identifying shortages and means of sharing resources across the Areas. Resources like residential units or fostering were still available to any social worker in Shire, and, on occasion, severe shortages meant placing children far from home. The aim of the Divisional discussions was, wherever possible, to enable resources to be made available locally, first in the Area, and then, if not available or appropriate, within the Division.

In management terms, however, the authority and status of the Division were ambiguous, lying as they did between two separate management systems – one for the Areas, and one for client groups. At the operational level, Area Managers were responsible for all client services – field, day and residential – within their Area, and specialisation by client group occurred at team level, within their Area. Area Managers were directly accountable to an assistant director at Shire Hall who was responsible for all Area Managers in a Division. There was no intermediate manager at Divisional level. In parallel, there was a similar structure for client groups. Thus, one Area Manager in each Division was made responsible for all services for children within the Division. Again, that manager was directly accountable to an assistant director at Shire Hall, carrying the same specialist brief. For the Division in which our study took place, the same assistant director fulfilled both roles.

The twin responsibilities of Area Managers had to be balanced, and one of them felt that more of her time was spent on Divisional/client issues than on Area management issues. The Area Manager with responsibility for children's services in the Division was therefore expected to act as a bridge between central policy and Divisional and Area implementation. S/he would report to the Assistant Director (Children) and also attend county-wide meetings with other managers with the same specialist brief, and with the Shire Hall Advisers. Such meetings were becoming one of the main forums of policy-making for children's services during our study, but the precise lines of authority were still being negotiated.

In the Division in which we worked, the Area Manager responsible for children's services began gathering together the other service managers to form a Divisional Children's Managers Team. This team was able to consider overall policy and procedures within the Division, and to assess whether the resources were appropriately distributed and allocated. Although this was a team of managers rather than a team with management responsibilities, regular contact between those attending its meetings had begun to initiate important developments in policy and resource distribution. Regular reports from the central meetings meant that local managers had rapid access to county-wide discussions, and the opportunity to respond. The Divisional Children's Managers Team had produced divisional policies, objects and plans which local service managers were able to interpret in terms of the teams they managed. This document was developed within the overall framework of a recent Shire policy on children's services, and was able to consider the priorities in that document in terms of their Divisional concerns. They had also considered a number of significant changes in staff and resources management. Out-posted child guidance teams were brought into the Area management system, and various plans were made to close projects and redistribute the resources (in particular, consideration was given to whether residential resources could be freed to enable the development of fostering). However, the authority to proceed with such initiatives was unclear, and could be overturned by county-wide developments.

As we saw in Chapter 3, the first published statement of Shire's Child Care Policy after the Children Act was passed came in the autumn of 1993, when the first stage of our monitoring exercise was almost complete. It refers back to Shire's radical Child Care Strategy of the mid-1980s, with its aims of 'turning existing resources into a range of community based preventative services . . . [which] helped support children within their families, reduced the number of children looked after by the department and successfully diverted young people from the negative influences of the Courts and the legal system'.

From that foundation it welcomes the Children Act and claims that 'current child care services are of a high quality and are in full accord with the substance and the spirit of the Act'. Emphasis is given to an amalgam of Children Act and Community Care principles (child-centred practice, partnership with parents, cost-effectiveness, and encouragement of the independent sector, for example). There are short statements of policy and the strategies which follow from them for different groups of children (those with disabilities, or in need of protection, or 16–21-year-olds, for example) and children in different situations (in day care, foster care, residential care, and so on). For all children looked after, there is emphasis on early planning for the child's return home, maintaining contacts and meeting health and educational needs. There is also the intention of extending foster care services by developing more respite and shared care facilities. There is one oblique reference to the role that Section 20 might play: 'Voluntary arrangements will be made whenever possible and legal intervention only used as a last resort.' Elsewhere, so far as our own focus of interest is concerned, the Act and its Guidance are left to speak for themselves.

Summary

As we have shown, during the span of the research project both social services departments continued to develop and change, though much more radically in County than in Shire. Chronic organisational turbulence is clearly not atypical (Challis 1990), and sensitises us to the unstable and surely stressful environments within which social services staff must operate and their clients or users must negotiate. Appreciating the tensions and instability that appear endemic gives us a more realistic (and perhaps sympathetic) view of the context in which a massive piece of new legislation was being implemented.

Local child care policies were also developing during our research, and the Children Act as a whole had received warm endorsement in both authorities. But apparently, little clear direction was being given in either authority to our specific area of interest: the use of voluntarily negotiated accommodation. This is the background against which our monitoring exercise to study admissions to accommodation over a period of eight months is set.

2 The monitoring exercise

5 Who needs accommodation?

In Chapter 1 we gave a brief description of the means by which we gathered data on a cohort of admissions to accommodation. In five Area offices in County (four in Clayport, covering half the city, and one in an adjoining rural area) and in the three Shire Area offices that constituted the whole of the city of Shiptown we attempted to examine all admissions to accommodation over a period of eight months, from October 1992 to May 1993 (for convenience, we will refer to the two sample areas as 'Clayport' and 'Shiptown'). From social services department figures for the previous year we calculated that this should provide approximately 200 cases. In reality, a dip in admission figures in the early part of 1993 in both authorities gave us a total of 177 admissions involving 153 children from 116 families; 24 of the children were admitted more than once during the eight-month study period.

It is difficult to be sure that every admission to accommodation within our sample areas during the monitoring period was included in the data. In many instances we were gathering information after the event, when accommodation had been offered or the child had already been admitted. Because some arrangements were very short-lived, the episode was often over by the time we conducted interviews and read the files. For these reasons we relied on record systems and the memories of team social workers and clerical staff to lead us to the relevant cases. But systems proved unreliable – particularly in Shiptown, where there was quite often a failure to record entries in such a way that they reached the social services department's client record system. This meant we had to double-check to try to ensure we included as many cases as possible, and we cannot be certain that we were successful in every instance.

More fundamentally, it became apparent that there was considerable ambiguity about what counted as being 'accommodated'. Not all arrangements to look after children that were made on a voluntary basis in collaboration with families and with financial and practical support from the departments were necessarily Section 20 cases. Short periods of full-time care with child-minders, for example, were sometimes translated into full-blown 'accommodation' and sometimes not. Similarly, some children placed with relatives were assisted by payments under Section 17 of the Act, whereas others were accommodated by relatives, who were treated as foster parents (which may account for the surprisingly low number of such placements within our sample). Another group targeted by the legislation, those aged 16, rarely appeared in our sample (six cases in all), but arrangements to place them in assisted lodgings and other forms of accommodation were clearly being made, with support from the social services department.

Being 'looked after' as a form of support for children and families does not always mean the use of Section 20. For team managers the decision may depend on which budget heading shows a surplus, or the smallest deficit, at a certain time. If nothing else, this taught us to be cautious in drawing conclusions from any comparisons of the numbers of children 'accommodated' in different Areas and in the two authorities. It also underlined the constraints of our research design. Had we had the time and resources to encompass the provision of *all* support services under Part III of the Act (see Chapter 1), we might have discovered the extent of their use as *alternatives* to accommodation and their consequent effect on the numbers accommodated.

Data was collected in two main ways. Our primary source of information was the social worker, usually the one who had assessed the needs of the child and family, and who had been instrumental in arranging an admission. Sometimes, as when a child was admitted by the emergency duty team, we relied on the worker who had taken over the case immediately afterwards. Occasionally, more than one worker was involved, and both would contribute. A second source of information was the child's (or family's) file. This was especially useful in checking details of events in the past, and gave us an opportunity to read minutes of meetings, accounts of interviews, written assessments and care plans.

The research schedule

The interviews with social workers were based on a research schedule (see Appendix) which aimed to explore in some detail:
- the basis of the social worker's assessment that accommodation was necessary and appropriate
- the processes by which decisions had been made

- some of the immediate and longer-term consequences of those decisions.

Assessment of 'need' was explored through questions on:
- family background and household circumstances
- family relationships
- the parents and their parenting
- the child and his/her health, education/employment and behaviour
- any history of separation or care
- the precipitating reasons for referral or concern leading to the arrangement of accommodation.

Descriptions of the assessment and decision-making process covered:
- any contacts and services offered in the past
- the role family, friends and other services played in the referral and through participation in planning
- the timing, nature and locus of planning
- the part played by parents and children in the process.

Immediate outcomes concerned:
- the placements used and the details of the care plans made – their purpose, time-scales, contact arrangements and parallel services offered
- any measures to achieve 'shared care'.

Finally, two follow-up exercises, approximately six months and two years after each admission, looked at the extent to which these plans had been achieved or modified and what changes had occurred for the family and the child within and beyond the care system. A summary by the social worker estimating the extent to which admission to accommodation had met the child's needs completed the schedule.

As can be seen, the schedules provided information ranging from 'hard' facts to sometimes very 'soft' estimates and opinions. It is also important to stress that we have elicited the professionals' view, seen through the researchers' lens, and we have only a small proportion of family versions (approximately 15%) for comparison. Nevertheless, the schedules provide a picture of 'need' and response, as seen by those who play a central role in the decisions which bring children into the newly constructed category of the 'voluntarily accommodated'.

The cohort

We begin with an overview of the children who were accommodated and their families, and we draw on the information that formed the basis of the social workers' assessment of the need for accommodation. In addition to setting the scene, this enables comparisons to be made with the families and children in the *Who Needs Care?* cohort a decade earlier: those who entered the care system by the 'voluntary' route (Child Care Act 1980, Section 2) and were labelled the 'volunteered' (Packman et al. 1986). This enables us to explore changes and continuities in the use of a resource which the Children Act 1989 has recast in such potentially important ways. Does the new emphasis on voluntarily agreed arrangements in preference to legal orders, and on looking after children on behalf of their parents as a positive *support* for the family, rather than failed 'prevention', have an impact on the profile of the children and families involved? From our data there is evidence of familiar and enduring patterns, as well as some striking changes.

Household composition

Family structures and the identity of the carers of the children concerned presented no surprises. Nearly half the children (46%) came from lone-parent households, a similar proportion to the *Who Needs Care?* cohort, and in all but two cases the lone parent was the mother. A quarter were living in stepfamilies, where one of the adults (nearly always the father) was not the birth parent of the child, and a similar proportion (28%) were living with both their birth parents. The complications of restructuring in many families also meant that 2 out of 5 children had step- or half-siblings in the household. The similarities with the *Who Needs Care?* research are striking, and this mirrors the findings of numerous child care studies (see Bebbington and Miles 1989) and reflects the vulnerability of what might still be termed the 'atypical' family unit.

Material circumstances

Measures of deprivation and disadvantage are also revealing. In just over half the households a father figure was present (though not always full-time, or for long), but more than half of these were unemployed. The 53% unemployment rate for the present cohort was well over twice that for the fathers of the 'volunteered' children in the *Who Needs Care?* cohort, reflecting general trends. Mothers were even less likely to be in employment – only 1 in 5 had any kind of job, and many of these were part-time and poorly paid. In consequence, a prime source of income for 7 out of 10 families was state benefits, and maintenance payments from absent partners were extremely rare. The inevitable result was that financial difficulties were judged to be a significant issue for more than half the families (56%).

Housing also reflected the social and economic position of families. A majority (60%) lived in council accommodation, and comparatively few (17%) were owner-occupiers. The rest were housed in privately rented flats or in other forms of accommodation, and 4% were classified as homeless and were lodged in bed and breakfast accommodation. The trend towards owner-occupation that had been apparent during the 1980s had obviously by-passed most of the families in our study and, although they had escaped some of the difficulties it later caused, they had problems of their own. For 2 out of 5 families, their accommodation was in poor condition or overcrowded, or sited in run-down or notorious neighbourhoods, which added to their difficulties.

Parental health

Within the generally deprived and complex living situations of the families in the cohort, the personal problems which beset parents and which contributed to their need for support in caring for their children were wide-ranging and often chronic. Parental ill health, particularly mental health, was a major problem in half of all cases, and the vulnerability of the mothers was clearly of great significance: 12% were disabled, chronically ill or were suffering an acute physical illness at the time their child was admitted, and 1 in 5 were said to suffer generally poor health; more than half (54%) were mentally stressed, and of these, 1 in 5 were suffering from a chronic or acutely disabling condition. Lone-parent households were obviously more vulnerable if the parent became ill or was hospitalised.

Relationships

Given the degree of stress among mothers, and the fragmented and complex family structures that were so evident, it is not surprising that family relationships were often strained – for example, marital problems (or perhaps more accurately, partnership problems) were prominent. According to the social workers, over 70% were under strain, and marital conflict, sometimes erupting into violence, was seen as a precipitating cause of the child's admission in a third of all cases. Parent–child relationships were also at the heart of assessments of family difficulties, and in nearly 4 out of 5 cases they were judged to be strained. Indeed, tension and conflict between parents and their children was the most common element among the reasons given for providing accommodation, and was evident in two-thirds of all cases.

Parental behaviour and parenting

Problematic behaviour on the part of parents was another dimension that was explored. It should be remembered that our informants were social workers, and their evaluation might be challenged by parents and children, whose detailed perspective we have in only a minority (approximately 15%) of cases. Nevertheless, the professionals' viewpoint is clearly powerful in defining a 'need' for accommodation, and from their perspective parental behaviour was an important factor.

Anxiety was expressed about inconsistent or poor parenting in terms of physical care of the child in a third of all cases, and there was concern about emotional care in no less than 4 out of 5. Mostly, this was described as 'inconsistency', and this reflected a sense that the chronic strains and intermittent crises that the families faced had almost inevitably taken their toll, upsetting the child's sense of security and safety.

Such general concerns about parenting standards are sharpened when neglect or abuse may have occurred. In almost two-thirds of cases, allegations or suspicions had been voiced at some time – not necessarily recently, and nor were they always accepted as valid by the social workers themselves – so the shadow of suspicion had hung over a majority of the families at some point. A more precise measure is the Child Protection Register, where suspicions are at least examined and tested by a multidisciplinary conference. In all, 35% of the accommodated children had been placed on the Child Protection Register at some stage of their lives. Here, the 'profile' of the accommodated child departs dramatically from that of the 'volunteered' in the *Who Needs Care?* cohort – a point to which we will return.

More general concerns about the lifestyle of parents and their impact on child care were less prominent, but nevertheless a substantial minority were said to be violent, criminal and/or heavy drinkers, and 1 in 10 was believed to be a regular drug-user. Parental behaviours of these kinds were thought to have been a contributory reason for admission of the child to accommodation in 1 in 8 of all cases.

Support networks

The Children Act and its volumes of Guidance have given special emphasis to the importance of kin and friendship networks in helping families to weather crises and in keeping children within a familiar environment. Few families were thought to be totally isolated, with no such network (7%), but for many there was limited support. Given the high proportion of lone-parent families, for example, the role of absent partners could be crucial, but only 2 in 5 of them were still in touch with their families, and only a quarter had any dealings with the social worker. Indeed, social workers believed that at least some absent partners were part of the problem, rather than its solution.

Within the wider network of kin, grandparents were the most likely sources of support to half of all families, with aunts and uncles lending some assistance to 2 in 5. Less than a third of families were thought to have friends who could offer support, and again, the social worker sometimes believed that this was likely to do more harm than good. It must be reiterated that our main informants were social workers, so the scale and usefulness of these networks may be underestimated. Nevertheless, lack of an adequate family support network was judged to be a contributory factor in 2 out of 5 admissions.

Family histories

The existence of inadequate support networks and the difficulties which need to be prevented or overcome may sometimes be linked to the childhood experiences of the parents themselves. We did not attempt to explore their histories in any depth, knowing how rarely they had been recorded in any detail and how mobile some families can be. Only where families had stayed put and files had accumulated over the generations (or where there were a few long-serving social workers) was such information likely to be readily accessible. However, we asked social workers whether it was known if parents had been in care themselves, and also if they had been abused. Despite uncertainties in many instances, a quarter of mothers were known to have been in care, and 15% were thought to have been abused. Figures for fathers were much lower – 6% had been in care, and 4% had been abused – but the uncertainties here were much greater. For the mothers, at least, this suggests a special degree of vulnerability, and perhaps a greater need (and willingness?) to turn to official sources of support when crises occur. For them, the social services department may be the only 'family network' they have.

Characteristics of the children accommodated

Our present study's composite profile of children who were accommodated diverges from that of the 'volunteered' in the *Who Needs Care?* study in several ways. Boys and girls were admitted in almost equal numbers, as they had been in the past, but the age structure of the two cohorts was quite different. In 1982, over half the children entering voluntary care in the same two authorities were under 5 years of age; in 1992, that proportion had dropped to 29%. In contrast, the proportion of teenagers (only 17% in the *Who Needs Care?* study) had more than doubled, and 38% were 13–16 years of age.

Ethnicity

Some ethnic minority children, but more particularly those of mixed race, have been shown to be especially likely to be looked after by social services departments (Rowe et al. 1989). However, our two sample authorities were situated in areas with very small non-white populations (in County, for example, the 1991 Census recorded little more than 1% of residents in ethnic minorities in any of the five localities we studied), so the number of such cases is too small to be very informative. Only two black children were admitted (one of whom was in a private foster home and came from a distant urban area), one Asian child, and 11 of mixed race, but nevertheless, together they represent 9% of the sample.

Children's health and development

Issues concerning the general health of the children were rather less prominent than was the case for their parents. Only 1 in 10 children were said to be suffering from varying degrees of poor health, but twice as many had special, quasi-medical needs – as a result of hearing loss, poor sight or impaired mobility, for example. However, the very small number of children described as having 'disabilities' (five in the whole sample) does require comment. Such children are now incorporated in the Children Act's definition of 'in need' (Section 17(10)(c)) and are eligible for all forms of family support services, including accommodation, yet only 3% of all the admissions in our study involved such children.

One reason may be ambiguities in defining 'disability'. Although only five children were described as 'disabled', we have seen that larger numbers were said to have special medical needs, and some of these could have been quite disabling. Also, 16% were said to have learning difficulties, and almost as many exhibited behaviour problems associated with their health and development, with a considerable overlap between these two groups. More precisely, 15% of the children in the sample were the subject of a Statement of Special Educational Needs, so larger numbers of disabled children may be entering accommodation than are currently recorded.

Care histories

Like their parents, a substantial proportion of the children were no strangers to the care system: 62 of the 153 children were known to have been in care before – 40% of all the children accommodated, compared with 30% of the 'volunteered' in the *Who Needs Care?* study. We were able to obtain information about these earlier admissions for 55 children, but we are aware that where files were particularly bulky or a family had moved into the area from elsewhere, some of the details of their histories may have been missed. Our data will therefore tend to underestimate the extent of their previous care experience.

As it stands, 55 children in our sample were known to have accumulated 84 previous admissions to care or accommodation between them. The majority were relatively recent entries, but 36% had been in care before the Children Act 1989 was implemented. Perhaps surprisingly, the younger children were almost as likely to have a care history as the teenagers (the proportion in each age band who had previously been in care was: pre-school 33%, primary school 36%, secondary school 38%), but this may be a distortion arising from the problems of relying on old records. It may also be a reflection of an expanding use of respite care. Girls were apparently more likely than boys to have experienced being in care before (58% of those with a history were girls), but we have no explanation for this.

Of the children with care histories, 64% had only one previous period in care, and the largest number of admissions recorded was four (experienced by four of the children in the sample, only one of whom was being offered planned respite). The rest were clearly the result of serious and escalating problems at home.

The majority of past episodes of being in care were relatively short-term: 42% lasted less than a month – some of these for a matter of only a few days – and 80% were less than four months in duration. Only four of the recorded episodes of care lasted more than a year, and the longest of these, which spanned almost the whole of the child's lifetime, was an anomaly, as most of it had been spent 'home on trial' with a court order still in force. On the whole, therefore, these were not children who had 'drifted' for long periods in the care system; rather, most appear to have been offered short-term accommodation at crisis points, and for a few a pattern of respite had been established.

Entering the care system was not the only form of disruption experienced by children in the cohort: 26% of all those accommodated in the eight-month monitoring period had lived away from their homes in the past, in other forms of care. Mostly this was within their family network – with relatives or with a parent who had separated from their usual carer – but for a minority there had been experiences of long stays in hospital, in boarding schools, private foster homes or other care arrangements. Two in five of the children with care histories had experienced disruptions of this kind, and no doubt it had sometimes been the collapse of these alternative forms of help that had finally propelled them into the care system itself.

Education

For those of school age, 70% attended mainstream schools, and 16% attended special and residential schools. A worrying group were the 5% who were attending alternative teaching units or receiving home tuition: in either case, this was a matter of only a few hours a week. Most worrying of all were the 8% who were suspended or excluded from school and were receiving no education whatsoever, yet this 8% was in some senses the tip of the iceberg, for no less than a quarter of the children had been excluded at some time in their school careers. Not surprisingly, a quarter of all the children were said to be poor performers at school, and according to their social workers, another third were not achieving their potential. On this basis, more than half the school-age children entering accommodation were already suffering from serious deficits and disruptions in their education which the care system was unlikely to find easy to overcome.

Behaviour

Educational difficulties did not stand alone, and were often associated with a further striking feature of the children accommodated: the degree to which their own behaviour was problematic, and how often this was seen as a precipitating factor in their admission to accommodation. This presented a sharp contrast to the 'volunteered' children in the *Who Needs Care?* study, and it was evident that the much higher proportion of teenagers in the present cohort played a significant role in this. Troublesome behaviour was apparent at every age, but was associated disproportionately with the adolescents.

Complaints came thick and fast from parents, teachers, the police (and social workers). Nearly a third of all the children were alleged to have truanted or run away from home, or both, and three-quarters of them were teenagers (the fact that there were five runaways under the age of 10 was no less disturbing). A quarter were said to be aggressive or actively violent, and 2 out of 5 were arguing and testing the boundaries with parents and others to an apparently unacceptable degree. Only 1 in 10 were said to be persistent offenders, who habitually tangled with the police and the courts, but a larger proportion had occasional brushes with the law, or were accused of stealing, violence or other misdemeanours within their own homes. The links between such behaviour and the often fraught relationships with parents were obviously strong.

Predictably, boys were more likely than girls to be offenders and to be aggressive and violent, and they were slightly more inclined to truancy; but girls were just as likely to be runaways, and they caused rather more concern about the risks they ran through their sexual activities. Indeed, among the adolescents whose acting-out behaviour had triggered an admission, girls slightly outnumbered boys (53%, compared with 47%). This was in considerable contrast to the situation in the *Who Needs Care?* study, where girls represented only a third of the so-called 'villains' who were propelled into care through the courts.

Other behaviour difficulties were not so numerous, though not necessarily any less significant or worrying. For example, 1 in 8 children was accused of having 'tantrums', but three-quarters of them were well past the 'terrible twos' stage of development (more than two-fifths were aged 10 years or older). A similar proportion suffered from behavioural problems associated with medical or developmental difficulties. Ten per cent were enuretic, and the distress and embarrassment for those (a half) who were over 10 or teenagers and suffered this complaint can be imagined. Reckless behaviour amounting to self-harm was attributed to 8% of children (most of them teenagers), and a similar proportion were said to be unusually withdrawn. Sleeping problems afflicted another 8% and these were equally likely to be suffered by pre-school children and those in secondary education.

The picture that emerges consists of a substantial proportion of troubled and troublesome children and young people, a large proportion of whom were either verging on or were actually described as being 'beyond control', or in more modern terminology, were exhibiting 'challenging behaviour'. Difficult behaviour within their families was regarded as a significant factor in nearly half of all accommodations, and their behaviour beyond the home, in school and the community, was a major element in the admission of a third of the cohort. In effect, there were strong indications that the so-called 'villains' of ten years earlier (most of whom, if they had been removed from home, would have been taken in on police Place of Safety Orders or brought to court and remanded or committed to care) were now being looked after under the new-style voluntary arrangements.

Risk

We have already indicated that there were widespread concerns about the physical and emotional care the children were receiving, or were likely to receive, given the family difficulties that were so apparent. A substantial proportion were also regarded as being 'at risk', and suspicions and allegations of abuse and neglect had been voiced in relation to a majority of them at some stage in their lives. This was in sharp contrast to the minority who were subject to similar suspicions in the *Who Needs Care?* study – perhaps a reflection of raised levels of consciousness, or a hypersensitivity to risk. More specifically, 12% were known to have been on the Child Protection Register in the past, and 23% were either on the Child Protection Register at the point of their admission to accommodation or were registered soon after they entered it – a total of over a third of the children in the cohort. Again, this is in sharp contrast to the situation in the *Who Needs Care?* study, when only 1% of children entering *voluntary* care were registered. Despite developments in the child protection system and a steady increase in numbers registered over the intervening decade, such a contrast is nevertheless significant. It is clear that children and young people who are thought to need protection, if they leave home at all, are now much more likely to be cared for on a voluntary basis. The 'victims' in the *Who Needs Care?* study were nearly always removed from home on Place of Safety Orders, to be followed in many cases by a Care Order. From the present study, it appears that they, together with the 'villains', were just as likely to be accommodated on a basis of negotiation and 'partnership'.

The first indications from our quantitative data are therefore twofold. The widespread deprivations and difficulties which beset the families and children to whom accommodation was offered are manifest and familiar from many other studies, both past and present. The emphases may vary, and some problems (unemployment, for example) were more prominent than before, but there can be little doubt that these were families and children 'in need' of assistance and support, who fell well within the parameters of Section 17 of the Children Act.

There is also evidence that the Children Act's declared preference for negotiated solutions to family problems, rather than court orders, has had a marked effect on practice. The profile of the accommodated children contrasts with that of the 'volunteered' in the *Who Needs Care?* study in two major ways: the extent of children's behaviour difficulties and their role in precipitating admissions, and the degree of 'risk' apparently threatening so many children. In consequence, the previously distinctive profiles of the 'villains' and 'victims' who normally entered the care system via Place of Safety Orders or direct from court have now been superimposed on the profile of the 'volunteered' children. In the chapters that follow, we will seek to disentangle these elements and explore the implications of these changes. In the mean time, we offer an overview of the ways in which accommodation was planned and effected, as revealed by our monitoring data.

Planning accommodation

The 'planning process', as described in the volumes of Guidance accompanying the Children Act, is conceived as a measured, step-by-step approach of crucial importance. The sequence moves from initial inquiry through extensive consultation to a comprehensive assessment. This, in turn, leads to the eventual decision and the making of a clear plan for implementation.

Volume 3 of the Guidance (DoH 1991b) addresses the issue concerning all children who may be 'looked after', and requires planning to begin 'from the earliest possible time after the recognition of need or referral, where the provision of accommodation is likely to be necessary' (DoH 1991b, para.2.9).

The importance of consultation with all other agencies or individuals who may know the family and/or the child is stressed, so that all relevant information can be pooled. The vital involvement of parents, children and other family members in the consultation process is repeatedly emphasised, and there are strong messages about their participation. Parents, grandparents and other concerned relatives 'should be invited to participate actively in planning and to make their views known'.

In addition, and in accordance with the legislation, the child's own wishes and feelings must be sought and 'given due consideration' in the light of his/her age and understanding.

The means by which the required degree of consultation and participation may be facilitated are hinted at rather than spelled out in Volume 3 of the Guidance. As in child protection work, meetings that bring together many of the interested parties are likely to be at the heart of the process, but are referred to somewhat obliquely: 'nor should they [the children] be forced to attend meetings if they choose not to do so' (DoH 1991b, para.2.48).

However, the two sample authorities had developed their own practice guidelines in this regard. County's procedures state:

> ♦ All children subject to a care order, who are accommodated or looked after or who receive a significant level of service must have a Care Plan. The Care Plan will be formulated at a planning meeting. Planning meetings may only be chaired by a social work supervisor/team manager grade (qualified in Child Care) or an equivalent or higher grade.

Further, participation of the parents, child and others in the planning meeting is expected:

> ♦ A planning meeting must always include the child (when of sufficient age and understanding), their parents, anyone with parental responsibility, unless they do not want to attend.

What is missing is specific reference to multi-agency involvement in the planning meeting.

In Shire, there was also guidance on the planning process, which echoed the Guidance to the Children Act. As in County, the planning meeting was a given a central role:

- ♦ When there is a request from a parent, other person with parental responsibility or a member of the Department for a child to be accommodated, this will be considered by a planning meeting or resource group chaired by a Team, Unit or Service Manager. The child, parents, others with parental responsibility, others with knowledge of the child and with control of resources will be invited.

Unlike County, the attendance of other professionals 'who know the child' and those who 'control resources' suggests a multi-agency/multi-professional approach to planning meetings in Shire. The involvement of 'resource providers' who can contribute to a care plan for the child suggests a large forum for linking a child's needs to a strategy with particular resources.

The timing of planning was also important. In County's guidelines it was expected that a planning meeting would normally be followed by a contract meeting, and that both would precede admission. The likelihood that there would be some emergency placements was acknowledged, but 'only where a child needs to be looked after immediately', in which case the appropriate planning meeting was to be held within five working days. An interesting footnote adds:

- ♦ No more than 25% of placements in any year by an Area are to be without care plans and agreements being made beforehand.

In Shire's guidelines there was also an expectation that the planning meeting would take place before the admission, but they allowed for exceptions:

- ♦ When a decision about accommodation of a child has been made in an emergency, a case planning meeting or resource group must be held within 2 working days to reconsider and confirm the plan.

Thus, although it was hoped that planning meetings in both authorities would precede and direct the admission to accommodation, it was acknowledged that emergency admissions would inevitably occur.

The monitoring data

How does practice in Shire and County measure up to the planning models at central and local government level? In the first place, most of the families of children accommodated were already known to the social services departments and had received some form of service before. Only 17% were described as truly 'new' cases, unknown to the department before the events leading to the admission. The rest were either open cases, where work was in progress when the issue of accommodation arose (53%), or had been known and worked with in the past but their case had been closed, and it was the events or issues that suggested a need for accommodation which had led to a reopening of contact.

There is also evidence of a considerable history of a range of services of having been offered in the past to most of the families concerned. More than three-quarters had previously received social work support and advice. Substantial minorities had received practical help in cash or kind (46% – a clear reflection of the poverty of many of the families), counselling (39%), day care for younger children (29%), home helps (27%) and psychiatric services (25%). A wide range of other services had also been offered to much fewer families. Some families had received a whole package of supports over long periods. As a result, assessments were not starting from scratch in a majority of cases, and accommodation was not often a service of first resort.

Despite this background knowledge, however, 47% of all the admissions to accommodation were 'emergencies' – a far cry from the measured ideal of the Guidance. One in five admissions occurred out of office hours (mostly overnight) and were fielded by the emergency duty team. A further 29% were effected on the same day that a request or referral was made – almost twice the rate of emergency admissions to voluntary care reported in the *Who Needs Care?* study ten years earlier. In fact, the rate of emergency admissions in the present study closely resembles that of the precipitate entries by means of Place of Safety Orders in the *Who Needs Care?* study.

At first sight, it appears that whilst the numbers of modern Emergency Protection Orders have been drastically reduced as a result of the Act, the unplanned scramble and potential trauma of the admission process with which they were associated remains intact. This is not to say that good assessment cannot be carried out under pressure and in a hurry.

Some practitioners – especially those in emergency duty teams – would argue that high-quality work can be achieved in a crisis, when problem issues are at their most dramatic. In the mental health world, 'crisis intervention teams' are (or were) an example of such an approach (Scott 1974). However, one consequence of the high rate of emergencies is that more overt planning occurs *after* the admission than before.

Meetings

Our evidence was that meetings have indeed come to play a prominent role in the process of local authority planning for children. In 83% of cases a meeting of some sort had been held where the issue of accommodation was addressed. 'Planning meetings' predominated, and occurred in half of all cases, but a further 1 in 5 were so-called 'contract' meetings, where details of placement aims and the means to effect them were discussed once a decision to accommodate had been made. A final 11% were child protection conferences – a small illustration of the overlap between protection and support that was so evident throughout the study.

The emergency nature of a high proportion of admissions to accommodation was reflected in the timing of these meetings. Only 38% were convened *before* the admission took place; the rest were held in its aftermath. Planning had to catch up with decisions already taken. Nevertheless, emergency admissions were no less likely to involve a meeting at some stage than those that had been planned in advance. In some cases, however, where a routine stay was anticipated as a response to an unambiguous and time-limited need for care, a formal meeting was avoided altogether. If no change of circumstances was foreseen, and if the return home seemed unproblematic, the formalities were sometimes sidstepped. A mother of four, well known to a County social services team, made an early request for accommodation when she knew she was to be admitted to hospital for an operation. Details of the accommodation arrangements were 'worked out with the mum beforehand, with no formal meeting'. The children were introduced to the foster parents in advance, and the return home also took place without a meeting. The mother expressed her appreciation with bouquets for the foster parents. The rules had been broken, but the outcome was highly satisfactory. Ironically, then, where there was no meeting the admission was sometimes 'planned' well in advance.

Attendance at meetings by parents and children has been an important feature of recent debates on child protection conferences and reviews (Gardner 1985; Lewis 1992; Thoburn et al. 1995; Farmer and Owen 1995; Sinclair 1984). It has been regarded as a matter of principle that such attendance is encouraged, although, as Petch (1988, p.1) notes, there has been an element of tokenism in adding the client perspective without recognising the potential conflict in such encounters. Both social services departments in our sample considered that parents should be invited to all planning meetings and case conferences, and that children should be invited if they were considered mature enough to contribute.

Parents attended 84% of meetings. Non-attendance at a meeting appeared to be a result of strained relations with social services rather than not having been invited. Parental participation in the planning process was said by social workers to be 'easy' for half those who attended meetings; for a quarter it was 'difficult', and for the remaining quarter it was 'mixed'. In contrast, of the minority of parents who did not attend, participation for 9 out of 10 was either 'difficult' or 'mixed', and only two were seen as 'easy' to work with. Attendance at the meeting also meant greater involvement in a working relationship, and more parents who attended were given tasks in relation to their child and the placement than those who stayed away. Not surprisingly, the parents of children involved in child protection meetings were the least likely to establish easy working relationships with the agency, and participation for them was said to be 'difficult' or 'mixed' in 4 out of 5 cases.

Overall, then, a large proportion of parents were present at the various types of meetings, and professionals were given the opportunity to listen to their views and concerns within a formal setting. But the meetings were also a forum in which parents heard, in a very public way, the accumulated concerns (and complaints) of the professionals, so merely attending a meeting need not necessarily indicate an easy working relationship – something we will discuss further in Chapter 12.

In contrast to their parents, the children attended only half the meetings, but this was related to their age. Teenagers attended almost as many meetings as their parents (77%, compared to 84%), and 43% of children aged 10–12 years also attended. Even a small proportion (8%) of children aged under 9 were present at the meeting, but in these cases they were likely to be less formal occasions, such as 'contract meetings'. For example, in an emergency a social worker took two brothers of 8 and 9, along with their parents, on an introductory visit to the foster home where they were to live during their mother's stay in psychiatric hospital. The reasons for the arrangement, their likes and dislikes, the routines of the family, plans for their schooling, and contact with their father were all discussed, and although the boys were obviously anxious, they 'spoke up well'.

Social workers found that, in general, children were rather easier to work with than their parents, but like their parents, their participation in the decision-making process was further improved if they attended the meeting. Even in child protection conferences, the majority were said to co-operate well – presumably because they felt less under attack than their parents. More children who attended meetings actually wanted to be accommodated, and, like the parents, attendance led to the allocation of more 'tasks' as part of a working contract. However, unlike the parents, the participation of children was apparently easier if the meeting took place *after* the admission to accommodation. Perhaps such a meeting offers some youngsters their first opportunity to express their point of view regarding the family crisis which resulted in the admission. In some cases, where social services has only recently become involved, it is the parents who will have been the main 'complainant', and the meeting might be the first occasion on which the child's voice is heard. The rather different perspective of the young people is discussed in Chapter 14.

Overall, analysis of the data from the cohort of 177 admissions to accommodation suggests that meetings had played an important part in the communication between children, parents and the social services. However, because two-thirds of meetings took place after the admission, they appear to be less an occasion for arranging accommodation as part of a planned package of intervention and more an occasion to sort out what to do after the crisis of the admission. It poses the question, not whether meetings monitor events and social work activity or make decisions, which concerned Sinclair (1984) and McDonnell and Aldgate (1984), but how meetings catch up with events.

Other aspects of the planning process concerned the placement arrangements that were made, the purposes and likely duration of the spell in accommodation, and the means by which placement aims might be met.

The choice of placement

In our cohort 81% of children and young people were fostered, and 16% went into residential care. These proportions were very different in the two authorities – this reflects the different balance of provision discussed in Chapter 3 and is explored further in Chapter 9.

A more surprising finding was how rarely relatives were used to look after accommodated children. Volume 3 of the Children Act Guidance (DoH 1991b) states: 'placement with a relative will often provide the best opportunities for promoting and maintaining family links in a familiar setting' (para.3.33). Taken at face value, our finding that only 4 initial placements out of the 177 which took place during the monitoring exercise were with members of a child's family is extremely disappointing. The Act puts special emphasis on the value of intra-familial relationships to an individual's sense of security and identity, and there is perhaps an assumption that there is untapped potential for help within many family networks. If so, our two authorities appeared to be failing to exploit it.

However, to set against this rather bleak picture, we have a number of indications of why this may be so. First, it was clear that for a substantial minority of children the extended family had already been used in the past. In 1 in 5 cases the child had spent considerable periods of time away from home, either with a separated parent (10%) or with members of the extended family (11%). For children where risk was a key element in the admission, 27% had been looked after by relatives in the past. By the time admission to accommodation was being discussed these sources of help had often been exhausted.

A second factor was the absence or inaccessibility of such a network. A small proportion (7%) had no 'significant others' they could approach. The use of relatives who lived at a distance could also militate against maintenance of contact with parents and friends, and continuity of schooling – one 'good' driving out others. Another complication was that the relatives sometimes had problems of their own, or were considered inappropriate carers by the social services department, the parents, or both. As mentioned earlier, a considerable proportion of the parents, and the mothers in particular, had been in care themselves and/or had been abused as children. Kin who were able and reliable were often no longer in touch, or were in very short supply.

In addition, even where relatives were apparently able and willing to offer accommodation, parents would sometimes veto such arrangements. Failure to control one's own rebellious teenager, for example, may mean it is easier to hand him/her over to strangers or 'experts', rather than risk seeing an uncle or a grandparent succeed where you have failed. Family dynamics could be strained or fractured as a result. The many excellent aims of the legislation and Guidance may not be compatible in any particular case, and parental responsibility and choice can sometimes override some aspects of the welfare of the child.

Another reason why so few intra-familial placements appeared to be made concerns the use of alternatives to Section 20. Earlier in this chapter we noted the use of Section 17 monies to support extended family members in caring for separated children. The benefits of such arrangements were that there was no need to approve them as official foster carers, which saved considerable work and time, plus the potential embarrassment of finding that they failed to measure up to the properly strict criteria of suitability. It was also likely to save money, as relatives were sometimes willing to help for minimal remuneration. In some cases the Section 17 budget might have been healthier than that for Section 20 at that particular time. The extent of such informal arrangements to care, encouraged or actively assisted by the social services departments, is not measurable in our data because our starting point was not referrals, but admission to accommodation.

Use of supported lodgings for teenagers entering accommodation was also apparently very rare: only one young person appeared in this category at entry. At first sight this could be interpreted as a welcome recognition that semi-independence at such an early age is rarely appropriate, but again, we became aware of numerous arrangements made outside the remit of Section 20. Both authorities had local agreements with voluntary agencies which found or supplied lodgings for 'homeless' youngsters on their behalf, and with the Department of Social Security, which undertook to provide the necessary income support. This may well have accounted for the surprisingly small number of 16-year-olds (six) who were admitted under the new provisions of the Children Act. We were also aware of some young people in the cohort who were placed initially in foster homes or children's homes but then moved to lodgings soon after their sixteenth birthday. Our snapshot at entry does not therefore reflect the true scale of this form of placement, either within or outside the care system.

Finding a placement was evidently far from easy, whatever the administrative mechanisms for doing so (these ranged from home-finders in each Area, to a centrally organised system). For a third of all admissions, securing a placement was said to be a problem, and for nearly three-quarters (73%) there was no degree of choice. Given such constraints, the social workers were surprisingly optimistic about its suitability, and in the vast majority of cases (84%) they felt that the placement was appropriate for the child in question.

There is considerable evidence to support such optimism. Preserving continuity of relationships and experience is a crucial part of the Children Act and its Guidance, and strenuous efforts were made in this regard. Most siblings were placed together, and in only seven admissions did separation occur. Even in these instances, where large families were involved, care was taken to select the right combination of siblings for each placement and to keep them in touch with one another.

Education

There was similar attention to preserving continuity of schooling, wherever possible: 86% of those who were in school at admission and who were accommodated during term time were able to go on attending the same school. This was achieved by placements that were near their home area, or with the help of carers, social workers, family aides and taxi services when they were placed at a distance. Considerable time, effort and resources were expended to avoid disrupting their education. However, for those who were excluded and had no current school, admission could mean perpetuation of a school-less limbo, or a long and difficult search for an acceptable alternative. For some, the placement was too short for such arrangements to be made.

Contact with families

Systems for maintaining family contact were also set in place in two-thirds of all admissions to accommodation. Where this was not the case, there were three main reasons. Some admissions lasted only a matter of days. In others, the purpose of the admission was to give the parent(s) and child a break, or 'respite' from one another. Contact would be resumed through the child's return home. There were also situations where relationships between children and their families were so hostile that contact was refused by all parties, and attempts at reconciliation were postponed for the time being.

The purposes of admission to accommodation

Care plans were also concerned with the purposes of the admission, and with what it was hoped to achieve. Aims were often mixed, but four main categories emerged.

The first, 'temporary care', applied, in a sense, to all admissions, but for about a quarter of them it was the only reason given. In these cases, for one reason or another – often parental illness – the care of the children had to be entrusted to someone else, and the social services department took on that responsibility.

More frequently, accommodation was arranged in order to allow a period of 'cooling off' or 'time out' in situations where relationships between parents and young people were extremely tense or hostile, and where separation seemed a necessary, if temporary, answer. No less than 43% of admissions fell into this category, but there was also a significant overlap with a third purpose of admission – 'protection'. This applied to 41% of all admissions, half of which were also for 'time out'. The 'protection' cases were thus a mixture of younger children where neglect or abuse was proven or suspected, and older ones at risk, whose own behaviour was contributing to their vulnerability. Protection for the latter group was often conceived as protection from *themselves*, rather than from other family members.

The fourth category of admissions was for 'respite', and a quarter of all cases included this as an element. Although there were some similarities with the notions of 'time out', children in this category were generally younger, and were sometimes disabled. Planning took place in advance of admission (unlike most of the 'time out' cases), and for a small number admission was one of a sequence of entries to accommodation.

Admissions for the purposes of 'assessment' and in order to effect 'behaviour change' in the child, parents, or both, were two remaining reasons given, but neither stood alone, and they were generally linked with 'protection' or 'time out', or both.

The thinking that lay behind an admission and the strategies for achieving its purposes were sometimes easier to appreciate through our interviews with the social workers than by perusal of their records – in the words of one social worker: 'I don't do care plans – they are too long-winded!' – but in most cases (81%), some of the means by which the goals of the placement might be achieved were recorded. Tasks were allotted to social workers, carers, parents and children, and where appropriate, to other agency staff. Most involved routine care tasks and who should undertake them, but work on behaviour was expected in two-thirds of all admissions, and on relationships in more than 2 in 5.

The planned duration of placements

Finally, we turn to the estimates of how long each period of accommodation would last. Projected time-scales varied widely, but the balance was towards relatively short periods in accommodation: 45% of placements were expected to last for no more than a fortnight, and some of them for a matter of only a few days; a further 28% were likely to last somewhat longer, but no longer than three months; the rest were either 'open-ended', in which case estimates were reserved 'until the next meeting', or were expected to involve a longer stay. No instances of accommodation were intended to be permanent at the point of admission.

Summary

Initial scrutiny of our quantitative data on planning and the processes involved shows that some strenuous efforts were being made to practise what the Children Act and its Guidance preach. Accommodation was being used in a variety of circumstances and for a range of different though overlapping purposes, as the Act suggests it should be. In a majority of cases parents and children appeared to be actively involved in the assessment process, and more often than not they were present at the meetings which have become a prime site for planning. (Indeed, meetings of many different kinds have become such a prominent feature of the planning process that we look in more detail at the way they operate in Chapter 12.) In most cases tasks were conceived that matched the purposes of the admission, though it was not always clear how well they were articulated or followed through.

Despite placement shortages, family groups were generally able to stay together, and continuities were supported by maintaining the child's contacts with home and neighbourhood, and by continuing attendance at a familiar school. From our data, it appears that there is still room for improvement, but the intentions of the legislation were adhered to more often than not. So, given that our study was conducted only twelve months after implementation of the Children Act, the fact that accommodation is just one of a whole range of support services, and that changes in every other aspect of child care services had to be absorbed, such findings are encouraging.

Of more concern, however, is the ubiquitous emergency admission to accommodation. Far from declining in proportion to the reduced number of Emergency Protection Orders, such precipitate and potentially traumatic admissions were apparently at least as numerous as they were before the Act. Some of the reasons for their survival and the implications this has for practice will be explored in the chapters that follow.

The monitoring exercise also indicated that accommodation was being offered to a more varied and challenging group of children than was the case under previous legislation. Many modern counterparts of the old 'villains' and 'victims' of the past – youngsters whose unruly behaviour is regarded as unacceptable and those who are thought to be at risk of significant harm – were being admitted to the care system on a voluntary basis rather than via the courts. In the next three chapters we look more closely at these new entrants alongside the more traditional voluntary cases, and examine what distinguishes them and how the services are responding to them.

6 *Difficult adolescents*

Developments in the criminal justice system, as well as changes in the Children Act, have had a marked effect on how difficult young people are handled by social services. The 1970s and early 1980s saw both a rise and fall in the numbers of delinquents within the care system. The rise was encouraged by the Children and Young Persons Act 1969 and its incorporation of Approved Schools into the care system. The fall came with disillusionment and competing critiques that suggested that 'care' was unjustly imposing a higher tariff of sentences on young offenders, or was contaminating the 'deprived' with the 'depraved'. In some respects, the Children Act 1989 reinforces this downward trend by removing truancy, moral danger and offending as specific grounds for a Care Order, and replacing them with the generic 'significant harm'. On the other hand, a child who is 'beyond parental control' may be regarded as suffering 'significant harm', warranting a Care Order. In addition, social services must cater for children and young people on remand and on Supervision Orders with a condition of residence. Furthermore, under Part III of the Children Act, local authorities are obliged to support families of children 'in need', and are expected to 'take reasonable steps' to reduce the need to bring care and criminal proceedings against children, and 'to encourage children within their area not to commit criminal offences' (Children Act 1989, Schedule 2). The role that voluntary accommodation may play in this rather complex picture is therefore of special interest.

Our research data shows that the behaviour of the children and young people, more often than not, caused concern, and in a substantial minority of cases it was regarded as a major reason (though not necessarily the only one) for offering accommodation.

We have chosen to focus on difficult adolescents because they were the least likely to be cared for voluntarily in the past, and because their difficult behaviour was much more likely to spill out into the community. Also, although they represented approximately a third of the cohort, they accounted for two-thirds of the admissions resulting from bad behaviour. Since adolescence is defined in terms of normal developmental change, maturation and rebellion it is difficult to relate it to specific age-bands, but for simplicity we have concentrated on the 13-plus age group, whilst recognising that there were younger children whose behaviour also caused concern.

Problem behaviour

What do we know of the behaviour of the difficult teenagers who were accommodated? The first and most striking point is that there were very few teenagers (eight) whose behaviour did *not* provoke complaints, and the 51 'difficult adolescents' represented 86% of all adolescents in the cohort. This suggests either that being a teenager, and being difficult are virtually synonymous in the eyes of most adults, or that accommodation as a service for youngsters of this age is hardly ever offered unless there are behavioural difficulties. There is probably truth in both propositions.

Perhaps more surprising, at least at first sight, is the gender balance among difficult adolescents. A slight majority were girls, in a cohort which had an even distribution of the sexes, but the nature of their problem behaviour was generally different to the boys. The traditionally male preserve of delinquency, which had marked out the 'villains' of the 1980s, was evident in this cohort, but was not the most prevalent among the long litany of complaints about these young people. One in five were said to be persistent offenders, and a rather larger proportion had had occasional brushes with the law or had pilfered from home. The most common complaints were of challenging behaviour that could be characterised as being 'beyond control', and these applied to girls as much as boys. Eight out of ten of the young people were described as 'excessively argumentative' and 'chronic rule-breakers', 7 out of 10 were runaways, 6 out of 10 truanted from school and 45% were described as 'aggressive' and sometimes 'violent'. The effects of their behaviour were not only seen as troublesome to those around them, but frequently as harmful to themselves. For example, half the youngsters were believed to be putting themselves at sexual risk, and here the concerns were mostly confined to the girls, whose recklessness and promiscuity were regarded as unacceptable and sometimes dangerous. In the legal language which preceded the Children Act, they would have been described as being 'in moral danger'. In contrast, the sexual behaviour of the boys rarely raised anxiety levels to this degree, except where they became involved with convicted child abusers.

Transgressions were generally multiple: only one adolescent was criticised for a single aspect of his behaviour. By the same token, there were a large number and range of complainants. Since the youngsters' difficult behaviour was often apparent in the home, parent–child relationships were usually under strain, and quarrels with siblings added to the tension. Despite the relatively low proportion of persistent offenders, the police were also involved in a majority of cases, and youngsters who ran away and put themselves at risk were specially likely to draw the police into the arena of family disputes. Schools were another major source of complaints, especially about truancy and disruptive behaviour in the classroom. A measure of the staff's concern (or exasperation) is the fact that no less than 45% of the difficult adolescents had been excluded at some stage in their school career.

Another distinctive feature of the 'difficult adolescents' was the fact that all but two of them were admitted on their own, without siblings, in contrast to the rest of the children accommodated, more than half of whom entered accommodation in sibling groups. In other words, the problems for which accommodation was seen as some kind of solution were much more likely to be construed as residing in the young person, the behaviour, and its effects on the rest of the family, and hardly ever as a family crisis shared with brothers and sisters.

But the concerns expressed were not solely about the effects of their behaviour on others. As we have indicated, there was also considerable anxiety about their own welfare, and for over half of them there were suspicions of neglect or abuse: 16% were currently on the Child Protection Register, and another 14% had been at some time in the past. There was a large overlap between troublesome, acting-out behaviour and risk, so the two case profiles are not mutually exclusive.

Family structure

The families of difficult adolescents were distinctive in one particular way: they were significantly more likely to be two-parent households, and almost half the young people were living with both their birth parents, compared with only 1 in 5 of the rest of in the cohort. This greater degree of structural stability did not extend to marital relationships, however, which were just as likely to be strained as in the rest of the cohort. Perhaps triads are harder to handle than dyads at this stage of human development, and perhaps the presence of a father figure in the family increased the potential for friction when teenagers were bidding for independence.

'Difficult adolescents' versus 'villains'

Before leaving the composite profile of difficult adolescents who were offered accommodation, in Table 6.1 we compare some of their features with those of the 'villains' in the *Who Needs Care?* study (Packman et al. 1986) – those who were admitted to the local authority care system expressly because of their difficult behaviour, but in their case via the courts or by means of police Place of Safety Orders. Another distinction is that the 'villains' were of no particular age, and Packman et al.'s analysis was not confined to teenagers.

Table 6.1 *Comparison of* **Who Needs Care?***'s 'villains' and the present study's 'difficult adolescents'*

	'Villains' (n = 52) %	'Difficult adolescents' (n = 51) %
Boys	69	47
Girls	31	53
Teenagers	81	100
On Child Protection Register	4	16
Offenders	73	22[1]
Truants	42	71
Runaways	42	61
Unmanageable	71	80[2]
Neglect/abuse	8	57
In care before	33	47
Lone-parent family	21	25
Marital stress	35	69

Notes:
1 Adolescents displaying a *pattern* of offending behaviour.
2 Adolescents who habitually broke the boundaries of acceptable behaviour and were 'beyond control'.

The 'villains' of the past were dominated by offenders, and we have seen that throughout the 1980s the trend was to move them away from the local authority care system altogether. Nevertheless, some of the difficult adolescents in accommodation *are* persistently delinquent, but most are troublesome in other ways which aggravate their families, schools and neighbourhoods. In this sense they may well be at risk of offending, and their high profile among those accommodated may be one response to the requirement under the Children Act to encourage children not to commit crime, as well as to avoid criminal proceedings.

The link between their behaviour and risk to themselves was far stronger than in the earlier study, and this may be less a change in reality than in awareness and perceptions. Sexual abuse, in particular, was not officially recognised as a category for inclusion on the Child Protection Register at the time of the *Who Needs Care?* study. Difficult adolescents are much more likely to be seen as vulnerable as well as troublesome, compared with the 'villains' of the past.

Social services' responses

As mentioned above, difficult adolescents had often been in trouble with their schools and the police, and they may have made the referral to social services. A majority were already known to the social services departments, though over a quarter were 'new' cases with no known record of involvement with social services – a higher proportion than the rest of the cohort. Thus, they can perhaps be characterised as the 'erupters' that other studies have identified (for example, Bullock et al. 1994).

Their sudden appearance on the social services scene did not mean that their troublesome behaviour was always of recent origin, and although their family disputes came out of the blue as far as social services were concerned, this was not necessarily the case from the family's point of view. As with the parents in other studies (for example, Fisher et al. 1986), the families often reported a long history of difficulties that had built up to crisis point before a referral was made.

One 14-year-old boy is an example of a 'new' case with chronic problems. He was referred to the social services department after he had been reported missing overnight, and the police had become involved. His mother and stepfather claimed he had been dabbling in glue-sniffing and drugs, stealing from home and staying out at night. He had also occasionally truanted from school. According to the parents, he was 'not keeping the family rules', in contrast to his younger siblings. Relationships between the boy and his stepfather had evidently been deteriorating for years, and the boy claimed they had never got on. The family was comfortably off and 'respectable', and approaching the social services department had probably been a 'last resort'. The stepfather was adamant that the boy must go; the boy was equally determined that he would not return home, and his mother was supporting her husband's version of events and accepting the inevitable. Accommodation was arranged, in the hope that a period of 'respite' (or 'time out', in our terms) would allow the emotional temperature to cool, and relationships to be renegotiated. In the event, the boy was still living away from home eighteen months later, and hostilities between him and his step-father were entrenched.

In other 'new' cases, difficulties were apparently of more recent origin, but none the less extreme. The first contact social services had with the mother of two teenage daughters was when she sent them into the office to ask to be accommodated while she sat outside in a very distressed state. The elder daughter had only recently returned to live with her mother after several years with her separated father, and her previously good school performance had swiftly collapsed, she had become highly disruptive, and she was subsequently excluded.

Attempts to offer alternative forms of help were often made in these 'new' cases – placement with relatives, social work support and family therapy in the case of the two sisters – but escalating behaviour problems and the urgent demands of both parents and their adolescent children sooner or later prevailed. And whilst some admissions might entail a few days' breathing space and a quick return home, in others – as in the examples above – there was a serious breakdown in family relationships which no community-based alternatives were able to prevent.

As we have seen, however, the majority of troublesome teenagers were already known to the social services departments, and a high proportion of them had been in care or accommodated before. In the study by Triseliotis et al. (1995, p.39) the teenagers were similarly well known to the social services. For some this had been a short-term admission when they were younger; for others there had been behaviour-related admissions in the recent past. A range of other supports had also been tried – in particular, family therapy, activities and clubs, holiday schemes and group work – but few had experienced the juvenile justice system. Not all of these community-based alternatives related to the immediate past, and of the 'known' cases, only just over half were still open immediately before admission to accommodation. Thus, where the behaviour problems had been mounting up over a long period, attempts to offer help in the community were often episodic, and a planned programme of support in the run-up to the admission only applied in a minority of cases.

One 15-year-old boy, for example, had been involved in truancy and offending, as well as there being concerns about his sexual activities. He had received a wide variety of interventions, in particular, holiday activities. As the parents said:

> *Mother:* They were involved with [young person] because . . . he was doing a
> lot of stealing and this, that and the other, and they were taking him out
> on trips – all this sort of thing . . .
> *Father:* . . . and rewarding him for being a bad boy.

But when he was accommodated a year later, he had just returned from staying with an uncle (the family's attempt at a solution), and there had been no social services contact with the family for some time.

Cases where support services were offered in the period immediately preceding an admission were in the minority. One family was referred to social services by their GP because the mother was seriously ill. It seemed that the family was beginning to fall apart under the stress of her illness: they were not talking about the situation, and they had refused contact with Child Guidance. The teenage boy was opting out of the family, staying with friends and behaving aggressively towards family members. The social worker was able to offer counselling and support to the parents, and to make contact with the boy. When the admission took place two months after initial contact, the social worker was able to avoid an emergency response, and set up a planning meeting to make agreements about the purpose and length of the placement.

In general, however, it seemed that whilst some of the difficult adolescents may have received a wide variety of services before being accommodated, this was not necessarily part of a consistent strategy of community support. Nearly half had already been in care or accommodation, and a quarter were new cases, and this in turn had some bearing on the manner of their admission.

Emergency admissions

The most striking feature of the accommodation of difficult adolescents was the predominance of emergency admissions. For 3 in 5 of these teenagers an unplanned admission took place without a prior planning meeting and within 24 hours of the referral or the precipitating episode.

As we have seen, emergency admissions were a prominent feature of the cohort as a whole, but the rates for the younger children were considerably lower, and the adolescents clearly contributed disproportionately to the total picture.

The crucial point here is that, despite the dramatic fall in the use of emergency court orders since the Children Act came into force (the *Children Act Report* for 1993 (DoH 1994) suggests a figure less than half that of Place of Safety Orders in the year preceding implementation), the processes by which the troublesome young person was admitted – hastily, without prior planning, and therefore in a potentially more traumatic and unsatisfactory way – have not changed at all. The use of emergency orders had diminished, but emergencies had not.

Why were there so many unplanned emergency admissions? Clearly, in many cases the crisis was generated by the behaviour of the adolescents themselves, and by their parents' response. Where they were previously unknown to social services, or where contact had been terminated some time before, social services were often forced into emergency action, so the first contact with social workers might be when the young delinquent or runaway was at the police station, refusing – or being refused – a return home. A 15-year-old accommodated twice in the space of three months was admitted on both occasions by the night duty officer. On the first occasion he made the request himself, because his mother was away and had locked him out of the house. On the second occasion, exasperated by his behaviour, she made her intentions clear by leaving his suitcase at the police station.

In some other 'emergency' cases, parents alleged there had been ample warning – indeed, they might have been requesting help for several weeks, but social services had resisted the pressure to offer accommodation. This is an important feature of the provision of accommodation for adolescents, and suggests widely divergent perspectives on the nature and availability of the service. The parents felt that they had done all they could to sort out the problems, and a point had now been reached where something significant must be done. The social workers, on the other hand, were sceptical about what could be gained by such a move, and were reluctant to act without both trying out other options and getting to know more about the situation.

There were two major areas of contention:

1   Is the situation really so serious?

2   Does it need to be resolved by the young person being accommodated?

However, underlying these questions are wider issues of parental responsibility and the role of the state. At what point does an intra-family matter become the responsibility and require the action of social services? The parents were clear that they no longer felt responsible for their child's behaviour, and wanted others to take over. The social workers resisted such an assessment, claiming that the child and his/her behaviour remained unquestionably the responsibility of the parents. Whilst social services were prepared to offer help, it was on the under-standing that the delineation of responsibility remained clear. Fisher et al. (1986) noted that similar discrepancies of perspective required care-ful presentation of the problem by the parents to social services.

The mother of a hard-to-control 15-year-old requested 'respite' after their relationship had deteriorated into a violent confrontation, and the duty officer was called in. The girl had moved to friends her mother considered highly unsuitable, but still the social services department did not act. In the mother's view, only her daughter's return home and a further and more serious explosion of violence between them produced the desired respite. In her words: 'I have begged you lot for help with her. I don't seem to be getting the help that I want. I'm sorry, I'm not having her back. If she comes back I shall literally throw her out.' (The parents' view of social workers' reluctance are discussed further in Chapter 13.)

Social workers' reluctance to offer accommodation

In general, the parents were correct in identifying the social workers' sceptical view of the benefits of accommodation for difficult adolescents (Triseliotis et al. 1995, p.75). This was particularly the case if the first contact was a parent 'storming into the office and screaming "Take him away!"' Social workers were concerned that social services would be no more successful than the parents at controlling such young people, and many had developed a working philosophy that accommodation should be avoided at all costs:

> *Duty officer:* Half my job is saying 'no' to parents who cannot handle their teenagers.

> *Social worker:* It's very frustrating working with adolescents. When the family comes in saying 'Take him away', they are very hard to work with. I have resisted admission to accommodation and done some good work. But often we just send them away and tell them to come back and see the duty officer. It is a crisis waiting to happen. But then again, can we do a better job than them?

Some social workers had worked in residential care, and wanted parents to realise that this was not an answer. They were also concerned that once away from home, a long stay in accommodation was a danger. There was also a view that some young people were fascinated by children's homes and rather liked the idea of staying in one:

> *Social worker:* I have worked in residential work, and I think it should be avoided at all costs as it is dangerous to them.

> *Residential worker:* It is getting all round the town, and all the young people see how nice it is here. They are queuing up to get in from this area.

On occasion, the difficult adolescent was seen as a 'victim' rather than a 'villain', reacting in a normal way to difficult family circumstances. There was a reluctance to 'punish' him/her for the family's problems. Older teenagers were sometimes seen as beginning the normal process of breaking away from home, but social workers did not often see Section 20 accommodation as the appropriate way to achieve this.

In addition, in crisis situations there did not appear to be an opportunity to avoid accommodation by offering counselling or family therapy. It was sometimes difficult to find such a service quickly enough, or family members were reluctant to accept it as a possible solution. There was also scepticism about whether social work involvement would make a difference to what seemed like long-standing family positions. The case would often be closed when things went quiet, even after a period of accommodation. The parents were always told of the duty system, and it was thought that offering them a safety valve supported them in carrying on:

> *Social worker: No, we won't take them away, and we can't necessarily offer a social worker. But there is always the duty officer available to provide support, a chance to offload.*

The researchers did observe long and supportive telephone conversations with parents, which appeared to provide at least temporary relief and support for some families. However, once this view of a case developed, it seemed to be assumed that 'counselling out' was enough.

There was also a view that the parents were ultimately responsible for their children and their behaviour, and they should not be encouraged to abrogate such responsibility too easily. Some interpreted the Children Act as re-emphasising parents' responsibilities for their children:

Social worker: They were asking for permanence. The father had left home himself at 11. He did not realise that things have changed and you can't just chuck out your child. You never lose parental rights nowadays.

This did not mean that social workers were not prepared to help parents carry out those responsibilities, but the offer of help required some degree of agreement about how to proceed. In particular, it meant the parents looking at their part in the problem, and the changes that were necessary in family relations.

For a majority of difficult adolescents, their own precipitate actions and/ or the desperate measures taken by their parents were magnified by social services' reluctance to offer accommodation as an appropriate resource. There may have been good grounds for the families' sense of desperation on the one hand and for social services' caution about providing accommodation on the other. But the end result was admissions that were unplanned, hastily effected and far from the ideals of the Children Act Guidance.

Nevertheless, not all admissions of difficult adolescents followed this pattern. Some admissions *were* planned in advance, and some social workers were persuaded of their value before a crisis forced their hand.

The mother of a 14-year-old boy contacted the social services department, saying 'the police had told her if things get too bad they can sign something so he goes into care'. The initial response was defensive, if not deterrent, and the social worker explained, 'this wasn't so and if he needed to be accommodated it could be done by social services, but only in extreme circumstances'. A parallel referral from the police underlined that extremity by alleging that he was leading younger boys astray, and that his exclusion from school meant 'he has nothing to do all day but crime'.

Family therapy was offered but refused, but at the third request for 'a period of trouble-free living', a planning meeting was set up and a foster placement was arranged as 'respite for the parents and the boy'. The worker argued that he was clearly a 'child in need' because his development was being impaired through 'poor family influences' (it was believed that he was 'scapegoated' at home) and the 'labelling of the criminal justice system'. The plan was for two months' respite, with personal counselling for the boy as an additional support. Unfortunately, the respite arrangement was not successful and he had to be readmitted

– this time in an emergency – and placed in a residential home for further assessment.

Purpose and planning

Once accommodation became inevitable, what was its purpose and how were plans developed for the future? As we have noted above, in only a few cases were planning meetings set up before the placement began, but there was usually a meeting afterwards, and only rarely was there no meeting at all. Teenagers were usually present at the meetings, as were their parents, and a majority were given relevant 'tasks' to accomplish during their stay. But the conflicts inherent in their family situations were evident in the difficulties social workers faced in working with the different parties. Only a minority of parents were said to be easy to work with – perhaps because of the professional resistance to admission that so many had experienced. Nor were the young people much easier to engage, and working relationships were said to be easy with only half of them. Their 'stroppiness' was evidently not confined to their home territory. Triseliotis et al. (1995, p.78) also note the divergent expectations of social work intervention between social workers, parents and young people.

Accommodation as 'time-out'

The stated initial purpose of the placement gives an indication of how long and how serious a separation from the family was envisaged. For a large majority, it was viewed as 'time out' or a 'cooling-off period': separating the young person from the family in order to let things calm down. For some, this was envisaged as a very short break, perhaps a few days, in which the separation itself was what the warring parties needed. It was merely a period in which to re-establish relations after a serious incident in which the young person had been thrown out or refused entry (those who returned home the next day are not included in our sample, since Section 20 accommodation is only applicable after a 24-hour stay). Sometimes a time limit would be imposed on the stay at the planning meeting, and various sessions might be arranged between the family and the field or residential social worker to explore how relations could be improved when the young person returned home, as illustrated by the following extract from the minutes of a planning meeting:

◆   [Mother] said that when [daughter] said she was leaving, she agreed
    because she was at the end of her tether. Before she comes home she
    must realise that there will have to be some changes.

These short stays were in some ways similar to the relief envisaged as being offered by respite care, except they were not negotiated and agreed in advance. One 15-year-old girl was accommodated by the night duty officer twice within a month after being thrown out of home. The social worker said she would have offered a planned respite placement if the mother had been prepared to discuss it with social services and if a respite placement for a teenager had been available:

> *Social worker:* The problem is with mum. We needed to accommodate [daughter] but in the longer term we will keep her out and just muddle through the crises. Mum will not yet consider respite, so we have to wait for a crisis and accommodate [daughter] as we have to. If she would agree to respite, that would be the solution.

There was also the salutary effect on the youngster of a break from home: if not necessarily experienced as a punishment, the fact that the parents had done what they had been threatening to do came as something of a surprise. Also, the apparent freedom of the children's home was not all that it was cracked up to be:

> *Young person:* It was a nice place and all that, but because I didn't know anybody I was really angry and hurt and scared.

'Time-out' periods are complex, however, and should not be seen only as a short period away from home to let tempers cool. Even in short placements work was often necessary to re-establish relations and re-set boundaries. In nearly half the cases some degree of behaviour change was envisaged during the period in accommodation, and most of the tasks that were set concerned working on family relations.

Given the risks that many adolescents were exposed to, many admissions were also for 'the protection of the child'. This was a response not only to the violence and threat of violence that often accompanied (indeed constituted) the crisis that led to the admission, but also the sexual risks that threatened some young people who were on the run. One 14-year-old boy was constantly running away from home, and ostensibly accommodation was seen as a one-month break for his mother. However, as he was associating with a known convicted child abuser, and the police had considered an Emergency Protection Order because of their concerns, protection was also an aim.

Thus, although 'time out' was described as the most common purpose of accommodation for adolescents, this varied from a short break to let tempers cool to attempts to renegotiate family relations and to rescue young people from serious risk.

Longer-term accommodation

Accommodation could also be seen as a longer-term solution to apparently intractable relationship problems at home, and was sometimes regarded as a stepping stone to independence. This seemed a legitimate and potentially valuable use of the resource for some young people, where family rejection was extreme. The schoolboy who had 'never got on' with his stepfather ceased to behave anti-socially once he had settled in an accepting foster home.

However, the time-scales envisaged for the 'longer-term' accommodations were sometimes limited: 'I think he will stay in accommodation until he is 16 . . . He has always said he intended to leave home at 16.'

It was our impression that there was a high degree of 'accepting the inevitable' in these situations, and that social workers, as well as the families and young people themselves, regarded the school-leaving age, rather than 18, as the normal point of departure from the care system. This is borne out by the use of supported lodgings highlighted in Chapter 5, but seems at odds with the evident vulnerability of many of the young people, and this has been highlighted in other studies, (for example, Stein and Carey 1986).

Placement problems

Accommodation was a significantly different experience for troublesome adolescents compared to the other children in the cohort. Nearly half were placed in residential care, in comparison with only 2% of the younger children, though practice was very different in the two authorities, as we shall see in Chapter 9. The difficulty of finding placements which would take (or hold) teenagers was particularly acute, and for a quarter of them the social workers considered the initial placement inappropriate. The stage was therefore set for a turbulent stay in the child care system – a feature which will be highlighted in our follow-up data (see Chapter 10).

Summary

Young people whose behaviour caused concern accounted for a third of all admissions to accommodation during our study period – itself a significant change from a decade earlier – but they posed a challenge to the principles of partnership and planning which underpin the Children Act. Partnership was often difficult to negotiate because the adolescents and their parents were nearly always in conflict, and it required high levels of skill in mediation and conciliation to draw all parties into any kind of agreement.

Partnership was further complicated by a widespread reluctance on the part of social workers and their agencies to offer accommodation as a support service for these young people. Such reluctance was based on a complex cluster of reasons: shortages of placements that were considered suitable; a sometimes realistic pessimism about their capacity to control the adolescents' behaviour any more satisfactorily than their parents, and concern that they might do more harm than good by severing family relationships and exposing the teenagers to a 'rotten system' that more than one social workers described as 'dangerous'. But their reluctance was frequently met with urgent and desperate appeals for action by parents, young people, or both, creating a demanding and withholding interchange that did not make 'working together' an easy matter.

As we have seen, for much the same reasons careful forward planning was also difficult to achieve in these circumstances. The admission was frequently a last resort, and the precipitate behaviour of the adolescents (and sometimes their parents) contributed to the preponderance of crises and emergencies, which in turn increased the instabilities of the accommodation experience.

7 Children at risk

Children who were thought to be at risk of neglect or abuse were another prominent group within our cohort, again in sharp contrast to the profile of the 'volunteered' in the *Who Needs Care?* study (Packman et al. 1986) before the Children Act was implemented. Like the difficult adolescents, in the past those children and young people who excited serious professional concerns about the risks inherent in the care they were (or were not) receiving were much less likely to be received into care on a voluntary basis. Further, there had been significant changes in public perceptions of the nature and extent of risk in the intervening years. Although 'moral danger' had long been a label attached to young girls who were running wild, and cases of incest were sometimes brought to court, the 1980s can be characterised as the decade in which sexual abuse achieved the status of 'moral panic' (Parton 1985). Its recognition as a category for inclusion on the Child Protection Register dates from this period, as do the alarums of Cleveland and Orkney, when 'awareness' reached fever pitch. In addition, the research studies of the 1980s and 1990s (for example, DoH 1995) have suggested that child protection concerns have come to dominate the child care domain. The legacy of two decades of high-profile tragedies and public inquiries has sensitised professionals to risk, and a large proportion of their work revolves around these issues as a result.

Who were the children at risk in our sample? In Chapter 5 we indicated that suspicions or allegations that children were being neglected or abused had been articulated at some time by somebody in relation to nearly two-thirds of the cohort. That such a pervasive cloud of concern should have hung over the families is perhaps another indication of the extent to which protection issues tend to dominate the contemporary child care scene (Audit Commission 1994). But the social workers did not always share these concerns, and in any case some were no longer seen as relevant to the family's current situation. As a firm indicator of perceived risk, therefore, this particular measure was too wide-ranging and nebulous for our purposes.

Alternatively, we had data on whether a child had been, or was currently on the Child Protection Register, and those who were currently registered, where concerns were immediate and 'live', would have offered a much smaller but more precise group for study (1 in 5 of the cohort). However, it was apparent that many children who were not or had never been registered were nevertheless regarded as being at risk to a degree which influenced the decision to offer accommodation. Although, for many, the risk had not received the official stamp of recognition by means of registration, it was clear from our social work interviews and from perusing the files that it was a current concern in the minds of those offering accommodation.

Harm, or more often the *likelihood* of harm, was frequently a factor in the professionals' analysis of 'need'. Where this was so, either neglect, abuse or risk was identified as a key element (though not necessarily the prime or only element) influencing the decision to accommodate. We have therefore chosen to classify the children in this substantial group as being at risk for the purposes of analysis. Hence, the cases identified cover a wide range and degree of concerns, and overlap with the difficult adolescents, half of whom were also regarded as at risk. At one end of the continuum might be a newborn baby, placed on the Child Protection Register at birth because of the father's sexual offences against children, the mother's limited understanding and the couple's stormy and violent relationship. At the other extreme might be a healthy, apparently 'normal' adolescent, whose rejection by his mother and stepfather was so vociferous and unyielding that it was regarded by the social workers as amounting to emotional abuse, although no child protection conference was ever convened. On this basis, 74 children (half the cohort) form the focus of this chapter. We begin with the characteristics of the children themselves.

Characteristics of the children at risk

In most respects, the children classified as 'at risk', were very like the rest of the sample, and there were few significant differences. However, compared with others in the cohort, those in the 'at risk' group were rather more likely to be very young or to be teenagers, and the proportion of 5–12-year-olds was only half that of the children not at risk. In this respect they also departed from the 'victim' profile of the *Who Needs Care?* study, where pre-school children formed by far the largest group and only 1 in 5 were teenagers. As we have already suggested, the current increased concern about risk to adolescents is likely to be related to the massive growth in awareness of the extent of sexual abuse. It is also evident that some of the young people's recklessness –

particularly that of the runaways – was central to the perception of risk. They were seen to be at risk from their *own* behaviour as much as (and sometimes in spite of) the quality of care that was being offered by their families, and in a previous generation the girls at least might have been committed to care as being in 'moral danger'. Admission for the purposes of protection was also very likely to overlap with intentions to provide a breathing space and 'time out' both for the young person and his/her family.

More disturbing was the fact that children from ethnic minorities were clearly over-represented in the cohort. Both the black African-Caribbean children and the one Asian child fell into the 'at risk' category, as did 6 out of the 11 children of mixed race. The numbers are obviously too small to claim any statistical significance, but inevitably they raise the question of whether some form of discrimination was at work. Are agencies quicker to perceive risk when dealing with the unfamiliar (the sample areas included very small ethnic minority groups), or are such families only drawn into contact with social services when their problems have reached an advanced stage?

Table 7.1 *Comparison of* Who Needs Care?*'s 'victims' and the present study's 'at risk' children*

	Compulsorily admitted 'victims' (n = 38) %	Voluntarily accommodated 'at risk' (n = 74) %
Boys	46	47
Girls	54	53
Under 5 years	47	35
5–12 years	32	23
Teenagers	21	43
Ethnic minority[1]	—	12
Health problems[1]	—	12
Special needs[1]	—	20
Excluded (school age)[1]	—	20
Withdrawn	8	11
Runaway	13	28
Truant	16	25
Delinquent[2]	10	3
On Child Protection Register (ever)	26	58
In care before	33	38

Notes:
1 No comparable data available from *Who Needs Care?* study.
2 Present data refers to persistent offending outside home. *Who Needs Care?* data refers to any delinquent acts.

In most other respects, such as their health, behaviour, schooling and care histories, this group of children was not significantly different from those who were *not* at risk, and Table 7.1 compares their characteristics with those of the compulsorily admitted 'victims' in the *Who Needs Care?* study of the past. It is the proportion of teenagers which clearly distinguishes today's 'at risk' cases from those of the 'victims'.

Family profiles

We now turn to the children's families in a search for more distinguishing features. On many dimensions the differences are modest and not statistically significant. The 'at risk' group were somewhat more likely to come from lone-parent families and from intact households consisting of the birth mother and father; they were therefore less likely to live in stepfamilies. This is interesting, if only because it flies in the face of the age-old stereotypes of wicked stepmothers and stepfathers!

There were also indications that their families were among the poorest, with even more money problems and housing difficulties than the rest of the cohort. As recent studies of child protection indicate, 'families overwhelmed and depressed by social problems form the greatest proportion of those supported by child protection agencies' (DoH 1995).

It is not surprising that more striking differences were evident in terms of parental well-being, behaviour and family relationships. The physical ill health of parents was actually less of an issue for the 'at risk' group than for other cases (as it was for the 'victims' in the *Who Needs Care?* study), but their mental health, particularly that of the mothers, was twice as likely to be regarded as a problem, and affected 3 in 4 of these cases. Such a large proportion does not, of course, indicate that all these mothers were mentally ill or disabled, though a substantial proportion were. Two mothers of children at risk had learning difficulties, 1 in 8 were said to be suffering from a chronic mental illness, and for a similar proportion the illness was at an acute stage. This means that in a quarter of 'at risk' cases – twice the proportion in the rest of the cohort – the mother's mental state had been clinically diagnosed. An even larger proportion of mothers of 'at risk' children – more than 2 in 5 – were described as being in 'poor' mental health, but here we rely on the social workers' own estimates of the evident stress they were experiencing and the underfunctioning that was implied. Even so, this was twice the proportion of mothers of children not at risk.

The relationship between a mother's mental state and the stricter criterion of 'risk' embodied in the Child Protection Register is also evident. A large majority of 'well' mothers (4 in 5) did not have a child on the register, and neither did a smaller majority (3 in 5) of those in 'poor' mental health, but a clear majority of the mothers with mental disability or illness (3 in 5) *did* have a child on the register – statistically significant differences.

Similarly, deviant or anti-social behaviour of parents was much more in evidence among the 'at risk' group. All but one of the parents accused of excessive drinking, and the same proportion of those who were said to be drug-users, were parents of children in the 'at risk' group. Thus, a quarter of the children at risk had a parent who drank heavily, and 1 in 5 had a parent who took drugs, compared with only 1% of the rest of the children in the cohort. A similar and predictable relationship between parental violence and 'risk' was apparent (in a quarter compared with 1 in 10 of other cases). It is no surprise that parental behaviour that is perceived as unpredictable, anti-social and potentially alarming or damaging is likely to trigger concerns for the safety and well-being of children in the household. The earlier 'victim' profile showed similar concerns (see Table 7.2). However, it is also worth remembering that it is still in only a minority of cases that such parental behaviour is seen as a crucial issue.

Table 7.2 Comparison of family characteristics of Who Needs Care?'s 'victims' and the present study's 'at risk' children

	Compulsorily admitted 'victims' (n = 38) %	Voluntarily accommodated 'at risk' (n = 74) %
Lone-parent household	37	50
Stepfamily (father)	27	17
Financial problems	58	60
Parental health problems	30	37
Mental health problems	32	76
Offender/criminal	24	15
Violence[1]	—	25
Heavy drinking	46	25
Drug-using[1]	—	19
Marital problems	62	81
Parent–child problems[1]	—	92
Wider family problems	50	65
Mother abused	24	16
Mother in care[2]	26	21

Notes:

1 No comparable data available from *Who Needs Care?* study.

2 *Who Needs Care?* data includes separations other than 'in care'.

In contrast, fraught family relationships – between parents, between parents and their children, and with the wider family network – were a feature of most of the admissions to accommodation, but they were even more apparent where an element of risk was recorded. In 4 out of 5 such cases, marital relationships were said to be strained, and not surprisingly, parent–child relationships were difficult in 9 out of 10 cases of risk. Poor relationships with the wider network of kin also affected a majority of these families.

We did not ask whether these difficulties with kin had existed throughout the parents' lifetime, but we did attempt to find out if the parents had also had been in care as children, and whether they had been abused or neglected themselves. Too little was known about the fathers, and so many were absent that little confidence can be placed in this kind of data about them. There was much more information about the mothers' childhoods, but even so, the figures may not be comprehensive or entirely accurate, depending as they do on old records and social workers' memories. Nevertheless, as they stand, they show that the mothers of children at risk were no more likely to have been in care or abused themselves than other mothers in the sample. Indeed, the children at risk were, if anything, marginally less likely to have a mother who had been in care or abused than the other children accommodated, though the differences are far from statistically significant.

Although there were only modest differences between the families of children at risk and other families in the cohort in terms of family structure, degrees of deprivation and their own childhood experiences, there *were* features which were much more prominent where risk was an issue. Mental illness in a parent and a range of deviant or anti-social behaviours were much more in evidence among the 'at risk' cases, and although family relationships were difficult and strained for a majority of cases across the whole sample, they were even more widespread in the 'at risk' group. In essence, the families suffered a combination of deprivation and stress which was likely to lead at the very least to what Thoburn and her colleagues have termed 'emotional neglect' of their children (Thoburn et al. 1995). There is obviously nothing surprising in such findings, but if nothing else, they indicate something of the context in which special concerns about the children were being expressed by social workers, and a degree of rationality in the judgements of risk that were being made.

Social services' responses

There were a number of indications that children believed to be at risk triggered professional anxieties, and consequently received rather more attention than other children in need. A higher than average proportion of families were previously unknown to the social services departments, and the fact that a spell in accommodation so quickly became the service response is a measure of their concerns. The remaining majority of 'at risk' cases were already known, and half were open cases, receiving help before accommodation became an issue. The range of services they had been offered was no different from those devoted to other children and families in the sample, but certain forms of support were particularly prominent for this group. Among these were family centres and family aides – both generally focusing on supporting and improving home management and parenting skills in relation to young children. Given the vulnerability of so many mothers, psychiatric help was also frequently given. The families of children at risk were also especially likely to receive a mix of several different services, sometimes amounting to complex packages of family support. They were also better known to other agencies – health professionals, the police, the probation service, education departments and schools – and were clearly subject to the multidisciplinary approach that has become the hallmark of child protection.

Despite this degree of previous and ongoing involvement, however, cases where children were judged to be at risk were nearly twice as likely as others to result in unplanned 'emergency' admissions, which affected 3 in 5. In some other 'at risk' cases, the need for accommodation had been anticipated, but was unplanned at the point of admission. Planning then had to follow rather than precede the event. This meant that in only a quarter of 'at risk' cases was accommodation planned in advance – half of the proportion of the other cases in the cohort – despite the fact that they were better known by social services and had been worked more actively.

Explanations for this apparent paradox are complicated. A strong commitment to providing supports within the home to keep families together may make a shift in emphasis to the provision of substitute care hard to contemplate, except in times of crisis – for parents as well as workers. There is also the volatile nature of the 'at risk' cases themselves. We have noted a substantial proportion concerned teenagers at loggerheads with their families, whose reaction was to run away from home, often at night when emergency duty teams would be drawn in at crisis point. If the parents and young person could not be reconciled, or if the youngster was alleging abuse (as was often the case), accommodation could be seen as the only protective option.

One example was a teenage girl whose mother was well known to social services as a valued registered child-minder. The girl, who had only recently returned from her divorced father's home to live with her mother, ran away from home, stayed away overnight, and the family contacted the emergency duty team. When found, the girl alleged sexual abuse by her stepfather – which was vehemently denied and never proven – and her mother refused to have her back. Accommodation was arranged immediately, but on the understanding that the situation would be comprehensively reassessed within a few days.

Similar crises of care could erupt without warning in other situations. A mentally frail mother, receiving intensive support from a variety of sources, suddenly found herself unable to control the wild and dangerous behaviour of her 6-year-old, and he and his sister were admitted to accommodation the same day. Another couple, in an intense and fraught relationship, exploded into violence one evening, and their two small children had to be removed immediately for their own safety. Under previous legislation, these children might well have been removed from home on a Place of Safety Order. In our sample they and many others like them were now being handled without resort to the new-style Emergency Protection Order, but their admission was no less of an emergency. This issue was also highlighted in relation to difficult adolescents in Chapter 6.

Participation and partnership

Risk, like the troublesome behaviour of adolescents, sometimes challenged the principles of voluntarism and consensus that are central to the provision of accommodation. A quarter of the parents were said by social workers to be reluctant to have their child accommodated. Lack of agreement was further amplified (or exposed) when the processes of assessment and planning were under way. Compared with cases where risk was not an issue, parental participation, more often than not, was a difficult and uncomfortable experience. The quality of their care – or lack of it – was often the central issue, and the public debate about their shortcomings, at planning meetings or child protection conferences, could be a daunting and humiliating experience (see Chapter 12).

Children – and more particularly young people – whose own behaviour constituted the risk, were also sometimes very resistant partners. For example, a 15-year-old runaway girl who was living it up with Travellers and rock musicians twice her age was careless of the risks she ran and accepted the shelter of accommodation only on her own terms – occasionally, and very briefly, when she was tired and dirty and there was nothing more interesting to do.

Social services' stance – and that of other concerned agencies – was also problematic in terms of partnership ideals. In contrast to their marked reluctance to admit some of the difficult adolescents to accommodation, risk was more likely to provoke anxiety and an understandable and often appropriate desire to protect and reassure the child. Sometimes, therefore, it was the authorities who were exerting pressure on reluctant or ambivalent parents or young people.

A bright 12-year-old boy was thought to be at emotional risk from his lone-parent mother's unstable mental state. Her frequent threats of suicide and extreme volatility made him fearful, and he adopted a protective but angry role, truanting from school in order to keep an eye on his mother, but quarrelling and fighting with her as well. A child protection conference concluded that the boy needed to live away from home – something that mother and son were both highly ambivalent about – and that court proceedings would be avoided in favour of accommodation with long-term carers – something that not all professionals present believed would work. Intense conflicts of wishes, feelings and opinion were therefore built into the arrangements from the start, and partnership was bound to be difficult. Social workers expressed their discomfort with the difficulties of establishing a partnership in such circumstances, in strong terms. To them, the voluntary nature of the arrangement was a 'sham' – a pretence that parents felt obliged to go along with, for fear of something worse.

In some cases the threat was quite explicit. A child protection meeting, concerned with a mother's physical abuse of her toddler, reached a 'mutual agreement to admit', but the minutes 'advised that legal action was not possible while the child was in voluntary care [*sic*] but would be instigated if she attempts to remove the child in an unplanned fashion'. Another child protection meeting concerning a child suspected of having been sexually abused resolved that he should 'remain in voluntary care, but should the parents seek to remove him, a review is to be called to consider a Care Order'.

The social workers involved felt implicated in the perceived dishonesty of the arrangements. In a sense, the old power to assume 'parental rights' over a child in 'voluntary care' under the Child Care Act 1980 was being replaced by the threat of immediate protective action should parents fail to agree to admission, or should they attempt to exercise their right under Section 20(8) of the Children Act 1989 to withdraw their child whenever they wished. The effects were similar. An arrangement entered into 'voluntarily' could be converted into something that was essentially 'compulsory' if the child's welfare appeared to warrant it. So the arguments that had been used against Section 3 resolutions in the 1980 Act, which led to their demise – the apparent injustice of taking over parental rights without recourse to a court, and the erosion of parental confidence in the care system – still seemed to apply in such cases. The threat of applying for an Emergency Protection Order or taking the case to court was often sufficient to ensure that parental 'agreement' was maintained.

For the professionals working with these families, the dilemmas were manifold. Was such covert compulsion strictly legal? Was it, in any case, in the *spirit* of the Children Act? Was it qualitatively different from and in any way preferable to the earlier system? Did the ends, the protection of a child's welfare, justify the means? To what extent was their 'partnership' with such families compromised in consequence? And, for the families themselves, had anything really changed?

The challenge of working in partnership in the most difficult cases is obviously a crucial issue, and we will return to it in Chapters 12 and 13.

The purposes of admission

The main purpose in providing accommodation for children at risk – at least in the first instance – was for their protection, and this applied in the majority of cases. The fact that it was not a feature for a minority suggests that for some, although 'risk' had been clearly recorded on file or voiced by social workers, it was less a matter of immediate relevance in the arrangements for accommodation. For example, there were families where an underlying unease about parenting standards, together with intermittent crises of care, put them in the 'at risk' category, but only indirectly contributed to the 'reason' for admission, such as a mother's stay in hospital.

Because such a substantial proportion of 'at risk' cases were adolescents, at odds with their parents, 'time out' (a breathing space for all parties, in which to 'cool off' and renegotiate rules and relationships) was also a feature of nearly half the 'at risk' cases. (We have seen this association already, from another angle, in Chapter 6 on difficult adolescents.)

Using accommodation of the child as a means of arriving at a more comprehensive assessment was also quite common practice, and applied in a third of 'at risk' cases. The child's health and development, and interactions with parents could sometimes be observed more fully within the environment of a placement, though this was not always made clear to the parents themselves. The admission of a small boy suspected of being a victim of abuse was framed initially as a period of respite for his disabled parents, and the social worker was clearly uncomfortable with the half-truths involved – another instance of the 'sham partnership'.

The multidisciplinary attention paid to child protection was also evident in the range of other professionals who became involved with these families. For example, the two young primary school children, who had been admitted when their mother's mental health and the boys' wild behaviour were both at crisis point, were both to receive special medical attention for their hearing, eyesight and speech defects. Social workers and foster carers were to share the task of transporting them to school to try to re-establish a regular pattern of attendance, and were working in partnership with the teachers to this end. Intensive individual work on the children's feelings and self-image was to be undertaken, and shared between a specialist social worker in the department and staff from the local branch of the NSPCC, who knew the family well. The family's social worker would continue to support the mother, in conjunction with the mental health worker, and a pattern of 'shared care', in which the mother played a role in looking after her absent children – accompanying them to doctor's appointments, shopping with them for clothes, and so on – was to be established.

The targeting of whole 'packages' of support for 'at risk' cases alongside the provision of accommodation is also illustrated by our quantitative data. Other cases also benefit, but not to the same degree. Social work support, counselling, group work, home helps or family aides, holidays or playschemes, family centre places and psychiatric help all favour the 'at risk' cases above the rest. The logic is clear and can be defended as entirely rational, but it provokes unease among social workers and their fellow professionals. As the notes of one child protection meeting observed: 'the hospital social worker objected strongly to the principle of putting his name on the register to obtain necessary services', but in reply, the chair explained: 'registration will nail these down and a package of support can be formulated'.

The nature of the placement

Four out of five children at risk were placed in foster care or lodgings – the same proportion as the rest of the cohort. More went to relatives (therefore, a slightly lower proportion went into residential care), but numbers are so small for the former (only four children in the whole sample were officially accommodated with relatives, three of whom were 'at risk' cases) that the differences are of no statistical significance. More youngsters at risk were admitted singly, without siblings, but as we have seen from the total cohort, where more than one child in the family was admitted they were nearly always placed together.

Plans for family contact were made in 7 out of 10 cases – the same proportion as in the rest of the cohort – so there is no suggestion that perceptions of risk lead automatically to restrictions on access. Where there were some differences, however, was in the time-scale that was proposed for the child's stay in local authority accommodation. Very few placements were envisaged as lasting for a matter of only a few days, whereas twice as many were expected to be 'long-term' or were open-ended, with no firm prediction 'until the next meeting'.

Summary

Within the total cohort of children who were accommodated, we have identified a substantial group whose safety and well-being caused social workers and professionals from other disciplines particular concern, and there is a significant overlap with the difficult adolescents of Chapter 6. One in five was currently on the Child Protection Register; more than 1 in 3 had been on the register at some time in their lives; for nearly two-thirds, suspicions or allegations of neglect or abuse had been voiced at some time, and for half, concern about actual or likely abuse or neglect was an element in the decision to accommodate. It is on the last group that this chapter has concentrated.

The presence of so many 'at risk' children within a group of accommodated children contrasts sharply with the situation in the two authorities in the *Who Needs Care?* study ten years earlier, when concerns of this nature would have been expressed for very few of the children admitted to voluntary care. Instead, those at most serious risk (the 'victims') would have been removed on Place of Safety Orders and dealt with by the courts, and others were more likely to be kept out of the care system, receiving what was often experienced by the parents as inadequate or inappropriate help in their own homes. This change is in the desired direction so far as the Children Act is concerned, but is unlikely to have happened overnight. A study by Owen (1992), for example, showed that by the late 1980s a sizeable proportion of the children in voluntary care in one county authority were on the Child Protection Register and could be regarded as 'difficult cases' that had escaped court proceedings. The move towards the use of voluntary arrangements in more challenging cases has therefore probably been a gradual one, anticipating as well as reflecting legal change.

In most respects the family circumstances of the children at risk do not differ significantly from those of other children in the cohort. The widespread levels of deprivation and stress reinforce the findings of several recent child protection studies (DoH 1995) which emphasise the value of treating them, like others, as families of children 'in need'. That this course is being followed to some extent is evident in the wide range of support services being offered across the whole spectrum of families in the cohort, but special targeting of those at risk still occurs, and the power of the machinery of child protection to command resources is again underlined. Where the circumstances of the families of children at risk *do* differ from others is in the degree of mental and emotional stress, in strained family relationships and in parental behaviour which is considered dangerous or undesirable, and here the heightened concerns of the professionals clearly have a rational base.

Despite the greater concentration of support services on the families of children at risk, and the higher proportion of open cases, the majority of admissions were 'emergencies', and most planning occurred after the event. The reasons for this apparent paradox may sometimes lie in the nature of the cases themselves, where family dynamics generate crises that cannot be anticipated and which demand immediate action. But we will explore other reasons for such a large number of emergencies, and means of reducing their occurrence need careful consideration. Meanwhile, our findings suggest that the change in legal measures applied to children at risk, from Place of Safety Orders to voluntary accommodation, has clearly happened on an impressive scale, but the hurried, unplanned and potentially traumatic nature of admission to accommodation in an emergency has continued unabated.

8

The 'volunteered'

We have devoted considerable attention to examining the kinds of admissions to accommodation that were much less likely to have occurred before the Children Act came into force. We make no apology for this, because *change* is what the Act is about and is what we are attempting to evaluate. We have repeatedly emphasised that adolescents whose behaviour was causing mayhem, and children who were neglected or abused or were considered to be at serious risk in the past were, at least in our two sample authorities, more likely to be dealt with through measures other than voluntary admission to care, although a minority were looked after in this fashion.

To complete the picture of all uses of accommodation, we now need to look more closely at the cases that are left: the children who were *not* difficult adolescents, and those for whom concern about risk of neglect or abuse was *not* one of the reasons given for admission to accommodation. As we have indicated earlier, these two large groups overlap, but even allowing for this, they account for two-thirds of all children admitted to accommodation during the eight-month study period. The 52 children who remain (out of 153) were drawn from 30 families, and provide the focus for this chapter.

Characteristics of the 'volunteered' children

One immediately distinctive feature of the children concerned was their age. There was only one teenager among them: it seems that virtually all accommodated teenagers are perceived as troublesome and/or at risk. Apparently, a straightforward child care service for teenagers scarcely exists. In contrast, 3 in 5 of the group were primary school children, aged 5–12, and the rest were pre-school children. None of the small band of ethnic minority and mixed-race children was in this group but, again, because of the small numbers involved it is difficult to draw any firm conclusions from their absence.

The children in this group were different from the rest in other ways, but sometimes to a less marked degree. They had proportionately more health problems and more medical, educational and behavioural 'special needs' and a quarter of school-age children were attending special schools. Given their youth, school attendance problems were less in evidence, but their school attainments were often likely to be seen as poor.

A substantial minority, a third, had a Statement of Special Educational Needs or were being assessed. It is in this group in particular that we find some of the disabled children that the Children Act was designed to include. Although they were certainly not without behaviour problems, some of which were connected with their disabilities, this was a significant issue in a smaller proportion of cases than in the rest of the cohort, and the types of behaviour complained of were often age-related (such as tantrums, enuresis and sleeplessness), and were causing stress within the home rather than in the community at large. Nevertheless, 1 in 5 of the school-age children had truanted, and there were six runaways. That said, nearly half had no significant behaviour problems at all.

Regarding risk, current or past concerns had been expressed for a minority, although in no cases was it considered a contributory reason for the admission to accommodation under scrutiny, hence they appeared among the 'volunteered' category. Eight children had been placed on the Child Protection Register – four of them in the past, and four were still on the current register. In addition, this group of children were just as likely as other children in the cohort to have been in care or accommodation before – 2 in 5 had had previous experience. These similarities and overlaps remind us that none of our convenient distinguishing labels is 'pure' or exclusive, and we are therefore concerned with children at one end of a complex continuum.

Family profiles

The 30 families from which these young children came were rather different from those of the other children in the cohort on a number of dimensions. Very few were headed by both their birth mother and father, and more were lone-parent families. In addition, a minority of children were still in touch with their absent parents. But to offset this degree of isolation and potential vulnerability, these families were no less likely to be in touch with their wider family networks, with grandparents, as ever, providing the most significant support. Nevertheless, as we shall see, such networks were often insufficient to meet the needs of the families in times of crisis.

The average size of the 'volunteered' families was only slightly larger than the rest, but a much more significant difference was the number of children in each family who entered accommodation together. Whereas two-thirds of the 'volunteered' came in sibling groups of two, three or four, three-quarters of the difficult adolescents and the children at risk came in alone. In this sense, a *family* service was being offered, rather than a service for troubled or troublesome children.

Like other families in the study, a majority were unemployed and living on benefits or maintenance payments. But health problems were more prominent: twice the proportion of mothers were described as either disabled or chronically or acutely ill, and illness and/or hospitalisation was frequently a major reason for an admission. In contrast, the parents' mental health was much less likely to be an issue, and the apparent link between concerns about parental mental health and risk to the child has already been made in Chapter 7. Parents in this group were also much less likely to be known as excessive drinkers or drug-users – both factors which were also associated with 'risk' – though, paradoxically, they were more likely to engage in criminal activity. A handful of mothers were known to resort to occasional prostitution to supplement their meagre resources.

Social workers were not without concerns about parenting capacities and standards within this group of families, but levels of anxiety tended to be less than in either of the other two groups we have identified. At the extreme, we have seen that in around a third of cases neglect or abuse had at some time been alleged. More generally, standards of physical care were thought to be adequate or good in 4 out of 5 families, compared with two-thirds of the rest of the cohort, and satisfactory emotional care was attributed to over a third of cases in this group, compared with only 13% in the rest of the cohort. Where there *were* concerns, these were generally related to inconsistencies in handling the child, and were often specifically connected to the illness or incapacity of the main (often sole) carer and/or the developmental difficulties of the child. They were frequently framed in the future tense – 'standards of child care will be at risk if services are not provided' – a proposition clearly in line with the definitions in the Children Act (Section 17(10)).

In the same way, there were also widespread concerns about family relationships, though again, to a lesser degree than in the rest of the cohort. Marital stress figured less frequently – no doubt because so many partners had departed – but carer–child relationships were said to be under strain in 3 out of 5 families, compared with the almost universal problems perceived in the rest of the cohort. Once again, it is differences of degree and emphasis that distinguish this group of families from the rest.

In summary, therefore, this small group of families whose children were generally not old enough to be classified as difficult adolescents and who were not considered to be at immediate serious risk of neglect or abuse were no less disadvantaged and vulnerable than the other families in the cohort. Indeed, they were *more* likely to be beset by problems connected with the mother's health and the children's 'special needs'. But on the whole, these families were seen as coping rather better than the rest, at least in terms of relationships and standards of parenting: the former were somewhat less fraught, and the latter were more satisfactory.

The admission process

The relationships between the families of the 'volunteered' and their social services departments were also somewhat different from those experienced by other families in the cohort. There were greater continuities, rather better working relationships, and admissions were more likely to be anticipated and planned. For example, a lower proportion were 'new' cases, and more than a quarter of the mothers had been in care themselves and were therefore well known to social services. This in turn reflects the fact that County contributed a much larger proportion of cases to the 'volunteered' (34 children from 17 County families were admitted in this category, compared to 18 children from 13 families in Shire). In a sense, the department was acting as the substitute family network that was lacking for those parents. It was also the case that 9 out of 10 parents referred themselves to the social services departments, and their participation in the planning process was much more likely to be described as 'easy' because of this.

The 'need' for an admission was also more likely to be seen as self-evident – in over half of all cases in this group no other service option was considered as an alternative, compared with less than a third in the rest of the cohort. There was, therefore, less likelihood of resistance by the social services department, and the potential for conflict with the parents that might ensue. Related to this level of agreement was the greater degree of advanced planning which took place, so emergencies were very much in the minority.

The purposes and outcomes of admission

What were the circumstances which led to the admissions to accommodation for this group and what were the aims and outcomes? Three main factors stand out: the illness or absence of a parent for other reasons, a limited support network which was not able to fill the caring gap, and concerns about the child's health and development (these latter issues were often connected with their disabilities and associated behavioural problems).

There were two main scenarios that typified this group of admissions. The most common was where a parent's (usually, but not invariably the mother's) illness or hospitalisation created a need for temporary care of the children. Given the number of lone mothers and the size of many of their families, the need was obvious. The crisis of care combined with a limited family support network, which, as we have indicated, afflicted two-thirds of the families, meant that social services were stepping in to fill the gap with accommodation. The inability of the wider family to help was not necessarily due to poor relationships within the network (although in some cases it was), but more often related to their inaccessibility, or to the numbers of children involved. Nearly half these admissions involved two, three or four children, unlike the 'at risk' and 'bad behaviour' cases, where admission of a single child was more usual. The aim of the admission was therefore to provide temporary care in a crisis.

The four young H children, all aged between 3 and 12, typify this kind of admission. Their lone mother was due to have a hysterectomy, but had no near relatives prepared to take them all on, and she wanted them placed together to give each other support in her absence. All of them had some minor medical conditions that needed special attention, and the mother's past experience as a child-minder gave her confidence in the fostering system. In the event, two separate foster homes had to be used, but the eldest girl could be placed with her little sister, and all the children were able to keep in touch with one another and with their mother in hospital. Placement lasted a matter of a few weeks, and the children returned home when their mother was well enough to resume care.

The two B boys, both in primary school, were accommodated for much longer – three months in all – because their mother was severely depressed and had to spend a period of months in a psychiatric hospital.

Although they had aunts who had looked after them for short periods before, they lived a long way away, and the parents were anxious that their father should keep in close touch with them and their schooling should not be disrupted. Social services placed them together in a foster home, a taxi ferried them to their old school, and their father had them home each weekend. When their mother was well enough, they returned home full-time and the case was closed, but with the offer of planned early respite if the mother felt herself becoming ill again.

A second group of admissions aimed to offer this kind of 'respite' in cases where the child's own behaviour was causing stress. The parents had often been functioning reasonably (sometimes unusually) well, but there was concern that without some relief they would crack under the strain and their caring capacities – and therefore the welfare of the child – would suffer as a result. Some but not all of the children concerned were disabled.

Mrs F is an example: a competent and caring mother of two daughters, one a youngster with learning and behavioural difficulties that appeared to threaten both her marriage and the chances of giving a fair share of attention and care to her elder child. Regular respite care to give the family breathing-space to re-form and stabilise while the child experienced skilled and stress-free care was the service offered.

As a lone parent, Mrs K's dilemma was similar in some respects. The younger of her two children was not disabled, but was hyperactive and extremely difficult to control, and she, too, felt at the end of her tether and guilty that she was neglecting her elder child as she tried to cope with his wild behaviour. Again, regular respite care for short periods was arranged, which served the dual purpose of giving both her and her son some relief from the intense interaction with one another, and making space for her to pay attention to the needs of her other child.

Not every case within the group fitted neatly into either the 'temporary care in a crisis' or 'respite' categories that have been suggested. For example, a few breakdowns in parental caring were not because of illness or hospitalisation. Two brothers were accommodated for a matter of a few weeks at the request of their mother, because her husband was on bail for a serious offence, and the anxiety and strain in the household was making it difficult for her to cope with the boys.

The one teenager in the group defied classification. He came from a large lone-parent family where delinquency was the norm. He, too, had committed minor offences in the past, but had chosen to leave his family and live with a private foster mother in a quiet country town. The admission to accommodation was a means of securing the placement by guaranteeing payments, and making sure that he could stay and be the generally law-abiding 'country boy' he so evidently wanted to be.

Perhaps the thread that draws all the admissions to accommodation in this group together is that, as we suggested earlier, the prime intention was to support the family (or, in one case, the foster family) in its caring tasks. This is, of course, a central principle of the Children Act as a whole, and of Part III in particular, where accommodation is seen as one means of doing so. What is distinctive is the overriding prominence of this aim in this group, and the fact that any concerns about the risk of poor or damaging parenting or of seriously disruptive behaviour in adolescence were in the future rather than troubling in the present. In this sense, the admissions were perceived as truly 'preventive'.

This is not to say that children at risk and troublesome teenagers were not offered either temporary care in a crisis or respite in an occasional or regular form. Had our analysis begun from the stated purposes of accommodation, rather than from the characteristics of the families in terms of absence of risk or teenage behavioural difficulties, more accommodations of this kind would have been revealed. As it is, this group of cases shows that this form of support was being offered to some families *before* their situations reached breaking point, but they remained very much the minority (30 families out of 116).

The fact that more families were not offered this kind of service seems a pity, because as we have seen, the basis for a fruitful partnership between the parents and the social services departments was stronger in this group of cases than in the rest of the cohort. There were more mutually agreed needs and solutions to those needs, and a greater degree of planning accompanied the accommodation arrangements.

Partnership was also enhanced by the respect and admiration social workers often expressed for the parents in these cases, in terms of their caring capacities and resilience in difficult circumstances. Mrs H was 'brilliant'. Mrs K 'showed great fortitude – an incredible lady'. In the case of the B boys, it was 'a *good* partnership – better than normal. Dad has worked hard at it.' Work with Mrs F provided 'a rare occasion for complete partnership. She showed great tolerance of the complications and delays of the many systems involved.' No doubt much of the credit for this lies in the personalities and behaviours of the parents themselves, but some may also be due to the speed and quality of service response.

Temporary care and respite were the two main stated purposes of the admissions, as we have already suggested, together with the related aim of providing 'time out' or a 'cooling-off' period in some of the more tense situations. Assessment, protection and behaviour change rarely featured as aims in this group, and were clearly much more applicable to the larger group of admissions where parental and child behaviours were more worrying and were under scrutiny. Related to this was the proposed length of time to be spent in accommodation. For 3 out of 5 the period away from home was planned to be no more than two weeks, and in only three cases was a stay of longer than six weeks anticipated. This was in contrast to the rest of the cohort, where over a third of youngsters were expected to stay that long.

Nearly all the children were placed in foster homes, reflecting their youth, and although social services – like their own family networks – sometimes found difficulty in placing groups of siblings together, efforts were made to cause as little distress and disruption as possible. Most were able to keep in touch with their parents and with each other, most continued attending their own schools, and despite difficulties in finding placements, most were considered by social workers to be appropriately placed.

It is tempting to see within our rough, bipartite classification of admissions within this group of cases both old and new versions of the traditional form of 'voluntary care' that preceded the Children Act. Temporary care of young children in a crisis caused by a parent's ill health or hospitalisation was a familiar reason for offering care under Section 2 of the Child Care Act 1980 and Section 1 of its 1948 predecessor, and lone-parent families then, as now, were particularly vulnerable. The profile of the 'volunteered' in the *Who Needs Care?* study reflects this and bears some resemblance to that of the present group on several criteria (see Table 8.1), although the main emphasis seems to have shifted to primary school children rather than babies and toddlers, and the economic circumstances of the families are even more deprived. What has also changed is the relatively small proportion of cases within the total sample which can be classified in this way. The modern 'victims' and 'villains' – children 'at risk' and 'difficult adolescents' – outnumber the classic 'volunteered' by 2 to 1.

Table 8.1 *Comparison of Who Needs Care?'s 'volunteered' and the present study's 'accommodated' children*

	'Volunteered' (n = 71) %	'Accommodated' (n = 52) %
Child		
Under 5 years	54	36
5–12 years	29	61
Teenage	17	2
On Child Protection Register	1	16
Family		
Lone-parent family	48	57
No wage-earner	51	70
Parental health problems	49	60

'Respite' care, on the other hand – especially that which is planned and repetitive, giving the child and parents some predictable form of relief from each other – was not a feature that was in evidence a decade ago, at least in these two sample authorities. Here, the Children Act's inclusion of disabled children (for whom there is a tradition of respite care) within its definition of 'need' and the Guidance (DoH 1991a) which suggests that such a service could equally well serve some non-disabled youngsters have had a positive effect, but on a very small scale. Part of this is due to the very slow incorporation of disabled respite schemes into the ambit of Section 20 admissions. (In County as a whole, only 27 (3%) of a total of nearly 900 admissions to accommodation were recorded as 'relief' for a family with a disabled child in the year March 1992–March 1993.) Numbers were slowly rising as our study progressed, and as existing arrangements were gradually being drawn into the larger 'accommodation' system. Some respite for other children was also being arranged with child-minders, and again, as long as stays were brief, Section 20 was by-passed. The extent of such support services was therefore greater than our figures suggest.

It is also evident that admissions of this kind are more numerous and put more pressure on the care system than might be immediately apparent. For example, the 30 families from whom the children came represented only a quarter of all families in the cohort, but their 52 children amounted to a third of those in the cohort. Furthermore, children who were involved in regular respite or whose families faced a series of crises of care were admitted several times. Their impact on placements and on the workload of the professionals and administrators was therefore disproportionately large.

Nevertheless, it was clear that social workers would have liked to extend the use of accommodation in this direction, in order to pre-empt and prevent much graver problems, and even total family collapse, but they lacked the resources to do so because placements in foster homes (and residential care) were scarce. It was argued that traditional foster homes could rarely be used for such short spells on a regular or reliable basis, because they were then unavailable for other children in more serious or urgent need. The high rate of emergencies put pressure on all placements and had a detrimental impact on admissions that could be planned. Regulations governing foster homes were also restrictive, preventing some willing foster carers from taking the occasional 'extra' child. Thus, there appeared to be no slack or surplus to allow for a significant growth in respite arrangements. The lessons from local authorities which have set up special, protected respite schemes (Aldgate 1992) would be of value to the majority which, so far, have not done so.

Comparison of 'difficult adolescents', 'children at risk' and the 'volunteered'

Finally, to round off our examination of the range of children who are accommodated, and the complex family situations from which they come, Table 8.2 summarises some of the key features of the three groups of cases identified. Analysis in the first instance was simply 'by eye', and this is what had been described in the last three chapters, but this was subsequently reinforced by the statistical technique of cluster analysis. This also identified a similar trio of dominant but overlapping groups for whom accommodation is now being provided. The challenges they pose to the principles of voluntarism, participation and partnership have already been touched on, and these are explored further in subsequent chapters.

Table 8.2 *Comparison of selected features of three case profiles*

	'Difficult adolescents' (n = 51) %	'At risk' (n = 74) %	'Volunteered' (n = 52) %
Age			
13+	100	43	2
5–12	—	22	61
0–4	—	35	36
Gender			
Boys	47	47	50
Girls	53	53	50
Behaviour			
Runaway	71	28	11
Delinquent	22	3	11
Truant	61	25	21
School			
Excluded (ever)	45	20	12
Risk			
On Child Protection Register (ever)	29	58	16
Household			
Both birth parents	45	31	13
Lone-parent family	25	50	57
Stepfamily	27	18	30
Ethnic minority	10	12	—
Parental problems			
Mental health (mother)	39	72	33
Drinking	14	25	3
Drugs	—	19	3
Violence	14	25	17
Parent–child conflict	96	79	27
History			
Mother in care (ever)	10	21	27
Child in care before	47	38	42
Admission			
Emergency	59	59	23

9 *Patterns of admission in the two sample authorities*

We have looked at our quantitative data as a whole, and at the emerging profiles of three distinctive (though overlapping) groups of cases which were offered accommodation. This chapter will compare experience and practice in the two sample authorities, but first we need to compare the two authorities and the sample areas within them to see how well they were matched, and to highlight features that differ and may, in part, account for any differences in practice.

The extent of the development of the city of Shiptown had been restricted. Inland and along the coast was large-scale suburban development, into which one of the sample Areas extended, but most of which was now outside the city boundaries. Even so, there was a strong link with many of these outlying localities, since a large number of council estates had been developed and were still administered by Shiptown City Council. The city was therefore a magnet for a large hinterland, and there was considerable movement to and from these outlying areas for commercial and entertainment purposes, as well as migration. Around the city centre there were housing estates, but these were smaller than those inland. There was a higher proportion of owner-occupied dwellings in Shiptown than in Clayport. Shiptown was both a port and a seaside resort, and this meant it contained a large amount of seasonal and bed and breakfast accommodation, which provided social services with the particular problems associated with poor and temporary housing and a transient population. As with other cities, Shiptown's population was declining, leaving elderly people and young families to face great social and economic deprivation.

Clayport had many features in common with Shiptown. It, too, was both a port and a resort, but it was much larger and less congested, and some wild countryside touched and even penetrated its boundaries. Four sample areas covered inner-city districts as well as outer suburbs, but the waterfront and a notorious red-light district were not included. A high proportion of council estates of varied vintage were included, along with some private housing and accommodation for service families, but bed and breakfast accommodation was less in evidence. In stark contrast, the fifth component of the County sample was the adjoining rural area, with a thriving market town at its centre, and a wide scattering of villages and hamlets beyond.

Socio-economic indicators

The cities of Clayport and Shiptown

Other studies have shown that rates of admission of children to care vary considerably between local authorities (Packman 1968; Bebbington and Miles 1989), with socio-economic factors as important, but not the only, factors influencing such variations. We found that the two cities were similar in their socio-economic make-up. An Office of Population Censuses and Surveys report (Craig 1985) based on the 1981 Census placed both cities in the same cluster, categorised as 'service centres with less industrial development'. More recently, Forrest and Gordon (1993) provided a detailed analysis of all authorities across a wide range of variables from the 1991 Census. They show that Clayport and Shiptown were similar on a number of key indicators of deprivation. Out of the 306 authorities in England, they both appeared among the top quarter, with a high proportion of lone-parent households, unemployment and lack of central heating. Forrest and Gordon also used cluster analysis, and again the cities were similar. Their material deprivation index is based on indicators of overcrowding (more than one person per room), lack of a car, basic amenities and central heating: both cities were ranked in the top 50, with Shiptown in the top 30. The social deprivation index is based on unemployment rates, youth unemployment, lone-parent households, single pensioners living alone, long-term limiting illness and dependants in the household. Again, both authorities were ranked in the top third, with Shiptown several places higher than Clayport. In yet another study (Wallace and Denham 1996) Shiptown and Clayport appear in the same cluster.

What this shows is that not only were the two cities alike on a number of key indicators of socio-economic need, they were also more characteristic of northern industrial towns than the rural and suburban areas that surround them. Both cities were characterised by older housing, mobile and disjointed families and high unemployment.

Table 9.1 *Socio-economic indicators of the sample areas*

	Clayport No.	Clayport %	Shiptown No.	Shiptown %
Age groups				
Under 5	9,276	6.9	12,267	7.2
5–9	9,329	6.9	10,431	6.2
10–15	10,695	7.9	10,482	6.2
16–17	3,633	2.7	3,539	2.1
Children of all ages	32,933	24.4	36,719	21.7
Total population	134,454		169,710	
Employment				
In employment	55,065	52.4	76,380	54.1
Unemployed	6,152	5.9	8,766	6.2
On government schemes	1,312	1.2	1,003	0.7
Economically inactive	42,627	40.5	55,164	39.0
Total adults over 16	105,156		141,313	
Household tenure				
Owner-occupied	85,003	63.5	118,487	69.9
Privately rented	13,662	10.2	19,552	11.5
Housing association	2,536	1.9	3,627	2.1
Council housing	32,612	24.4	27,853	16.5
Total residents	133,813		169,519	
Lone-parent households				
Households with lone parent	2,273	4.5	2,935	4.0
Total households	50,786		72,551	
Ethnic minorities				
White	133,477	99.2	165,297	97.4
Non-white	977	0.8	4,413	2.6
Households lacking amenities				
No car	15,546	30.6	29,067	40.0
No exclusive use of bath	261	0.5	1,327	1.8
No central heating	14,521	28.6	26,293	36.2
Mobility				
Recently moved into area	16,003	11.9	21,213	12.5

The sample areas

As we noted in Chapter 1, our sample areas consisted of a cluster of administrative Areas in each local authority. In Shire we concentrated on three Areas which comprised the whole of the city of Shiptown and covered a child population of 36,000. In County, where administrative units were smaller and more numerous, five Areas were included. Four covered approximately half of the city of Clayport, and the fifth was an adjoining rural area. The child population was approximately 33,000. For convenience, we will refer to the sample areas as 'Shiptown' and 'Clayport'.

A comparison of the socio-economic make-up of the sample *areas* is a more precise way of investigating factors which might affect numbers of children accommodated and their family profiles than comparing the cities themselves (see Table 9.1). These figures should be approached with some caution since they are the local authorities' own application of census information to social services area offices, and they may have used different methods of calculation. Even so, as with a comparison of the two cities, the sample areas suggest a similar socio-economic make-up, albeit with some important differences.

The age structure of the child population was similar, with proportionately more children in the Clayport sample. There were slightly more under-fives in the Shiptown sample area and more teenagers in Clayport, but the differences were small. There were similar proportions of households headed by lone parents, but there were more residents from ethnic minorities in the Shiptown sample, although there were few in either area.

The employment indicators were also similar, with slightly more both in employment and unemployed in the Shiptown sample, but there were more economically inactive (that is, elderly) people in Clayport. However, there was a difference in the proportion of households without a car. In both sample areas there was a similar level of household mobility.

There were more differences in household tenure, reflecting the balance between inner-city and suburban districts in the sample areas. The Shiptown sample had more owner-occupiers and more private rented housing, whereas the Clayport sample had more council housing. Housing in the Shiptown sample was more deficient in basic amenities.

Resources

It is not possible to make accurate comparisons of the resources available to social workers in the two sample areas because of the way they were managed, distributed and organised. For instance, in Clayport residential resources were shared with areas which were not included in our sample. In Shiptown, family placement was administered by a single team in a family resource centre, whereas in Clayport it was managed in the Area offices, which prevented a direct comparison of the two main means of accommodating children. Furthermore, social workers in Clayport were not all split into client-based teams, so it is not easy to compare fieldwork resources. These considerations mean that the overall child care budgets for the sample areas are difficult to assess and compare.

In Table 9.2, however, we can see that the *types* of resources available to the two sample areas were similar. Both had similar numbers of residential units, family centres and counselling services. The expenditure of the two local authorities on children's services was also similar, both in terms of the proportion of total social services spending and the amount spent per child (see Table 9.3). This displays remarkable similarity between the two social services departments' spending decisions, given that other authorities' spending varied between £52 and £308 per child in the same year.

Table 9.2   Resources available to the sample areas

	Clayport	Shiptown
Children's homes	6	5
Family centres	5	5
Counselling services	3	3
Juvenile justice schemes	1	1

Source: Adapted from CIPFA Statistical Information Service (1991–2).

This evidence suggests that the sample areas were similar across a number of important socio-economic indicators, and that the social workers had similar sorts of resources available to them. Whilst a number of indicators might be used to point out similarities and differences, we are suggesting that those described above are important pointers to social deprivation, family stress and mobility, and have a significant influence on the demand for and the use of local authority accommodation for children. Differences were relatively small, and other authorities in larger cities or rural areas displayed major differences across these variables.

Table 9.3   Child care spending in the two local authorities

	County	Shire
Number of children in area	217,000	353,000
Net expenditure on children's services	£21.1 million	£33.7 million
Proportion of total net social services expenditure on children's services	21%	22.5%
Expenditure per child	£97.23	£95.47

Source: Adapted from CIPFA Statistical Information Service (1991–2).

Profiles of those admitted to accommodation in Shiptown and Clayport

How did these two similar authorities respond to the challenge of Section 20 of the Children Act? As indicated earlier, there were 177 admissions to accommodation involving 153 children from 116 families. Despite a smaller child population, Clayport contributed the larger share – 96 admissions to Shiptown's 81. This difference should be treated with caution since, as noted in Chapter 5, there were problems in recording admissions and interpreting Section 20. Nevertheless, the comparisons that follow offer an insight into the families, children and the admission process in the two sample areas. The information is drawn from interviews with social workers, so it contains subjective evaluations as well as reported facts. We were also aware that differences in the researchers' interpretation in completing and coding the schedules might have an influence, so we were careful to scrutinise major differences between the two samples and to base discussion on more than one variable.

Family structure

The families in both samples were atypical of the general population of their locality. Comparison of the socio-economic indicators for the two sample areas shown in Table 9.1 with the family structures and socio-economic features of those children accommodated given in Annex 9.1 shows that these children were much more likely to be from lone-parent families, to come from ethnic minorities, to live in council accommodation, and that the fathers were more likely be unemployed. However, important differences between the two authorities are apparent. The Shiptown sample included a higher proportion of lone-parent families. A number of factors point to greater isolation and movement in Shiptown: more had moved into the area recently, were seen as isolated, and were homeless or lived in privately rented accommodation. There was a greater proportion of families from ethnic minorities and more owner-occupation, as reflected in the census data.

In the Clayport sample, families were more likely to consist of two parents, although more were stepparents. Social workers reported more problems of low income and unemployment, even though similar proportions were on benefits. The larger proportion in council accommodation reflects the large council estates typical of the sample area, and indicates a more traditional and stable working-class population.

We cannot tell, of course, how far the social workers' perceptions of these families were an accurate estimate of socio-economic characteristics. For example, in the two samples, similar numbers were on benefits, yet the social workers differed in their perceptions of the significance of low income, which may reflect different attitudes to coping in these circumstances. The much larger proportion of lone parents in the Shiptown sample could not be explained by there being more lone parents in the Shiptown area as a whole. Similarly, according to Table 9.1, there was higher unemployment in Shiptown than Clayport, but a higher proportion of the Clayport cohort came from families where the father was unemployed. The larger proportion in the Shiptown sample who belonged to ethnic minority families was also not fully reflected in the census data.

Therefore, even allowing for variations in social workers' perceptions, there were some evident differences between the families in the two samples that were not a reflection of the area from which they were drawn.

Family function and parenting

A number of questions were asked about the social workers' views of family problems and relationships, and here there was remarkable consistency between the perceptions of the two groups of social workers (see Annex 9.1). Similar proportions of families where issues like the health of the parents, concerns about physical and emotional care, and suspicions of abuse or neglect were prevalent occurred in both samples, and relationships between parents and between parents and their children were regarded as problematic in most cases. Concern about the families' care and relationships was expressed regarding most admissions to accommodation, suggesting that social workers in the two sample areas had similar perceptions of risk thresholds, which outweighed perceived differences in the families' socio-economic backgrounds. It might also suggest that the professional explanation of appropriateness for accommodation in research interviews was similar.

However, Clayport social workers displayed significantly greater knowledge of the parents' own childhood problems. In both authorities more was known of the mothers than the fathers, but in Clayport over a quarter of mothers were thought to have been abused as children, and nearly a third had themselves been in care. This may be linked with the smaller proportion of new cases in Clayport, and perhaps also reflects the greater mobility of Shiptown families.

Children's characteristics

There were some differences of age and gender in the two samples of accommodated children (see Annex 9.1), which would have implications for placements. The greater proportion of children from ethnic minority families in Shiptown (see Table 9.1) meant that Shire needed to be alert to appropriate race-sensitive placements.

The health, developmental and behavioural problems of the children, as assessed by doctors or psychologists, reveal few differences. In both samples a relatively small proportion of the children had physical health problems, learning difficulties or were disabled. However, significant differences were reported in terms of schooling and their behaviour. There were major concerns in Shiptown about the education service offered to children who were accommodated, compared with Clayport. For a number of reasons, more Shiptown children were not in mainstream education or had school-related problems (see Annex 9.1). Also, in the more subjective estimates of behaviour problems, the differences between Shiptown and Clayport are significant across a wide range of behaviours. The Shiptown children were seen as more violent and more argumentative, with more runaways and persistent offenders.

Surprisingly, however, the proportion of children who were reported as having no behavioural problems was similar in both areas, as was the proportion where behaviour problems were not an issue at the time of admission. Further analysis revealed that it was the number of different behaviour problems per child that was much greater in Shiptown, rather than the proportion of troublesome children. Also, analysis by age groups showed that the two samples had similar numbers of difficult teenagers (see Chapter 6), but there were significantly more complaints about badly behaved *younger* children in Shiptown: more of the pre-teenagers in Shiptown were runaways, truants and were said to be aggressive or even violent. On the face of it, and as far as social services were concerned, troublesomeness began earlier in Shiptown and came in larger packages – an interesting continuity with the *Who Needs Care?* study, when Shiptown's 'villains' were apparently more villainous than their Clayport counterparts! It should be noted that the social workers' evaluations were similar to those of parents and teachers.

Previous contact with social services

It was suggested above that the Clayport families were better known to social services, and this is reflected in the figures for previous contact with social services in Annex 9.1. More cases in Shiptown had involved other agencies, indicating the strong influence of the 'welfare network' and the extensive practice in Shiptown of planning meetings which included health visitors, teachers and so on.

A wide range of other services had been offered to the families before admission to accommodation (see Annex 9.1). We were not able to record precisely *when* such services had been offered – in some cases it could have been several years previously. What we were able to show, however, was the way the two areas offered rather different packages of services. Significant social work support to a majority of families had been offered by both social services departments. In Clayport, accommodation was offered to families who had been worked with consistently for some time. A higher proportion of families were offered psychiatric help, and there was a greater concentration on services which supported the family's material circumstances – more use of assistance in cash or kind, home helps, family aides and volunteers (this may be related to the greater concerns about employment and income problems reported earlier). In Shiptown, however, the services offered reflect the strong departmental commitment to preventing admission to accommodation established in the development of family centres and resources with a 'preventive' agenda – activities or clubs, playschemes or holidays, and group work.

Once the children were accommodated, many of these services continued to be made available, or were then offered as a part of a rehabilitation strategy. In general, the two authorities continued to offer the same range of services as before admission, although usually at a reduced rate. However, social work support and counselling were offered to a higher proportion of families in Shiptown after admission, perhaps signalling a reluctance to offer a service earlier. In Clayport, on the other hand, social work support and counselling were somewhat reduced after admission, suggesting that social services in County more frequently saw accommodation as a short-term service, where continuing support was not deemed necessary.

The nature of the admission

So far, we have found some differences between the two samples in terms of characteristics of the families and children, and features of the services offered. When we consider the nature of the admission process and the ways decisions were made, however, it is clear that there were major differences in practice between the two sample areas. As the social workers' comments reported later in this chapter illustrate, Shiptown was strongly committed to a 'last resort' response, whereas in Clayport there was a more positive view of accommodation as a planned family support service.

The admission to accommodation in Shiptown appeared to be hurried and unplanned. There was little warning that an admission was about to happen, and consequently little opportunity to plan the placement beforehand. Over a quarter were accommodated by the emergency duty team, and over a third at 24 hours' notice (see Annex 9.1). In Clayport, on the other hand, the majority of admissions involved over five days' warning. What constitutes 'warning' of an admission is, of course, a subjective evaluation: there are various positions between anticipating that a situation might result in an admission to accommodation and actually warning the relevant placements that a bed is needed. It might be that in Shiptown, because of the perceived resistance among managers to admitting children to accommodation, social workers were more reluctant than in Clayport to make decisions about admission at a relatively early stage. The response of the placement providers might also be a factor: if the fostering section responds on an emergency basis, giving social workers the message that they should only approach them when a bed is actually needed, then social workers are likely to be more reluctant to identify a situation as a potential admission. For example, in one Shiptown case involving the admission of three children, a mother was having a difficult pregnancy and it was unclear when she would enter hospital. The problem of placing three children together meant that the fostering team was unable to identify a placement in advance, and planning could not take place. Therefore, although this admission was expected, it was not planned. Whatever the strategy behind such decision-making, it is clear that planning admissions in advance was much more prevalent in Clayport.

Further evidence of the emergency nature of admissions in Shiptown can be seen in the social workers' categorisations of the types of admissions as 'planned in advance', 'emergency' or 'expected but unplanned' (see Annex 9.1). Again, the difference between the two samples was clear. In Clayport, over half the admissions were seen as planned, with a third seen as an emergency. Cross-tabulating the responses to questions about warning and planning reinforces the link. Shiptown's social workers' view of what constituted 'planned in advance' differed from that of Clayport's, since half the cases they saw as 'planned in advance' involved less than five days' warning, whereas in Clayport most planned cases involved more than five days' warning, as did most 'expected but unplanned' cases.

This longer period of preparation for admission to accommodation in Clayport was also evident in the way planning meetings were organised. Annex 9.1 shows that there were more planning meetings related to each admission in Shiptown, but in Clayport the majority took place before admission. Again, this reflects the fact that Clayport planned admissions to accommodation further in advance.

Thus, admissions in Clayport differed from those in Shiptown in a number of ways. Over half the admissions in Clayport were planned in advance, with over five days' warning and a meeting held prior to admission. In Shiptown, on the other hand, about two-thirds of admissions were emergency, with no more than 24 hours' warning, and the meeting took place after admission. Such major differences in the nature of admissions provide further evidence that the two sample authorities saw accommodation in a rather different light.

Partnership and planning

How did the differences between the processes of admission to accommodation in the two sample areas affect relations between social services and the families? What was the nature of the contract within which accommodation was offered?

There appeared to be better relations between families and social services in Clayport concerning admissions to accommodation (see Annex 9.1). Half the parents in Clayport were seen as 'easy to work with', and a high proportion of parents were thought to want the admission. Most social workers in both samples either supported the admission or felt that there was no alternative, but the proportion who did not support the decision was higher in Shiptown. A similar degree of reluctance to be admitted was shown by the children, but apart from those children considered 'too young' to have an opinion, the Clayport social workers found the children in their locality slightly easier to work with than was the case in Shiptown.

However, as we have already seen, in Shiptown parents and children became more involved in planning *after* admission (see Annex 9.1) – a higher proportion of meetings were held after admission, and higher proportions of parents, children and social workers were given tasks at meetings. Significantly, more tasks in Shiptown were concerned with 'working on relationships', perhaps a further indication of the greater involvement of parents and children at this stage, in contrast to Clayport, where there was more planning before admission, and less social work activity afterwards.

There were few differences in the intentions behind the period in accommodation, but respite care was more prevalent in Clayport (see Annex 9.1). In Shiptown there was greater emphasis on a rapid return home, with over half the placements expected to last less than two weeks, whereas Clayport more often anticipated a slightly longer stay, which may indicate that reluctance to admit a child to accommodation correlated with greater efforts to return the child home, and vice versa.

It seems that the Children Act model of partnership with parents in planned admissions was more a feature of the Clayport sample. However, after admission, planning got under way in Shiptown, and parents, children and social workers were more 'task-oriented' than in Clayport.

Placement

Having examined variations in the use and nature of admissions to accommodation in the two sample areas, we can now consider some differences in the accommodation experience.

Most of the children in the Clayport sample were initially placed in foster care, including a handful with relatives, whereas Shiptown placed over a quarter in children's homes (see Annex 9.1). In seeking appropriate placements there was clearly a commitment in both authorities to issues highlighted in the Guidance to the Children Act: finding accommodation near the child's home, not separating siblings, and keeping children in their schools. Few children changed schools because of the placement, although 1 in 5 of Shiptown's children had no school place to preserve at admission – an additional problem in finding a placement.

Shiptown was successful in keeping siblings together in every case, perhaps because of the greater availability of residential care. However, neither authority was as successful in placing children near their family home, underlining the acute shortage of places, and the difficulties this caused in maintaining family contacts and continuity of schooling.

Social workers' perceptions of the availability and appropriateness of placements differed slightly between the two authorities. A higher proportion of Clayport social workers described finding the placement as a problem, but they expressed more satisfaction with its suitability (see Annex 9.1). This could be related to the different systems operating in the two authorities at that time. In Clayport, finding placements was the responsibility of the Area Teams, and this may have enhanced their awareness of shortages but increased their investment in the eventual outcome. In Shiptown, keeping home-finding as a separate team may have had the reverse effect, shielding them from the frustrations of the search but reducing their investment in the placement. Also, the longer period allowed for planning in Clayport may have enabled more appropriate placements to be found, but it is not easy to separate these factors.

Differences in social workers' approaches to accommodation

Finally, in our interviews we offered the social workers the opportunity to suggest what influenced their approach to Section 20 accommodation, in the case under discussion and in general. We asked them the source of any guidance they received regarding when it was appropriate to offer accommodation. In particular, we were interested in the extent to which social workers felt they were constrained by Departmental or Area policy. As with the clear differences between the characteristics of the admissions to accommodation discussed earlier, there were notable differences between the two sets of social workers in how they viewed the appropriateness of accommodation.

Departmental policy in Shiptown

At the time of our interviews there had been no recent document in Shire which outlined departmental policy regarding accommodation and care (although a new Child Care Policy document was issued some months later). Particular policies were mentioned which were seen as 'carved in stone' somewhere – 'don't place children under 10 in children's homes; try the family first'. Social workers also referred to the existence of an overarching departmental policy, but usually with some reservations:

- There is the overall parameter of departmental policy, but it is very wide. It has to be refined locally, as it should be.

- Policies are fine, they do set the tone, but so much horse trading goes on over resources.

- Departmental policy is excellent in thinking, probably, but it falls down when it comes to procedures.

Only one respondent was unsure whether a departmental policy existed at all.

Accommodation as a last resort

The use of accommodation as a last resort was described as policy by a large number of respondents in Shiptown. It was not always clear where such a policy resided – some thought it was explicit or implicit departmental policy, others saw it as located in the local office or particular managers, whilst others described it as the approach of themselves and their colleagues. Not all social workers were happy about how it was negotiated in particular cases, but no one was unaware of its pervasiveness. There were some who saw it as a long-standing stance by the social services department, although no one linked it specifically to the developments in the 1980s described in Chapter 3:

- It is the department's policy to avoid accommodation at all costs. It's been that way for a long time.

- Shire's approach to accommodation? Remove children as a last resort, in a nutshell.

Some linked the present policy to a reaction against previous practice:

- We used to use residential accommodation a lot in the past, but now we avoid it. It is no longer seen as therapeutic.

- We avoid it now, as children have been stuck in accommodation in the past.

- There used to be a lot of children put in children's homes, but it didn't work. It says a lot about our previous practice.

However, although some saw the 'last resort' response as a county-wide policy, most respondents saw it as located in their Area Office, since it was here that they experienced its implications. Such a response was linked to trying other alternatives first:

- We do everything to avoid accommodating children. We explore every alternative.

- In this office we try to offer other services before accommodation. We do understand families' desperation, and offer a range of things rather than take the problem off their hands. Planning meetings are organised quickly, and we offer day care, counselling, activities, support groups. It often takes the heat out of the situation.

- We try the family first, and there are other ways, family centres, groups. It is not a last resort, but . . .

- We offer other provision to forestall accommodation – try the extended family and have a planning meeting. It's a last resort.

Some related the practice to their own experience of residential care or fostering, and to their interpretation of parental responsibility in the Children Act.

- We avoid accommodation at all costs, as it damages them. We try to place them in their own family. I've had experience of fostering and residential work.

- I worked in residential care previously, and I know that they only pick up more poor behaviour there.

- We try to tell parents that since the Children Act, you can't just get rid of your children. The social services department is not going to take away the parents' responsibility so easily. Accommodation is at the end of the line because of our experience of care. We try not to use it unless absolutely necessary. Social services is not the best way: it deprives families of their own resources.

Others, however, were critical of what they saw as a potentially rigid policy:

> *Social worker:* We are fairly strict about not offering accommodation here. But there are always risks when you say 'no'.
> *Researcher:* Is there agreement about when to say 'yes' or 'no'?
> *Social worker:* Not always. It is difficult. But it is better if you are clear about where you stand.

♦ The policy in this office is to say 'no' to accommodation. But what do you do when [child] starts acting out? Tell her to attempt suicide?

♦ It's avoided at all costs. That is the theory, but it's not practical. Not reasonable. Accommodation can meet a need.

Problems were sometimes experienced by social workers in negotiating with managers, who might be seen as rigid, or even as trying to impress their superiors:

♦ You are really up against it [when asking for a child to be accommodated]. You have to make a really strong case.

♦ The team leaders give as little as possible. It's got to be a last resort. They are not easily moved, even after the [mother's] overdose.

♦ You feel you have to justify your decision to management. I think accommodation can help to relieve situations, but we are told no, we must try other things first.

♦ You have to go through the team leader. It can be very stressful.

♦ It's a numbers game. You have got to keep them down. It looks good, but you can't always control it.

♦ The team philosophy is set up by the manager, the way they treat the workers. They enforce the policy to climb the ladder. Show that there's a decrease in the number in care, and you get more brownie points. It's very negative, sometimes care is the right option. But it looks good on paper. I don't really want to say any more.

As is clear from these comments, negotiating admissions to accommodation, both within departmental and Area policy and with managers' agreement, was a difficult, sometimes stressful process in which the 'last resort' response appeared to be overriding, and social workers sometimes found it hard to counter this when assessing the needs of families.

Assessment, colleagues and procedures

Most social workers felt that despite the strong departmental and Area policy, if they were clear about what was needed, then management could be persuaded:

♦   You have to see the duty manager, but they rely on the social worker's assessment.

♦   I base my approach on my ideas, colleagues and the team leader. But generally, it's my choice.

Others were guided by the parents and children:

♦   It depends on my own assessment and what the family are saying.

♦   The young people themselves should be the basis of my decisions, but it's usually too late. Parents and other agencies are more powerful.

Aspects of policy were also enshrined in procedures, which helped social workers. For example, planning meetings were seen as an encounter in which particular situations could be handled under the rubric of departmental policy, and meetings were held with family placement staff and residential managers. The process of completing particular forms was seen by some as structuring the agency's response:

♦   The guidelines are helpful. It is a structured, clear way of doing things.

♦   The paperwork itself forces you to consider the issues.

♦   It's a straightforward process: team manager, service manager, then a meeting. If the parents request it, you tend to go along with it.

Accommodation as a service

The last comment cited above was one of the few in Shiptown that hinted at the use of accommodation as a service to parents. Other social workers suggested that whilst all alternatives had to be tried, the parents could eventually get what they requested. We have seen earlier that some respondents felt that accommodation *can* help families in stressful situations, and that the 'last resort' policy was militating against this. A number felt that accommodation as a service would only be possible if there was a change in the public's perception of accommodation and how it was made available:

♦   There are a lot of preconceived ideas about social workers, that they take children away. They have reactionary, Victorian ideas on [estate] . . . Accommodation as a service can only work when it is offered through community organisations. Preventive work should be done outside this office, where it is not associated with the media view of social workers.

There seemed to be a view that accommodation in an emergency should be avoided wherever possible, but where it could be negotiated through the right procedures, like planning meetings, accommodation could be an appropriate response. A social worker described a family crisis where she had made strong efforts to avoid an emergency admission and the two children went to their grandparents. However, as she learnt more about what the family could offer and what the children needed, she recognised that respite care with foster parents was more appropriate:

♦   In the first incident, the first crisis, it was just the safety of the children. Mum was actually saying, 'You've got to take them 'cos I'm going to hurt them.' In which case, you're talking about a safe place, with a roof over their head. Further on, you get to see the problems that there are, see what the extended family can offer. Certainly, in my meetings with grandparents, they haven't got a clue where their grandchildren are coming from . . . And the support of a foster parent would be appropriate, that's what I would push for if it comes up again.

Three weeks later, the children were accommodated. In this case it is apparent that the 'last resort' response was sustained as a first reaction to the situation, but with subsequent information, planned and respite accommodation came to be seen as an appropriate response. However, this was not true of all such cases, and one social worker described a situation where a previous worker had appeared to deliberately avoid calling a planning meeting in order to prevent the mother having an opportunity to press the social services department to accommodate her child. Once a view of a case was established, it was sometimes hard to alter.

To summarise, in Shiptown a policy based on 'last resort' responses appeared to be prevalent throughout the sample Area Teams, and its rationale was accepted by many – but not all – social workers. Frequent explanations in terms of 'prevention' and 'parental responsibility' were bolstered by views of the damaging effects of care, and the belief that parents should be discouraged from offloading their problems onto social services. 'Last-resortism' also appeared to be embedded in ideas about good management of scarce resources. In addition, Shire's commitment to reducing numbers in care, which had been explicit since the mid-1980s (see Chapter 3), had generated decision-making systems and preventive resources which supported a view of accommodation as a service of last resort. However, as we saw earlier in this chapter Shiptown's 'last resort' stance appeared to be associated with emergency responses, which were *not* seen as being in accord with departmental policy. Where partnership and dialogue could be developed with families, accommodation as a support for families could eventually be accepted as an appropriate use of accommodation. After an emergency admission, positive planning of accommodation was more acceptable.

Departmental policy in Clayport

In answer to our questions about how each decision to accommodate was reached and what influenced or guided it, in County, departmental *policy* (as opposed to *procedures*) was scarcely mentioned. Rather, reference was usually made to the Act itself, and its Guidance, to colleagues and supervisors, and to the social worker's own experience and professional judgement:

♦ The Act itself – I have it bookmarked!

♦ A mixture of Guidance, seniors and experience.

♦ The Children Act Guidance, procedure book, supervisor and team.

♦ The team manager – after gathering ammunition from the Act and Guidance!

♦ My own experience and ideas, plus those of my supervisor. I look at the regulations and procedures after the decision's made!

The independence of the social worker's own professional judgement was sometimes emphasised:

◆ I follow my own instincts, and am clear about those who I'll talk out of admission, because there are viable alternatives.

◆ 'What does the child need?' is my frame of reference. 'When does accommodation become abusive in itself? Can there be long-term shared care?' Not really much reference to guidance or policy, I'm afraid!

◆ It's internalised. I observed the deterioration, and prefer co-operative solutions.

◆ It's basically built in. I go to the supervisor for the small print.

To some, the decisions were simply self-evident:

◆ It's fundamental – she needs accommodation.

◆ It seemed obvious.

The legitimate influence of the families themselves was also recognised:

◆ The boy's views, his mum's views and the foster carer's wishes.

◆ They're very responsible parents – thinking out their own plans. A wonderful family.

◆ I took the mother's request very seriously. There was self-evident need.

One social worker summarised a range of influences that shaped decisions:

◆ The Children Act and welfare checklist are there in the background, plus my personal values about honesty and empowerment. Then, protection is a departmental responsibility – it's in the bloodstream. There's the line manager to check with, and there's what you've seen before, and consultation and partnership with supervisor and colleagues which are good and trusting.

Some common themes that arose from these decision-making processes were the importance of attempting to preserve family responsibility, the seriousness of removing children from their family network, and the desirability of finding alternatives to accommodation wherever possible.

Accommodation as a last resort

The emphasis on accommodation as a last resort which was so evident in Shiptown was only articulated as strongly in one Area Team in Clayport:

> ♦ We only consider it if it's better than home. It's a last resort in most cases.

A team leader put it more strongly:

> ♦ The social services department makes a lousy parent. There's a mass of evidence of instability and the breaking of links to prove it, so social workers take a strong attitude and exert pressure to stick with the family.

In this Area, planning meetings were said to occur only if the team leader had already been persuaded by the social worker that admission was absolutely necessary, so in effect, the decision was made beforehand.

Elsewhere, there were only faint echoes of the 'last resort' slogan. One worker referred to the 'importance of not leaping to accommodate', but was 'not sure if it's departmental policy!', and we earlier quoted another referring to 'talking parents out' of an admission if he believed there were better alternatives.

Accommodation as a service

More social workers stressed the positive value of accommodating some children:

> ♦ This admission is an example of a preventive package which doesn't wait till there's a complete breakdown. We're gradually taking these decisions.

Some were more defiant:

> ♦ Accommodation is part of a package of prevention – and there's nothing wrong with that!

Therefore, in Clayport the combination of a considerable amount of delegated responsibility to small operational units and the perceived absence of an overarching departmental policy about admissions seemed to have generated a mosaic of approaches that ranged from hard-line resistance to a relaxed and even positive attitude to admissions. The Children Act and its Guidance were credited with an important role in shaping decisions, but given their many potentially conflicting principles – the paramountcy of the child's welfare, parental responsibility, the local authority duty to support families and to protect children – it should not be surprising that some are given more prominence than others by different teams and different individuals in different circumstances.

Where there was 'last-resortism', it was supported by an emphasis on parental responsibility, the value to children of continuity of family ties and community links, and the inadequacies of a care system that undermined these values. The proposition in the Guidance to the Act that 'accommodation of a child by a local authority is now to be viewed as a service, providing positive support to a child and his family' (DoH 1991a, para.2.13) was countered by a gloomy view of what local authorities could provide and what they did provide in practice. Where 'preventive accommodation' was promoted, it was seen as a positive support for families who lacked adequate networks of their own, and was intended to pre-empt deterioration and the crises of total breakdown that might occur with such support.

Summary

In this chapter we have identified some important differences between the two local authorities in terms of the social workers' attitude to accommodation and features of the cohort of 177 admissions studied. Given the similarities between the two sample areas in terms of socio-economic indicators and resources, we suggest that these differences are a product of policies, procedures and working practices.

The first important difference to note was in certain characteristics of the families of the accommodated children which could not be explained by features of the localities from which the samples were drawn. In particular, there were many more lone-parent households in the Shiptown sample, despite census data analysis indicating that there were more lone parents in the Clayport area. There were more unemployed fathers in the Clayport sample, although there was more male unemployment in the city of Shiptown. These characteristics are less open to interpretation than some variables, and suggest that to some extent social services chose different families to work with, or conversely, different families chose to approach social services.

Second, there were some differences in the characteristics of the children. Assessments of the children's behavioural problems in the two sample areas varied greatly but this could be the result of differing interpretations among social workers and/or researchers. However, in the Shiptown sample there were many more concerns with educational disruption. In the Clayport sample, more were open cases, and a greater proportion had been accommodated on previous occasions. This does suggest that accommodation was offered to slightly different categories of children. In Clayport, accommodation was more associated with regular contact with social services, hence the children were better known, whereas in Shiptown accommodation appeared to be justified in terms of serious behaviour problems, in particular educational disruption.

Third, the admission processes presented the clearest differences of policy, practice and philosophy about the provision of accommodation. The quantitative analysis of admissions earlier in this chapter is supported by the social workers' comments. Admissions to accommodation in the Shiptown sample were directed by an awareness of a departmental policy which was well established and in most cases internalised by practitioners: accommodation was viewed as a last resort, and there was an emphasis on preventive strategies and promoting parental responsibility. This reluctance to agree to an admission resulted in more emergencies, less agreement with parents, and more difficult working relations. In Clayport, however, departmental policy was not described as a major influence on decisions, hence social workers appeared to be directed more by their own professional judgement and interpretations of the Act, in consultation with colleagues. As there was less external pressure on their decision-making, Clayport social workers seemed more willing to consider admission to accommodation as an option. This was evident in their comments on the positive use of accommodation, and in the higher proportions of planned and agreed admissions.

There may be a link between these differences. The Shiptown sample area contained more children, and had slightly higher unemployment and poorer housing, so we might expect a higher accommodation rate than in Clayport. The fact that the rate was lower suggests that Shiptown social workers made more restrictive use of accommodation than those in Clayport. There was a higher threshold in Shiptown: the requirement to restrict offers of accommodation meant that a higher level of justification would be required to persuade managers that it was necessary – possibly characteristics like being a lone-parent family or a higher incidence of behavioural problems. However, we would only be able to test this proposition that different thresholds applied in the two authorities if a family with the same characteristics were treated differently when they approached the two social services departments.

The differences between the two authorities' approaches to accommodation seemed clear and well-established. They were a product of the histories of the two social services departments, the attitudes of the families who approached social services, and possibly pressure from other professionals. They were also rooted in the management processes and the structure of resources. For these reasons they are likely to be hard to change, particularly as both sets of social workers considered that they were interpreting the Children Act correctly: Shiptown's by emphasising parental responsibility, and Clayport's by emphasising parental support.

Annex 9.1 *Comparison of admissions to accommodation in the two sample areas*

	Clayport (n = 96) %	Shiptown (n = 81) %
Family structure		
Lone parents	36	59
Stepfamilies	30	22
Families with step- or half-siblings	51	28
Children from ethnic minorities	4	15
Families seen as isolated	4	29
Socio-economic factors contributing to admission		
Resident 'father' unemployed	58	34
On benefit	70	72
Low income	62	47
In homeless accommodation	1	9
In private rented accommodation	3	7
In council accommodation	67	53
Owner-occupiers	13	24
Family problems and relationships		
Physical health of parents	46	39
Mental health of parents	55	56
Concerns about physical care	33	32
Concerns about emotional care	83	75
Suspicions or allegations of abuse or neglect	61	67
Concerns about 'marital relationship'	65	78
Concerns about parent–child relationship	81	75
Mother known to have been abused	26	2
Mother know to have been in care	31	21

	Clayport (n = 96) %	Shiptown (n = 81) %
Children's characteristics		
Girls	45	53
Under 5	27	33
5–12	35	30
13+	38	37
Physical health problems	15	10
Disabled	4	2
Special medical needs	26	17
Assessed as having learning difficulty	16	17
Assessed as having behavioural difficulty	10	17
Education (age adjusted)		
School:		
Mainstream	80	65
Special	10	13
Residential	4	—
None (excluded or taught at home)	6	22
Problems:		
Attendance	39	52
Excluded (currently, or in the past)	15	37
Subject of Special Educational Needs Statement	13	31
Behaviour problems		
Violence	19	33
Running away	25	35
Persistent offending	6	12
Occasional offending	17	12
Temper tantrums	9	15
Sleeping problems	5	14
Self-harm	5	10
Sexual risk	17	17
None	26	21
Previous contact with social services		
New cases	11	25
Ongoing contact at admission	58	47
Known, but closed at admission	31	28
Child previously accommodated	55	41
Other agencies involved:		
Health	49	70
Education	34	51
Police	35	46
Services offered before and after admission		
Before:		
Social work support	81	72
Psychiatric help	39	10
Cash or kind	54	36
Volunteer/home help/family aide	31	22
Family centre	20	48
Activities/clubs	2	28
Playschemes/holidays	2	26
Group work	3	21
Day care	30	28

	Clayport (n = 96) %	Shiptown (n = 81) %
Services offered before and after admission – cont.		
After:		
Social work support	72	95
Counselling	33	51
Psychiatric help	30	12
Cash or kind	24	10
Activities	4	21
Family centre	6	33
Admission to accommodation		
Amount of warning:		
Overnight accommodation	14	28
24 hours	21	38
1–5 days	9	23
5 days or more	55	10
Type of admission:		
Emergency	33	64
Planned in advance	51	22
Expected but unplanned	15	14
Planning		
Meeting:		
Held before admission	42	19
Held after admission	33	64
Not held	21	11
Tasks set at meeting:		
For parents	46	64
For children	27	30
For social workers	60	84
Concerning 'working on relationships'	35	53
Anticipated length of stay:		
Less than 2 weeks	36	55
2 weeks–3 months	38	15
Longer	26	30
Purpose:		
Respite care	29	18
Partnership		
Who wanted admission:		
Parents	88	76
Children	37	38
Social workers (or saw it as inevitable)	92	77
Parents:		
Easy to work with	54	32
Difficult to work with	22	42
Mixed	22	26
Children:		
Easy to work with	46	39
Difficult to work with	8	9
Mixed	11	16
Too young	34	36

	Clayport (n = 96) %	**Shiptown** (n = 81) %
Placement		
Initial placement in residential care	6	28
Initial placement in foster care	90	70
Placed with siblings	82	100
Changed school at placement	11	7
Finding placement a problem	42	18
Placement appropriate	91	76

10 Results of the two-year follow-up study

The 153 children who were placed in accommodation were followed up six months after entry, and again approximately two years after they were first admitted (the timing of the second follow-up varied between 19 and 27 months after admission). Because they provide richer material and an extended perspective, we will concentrate on the later findings, but we will make comparisons with the earlier follow-up when relevant.

The picture that emerges is complicated by the diverse problems and experiences of the children concerned, so the general findings conceal vast differences. We therefore attempted to break down the data in three ways: first, groups of children with similar experiences of accommodation; second, case types of adolescents, children at risk and others; and third, the two local authorities.

The cohort was divided into four mutually exclusive groups, based on the different types of accommodation experience that the children and young people had had by the time of the second follow-up.

- Group 1 was the largest (37% of the cohort), consisting of those who had only been admitted to accommodation once, and had left before our second follow-up.
- Group 2 (25% of the cohort) was made up of those who had been readmitted for short periods, none of which had lasted longer than a month.
- Group 3 (28% of the cohort) consisted of those who had been readmitted for longer periods, at least one of which had lasted more than a month (many remained in accommodation for much longer periods).
- Group 4, the smallest (just over 10% of the cohort), consisted of those who had remained in accommodation ever since the initial admission, and were still there at the time of our second follow-up.

Some of those in Groups 2 and 3 were still in accommodation at the time of the second follow-up, whereas others had left it.

These groups were based on only rough outlines of the accommodation experience, so we also looked at the data in terms of 'case types'. Here we departed somewhat from our original analysis in Chapters 6–8 in order to avoid the large overlap between 'difficult adolescents' and 'children at risk'. Instead, we separated out *all* adolescents (all those over the age of 12), who represented 39% of the whole cohort. We knew from our earlier analysis that very few teenagers were considered to be untroublesome in terms of their behaviour and/or the risks they were exposed to, and they could therefore be treated as a reasonably homogeneous group. The pre-teenagers were then divided into those where risk had been a significant factor in the original admission (28% of the cohort) and those where it had not (a third of the cohort).

Finally, the data was also divided according to the two authorities in the study, so that comparisons of outcomes could be made and linked with our earlier findings which showed different intervention styles and practices.

Overview

Before we apply these criteria to the data, we will give a brief overview of what had happened to the cohort as a whole. The total amount of time the children had spent in accommodation or care during the two years varied widely, from less than a month (28%) to more than a year (26%), and nearly half had spent a matter of months in the child care system. About half the children had been accommodated intermittently (so the total time they had spent in accommodation was the sum of separate episodes). In terms of disruption and absence from home, being placed in accommodation is thus a very variable experience that touches some families very lightly whilst having a profound and lasting impact on others.

Accommodation was generally provided as just one element in a package of assistance for the families concerned, as we shall see later. Very few cases (12%) were open for less than three months, despite the very short stays of a substantial number of children, and 3 in 5 cases were open for more than a year.

Two years after the original admission, a rather slim majority of children (57%) were living with their original carers, or within the wider family network – a reflection of the often fraught and complex living situations from which they had originally been admitted. A small proportion were living independently (7%), and a handful were with friends, whilst an unfortunate quartet were in custody; the whereabouts of half a dozen young people were unknown, and the remaining (26%) were in accommodation or care.

We will now look more closely at the impact of the range of accommodation experiences on the children and their families, and at the inputs of social services as they attempted to meet their needs.

The types and stability of placements offered

What form of substitute care was being offered to these children, and how stable was it? We have already seen that the majority of children were fostered in the first instance (though more in Clayport than in Shiptown) and that residential care, boarding schools, hostels and lodgings were used for a minority of young people. At the six-month stage, 2 in 5 children had experienced at least one change of placement, and teenagers were especially likely to experience a series of different placements. At the two-year stage, these instabilities were amplified, both by the length of time some children had spent in the care system and by the additional number of readmissions that had occurred.

Thus, two years on, a majority of 3 in 5 of the cohort had been through at least one change of placement. The 153 children in the sample experienced 363 placements in the period from admission to second follow-up – an average of 2.4 placements per child. However, this average conceals a range of very different experiences, both according to the length of time spent in accommodation and the number of readmissions, and according to the case types we used for analysis (see below). It also conceals the different experiences of individual children, from the 42% who had only one placement to the 21% who experienced four or more (five young people underwent seven or more placements).

Table 10.1 shows that the children in Group 1 (those who had experienced only one episode of accommodation, which had ceased by the second follow-up) had by far the greatest chance of stability, with an average of 1.6 placements per child. Over three-quarters had experienced a single placement, but since half were in accommodation for less than a month, a reasonable degree of stability was to be expected. Nevertheless, for some their stay was protracted, and this is reflected in the small proportion who went through four or more placements during their time in accommodation.

Table 10.1 *Comparison of the number of placements for those in each group*

	Group 1	Group 2	Group 3	Group 4	All
1	77%	36%	5%	41%	42%
4+	9%	8%	44%	29%	21%
Average per child	1.6	2.0	3.6	2.8	2.4

Group 2, those children who had undergone repeat short-term admissions (no more than a month on any one occasion), was the next most stable in terms of the average number of placements per child. Nevertheless, only a minority avoided any change. Regular respite cases, where the child returned again and again to the same carer, formed part of this group, but were small in number.

Sadly, remaining in the care system for a protracted period did not guarantee placement stability for many children. Although 2 in 5 of those in Group 4 did remain in the same placement throughout, the rest did not, with one unfortunate teenager amassing 12 different placements.

Finally, Group 3 (those who had been readmitted for longer periods – substantial numbers were still in the system by our second follow-up) had the worst record of placement change of all. Only two youngsters were lucky enough to avoid a change of placement, whilst more than 2 in 5 had four or more.

Such instabilities can also be examined in terms of case type (see Table 10.2). As expected, adolescents suffered most changes of placement on average: 20 of them experienced at least four different placements, and all those who went through seven or more placements were adolescents.

Table 10.2 *Comparison of the number of placements for each case type*

	Adolescents	Those at risk	Others
1	34%	49%	48%
4+	51%	14%	12%
Average per child	3.1	2.0	2.0

By comparison, the children at risk and the 'others' in Table 10.2 were more fortunate, with similar degrees of stability and disruption. Nevertheless, half were subjected to change, and the likely effects of repeated disruption on young children cannot be overlooked. No less than 12 children who had not yet reached their teens had been through four or more placements, and half of them had been readmitted for longer periods.

Thus, the chances of having to change placement were increased by a combination of factors: the troublesomeness of the child, the length of stay and the experience of readmission. Children might have to enter a fresh placement if admitted more than once (unless this was part of a regular respite arrangement); they might have to change placements if the accommodation episode was prolonged, and there was a particularly high risk of frequent changes for acting-out adolescents.

Less obvious were the effects of placement choice. For example, it has sometimes been suggested that residential care can offer more stability than foster care. Rowe et al. (1989) found that 'premature endings' were less likely to occur in residential establishments than in foster care. It is therefore interesting to compare the degree of turbulence within these two placement systems in our own study. In all, 134 of the cohort (88%) were fostered at some stage. Of these, 48% experienced only one placement, but 1 in 10 had four or more foster homes. For the 47 (31%) who spent time in residential care (obviously, some experienced both forms of care) the figures were similar: 45% had only one residential placement, and 13% had four or more. Perhaps the steadily increasing concentration of adolescents in residential care since the 1980s combined with the reduction in the number of units from which to choose contributes to the apparently greater turbulence in the residential sector in more recent times.

Finally, we can compare placement change in the two sample authorities. Clayport's 86 children experienced 192 placements (an average of 2.2 per child), whereas Shiptown provided 171 placements for 67 children (an average of 2.5 per child). The greater degree of instability in Shiptown stems almost entirely from the children in Group 3: a higher proportion of Shiptown's cases fell into this group (34%, compared with 22% in Clayport) and amassed more placements in the process. The average number of placements per child in Group 3 was 3.2 in Clayport, but 4.1 in Shiptown. We will speculate on reasons for this discrepancy later in this chapter, when we discuss the differences in policies, processes and outcomes between the authorities.

Change of social worker

To a child, a change of placement may be more devastating than a change of social worker, but for families the latter may have a greater impact. Whatever the effects might be on individual cases, such changes are another aspect of instabilities in the accommodation experience. In our study, social workers were generally rather more long-lasting than placements: no child had more than four social workers during the two years of the study, but different experiences according to case type were very marked: 7 out of 10 children at risk had at least one change of social worker, compared with less than half the adolescents and only a quarter of the 'others'. It appeared that where child protection issues were the main concern, a deliberate policy of handing cases on to new workers once the delicate and disturbing phase of investigation and assessment had been completed was sometimes in operation.

Turnover of social workers also related to the length of time children were accommodated, and those who were continuously in accommodation or who had repeat longer-term admissions had most changes of social worker. Such changes were also linked with administrative systems – for example, the existence of intake and long-term teams, where there was a handover if the case remained open for more than a specified (though often quite flexible) period. Staff turnover frequently precipitated by organisational reshuffles (not least the impending moves towards 'purchasers' and 'providers') also played a part.

One mother had vivid recollections of such changes. Her first social worker, whose task had been to investigate allegations of child abuse, was characterised (perhaps inevitably) as 'horrible'. The second, who supported her through the trauma of discovering her husband was guilty, and the subsequent break-up of the marriage, was 'just like a mother to me'. The third, who responded to a request for respite for a difficult and damaged child, was 'very efficient' because she had found what was needed much more quickly than expected, and had left the mother and carer to make their own arrangements, to 'get on with it' with little interference. For her – and perhaps for some other parents – a change of social worker was seen as appropriate and beneficial.

The rates of turnover of social workers were similar in both authorities.

The work carried out during accommodation episodes

It was very clear that in all but a few relatively 'straightforward' cases, where children had been accommodated during a short-lived crisis of parental ill health (these were mainly Clayport cases), a variety of work was attempted with parents, children, or both. In effect, accommodation rarely stood alone, but was accompanied by other interventions aimed at supporting and improving the families' capacity to cope.

Whatever the nature of the accommodation experience, social services claimed to be working on family relationships in a majority of cases. This was especially true of Group 3 (those who had experienced longer-term readmissions), where in every case but two, family relationships had been a focus of work. Such work was least likely among Group 1, where some of the least complicated situations were to be found, but even in this group, 3 out of 5 families were subject to this approach. Working with personal problems was similarly high on the agenda for all, but again, especially for the continuous and long-stay cases.

Efforts to effect behaviour change in more positive directions and to assess risks to the child were most prominent among Group 3, some of whom were among the most troubled and troublesome in the sample. In a minority of cases, work had also been done to prepare a child either for permanence or for independence, and this was clearly linked to the severity of family difficulties and to the child's age. Obviously, longer-term cases were more likely to involve this form of work than those who were subject to short-term readmissions. Lastly, material help - to parents, young people, or both – was a feature in all four groups, but particularly for the families of children in Group 2, which included a high proportion of deprived and struggling young families.

The emphasis of the work attempted also differed according to the nature of the case and between the two authorities. Young children at risk and adolescents (many of whom were also at risk) were more likely to receive a greater breadth and intensity of intervention than the 'others', but the differences were not enormous. Only in obvious features like preparation for independence (reserved for adolescents) and permanence (largely for younger children at risk) were there significant differences. More striking were some differences of emphasis in the two sample authorities. Shiptown lived up to its more decisive image by accounting for the majority of cases that involved working towards permanence. Clayport, on the other hand, seemed more concerned with family poverty, and offered more support in material terms.

After-care

Supportive after-care services in those cases (the majority) where children had returned to their home or community were another measure of social services activity. The patterns that emerged after two years were similar to those detected at the six-month follow-up stage. Shiptown offered more activities, group work, holidays and playschemes, as well as 'family care' for the whole family unit. The crucial role that its family centres played in the range of provision was very evident. Clayport, for its part, was more likely to offer home helps and family aides within the home, and day care for young children. It also sought help from psychiatric services much more often than was the case in Shiptown. However, much group work for adolescents as well as individual counselling and family therapy were all on offer under the heading of 'psychiatric care' in Clayport, so some of the apparent differences between the authorities may have been exaggerated by a different mix and locus for similar resources.

There were predictably greater inputs of after-care services to the families of children who were readmitted than to those who were accommodated only once. Patterns of support also varied according to age. Finally, a small group of families in Group 1 received no further support services once the accommodation episode had ended. All were Clayport cases, and it appeared that this authority was offering accommodation to a few families in crisis whose normal functioning was seen as relatively unproblematic and therefore did not need further assistance. In contrast, Shiptown's 'last resort' stance did not offer scope for this type of admission, though other forms of support through its family centres may well have been substituted in such cases.

'Shared care'

'Shared care' was another feature of the accommodation experience – a style of intervention that assumes that the social services department will not 'take over' the care of the child, but will endeavour to include the family within the caring process. This is in accord with the spirit of the Children Act, with its emphasis on partnership with parents and its stress on the truly voluntary nature of accommodation. Indeed, according to the legislation, all accommodation should be a form of shared care. However, for our purposes we looked for parental participation beyond their involvement in the initial assessment and drawing up of care plans. How actively were they involved in the accommodation episode itself?

We proposed three levels of sharing that might all apply in some cases but would stand alone in others. At its most basic, parents could be encouraged to advise carers on an ongoing basis, sharing details of their child's needs and routines that would help shape their day-to-day care and provide some continuity. At the second level they might continue to take on some parental tasks while the children were accommodated: attending school functions, taking them shopping, to the doctors and dentists, and so on. The third level involved taking significant decisions. Did parents help choose the placement, for example, or decide exactly when and for what purpose the child entered and left accommodation? Were they in charge of the process in the way a parent placing a child privately might be – the consumers of a service?

On this basis we judged that in almost half of all the cases of repeat admissions (long- and short-term) sharing of advice and guidance was achieved: the parents were still very much in the picture. Proportions were lower for the children in Group 1 (just over a quarter), but a substantial number of this group were in accommodation for a very short time, and illness or incapacity of a parent was a reason for admission for many. Time or opportunity for regular exchanges would have been short. At the other end of the scale there was very little shared care of any kind for those in Group 4 (only 2 of the 17 children), and in this group plans were more likely to focus on independence or permanence and securing new ties.

The more comprehensive sharing of tasks and major decisions with parents applied to around a quarter of the short-term readmissions and to rather fewer of the long-term readmissions and those in Group 1. Sharing care on this more comprehensive basis also tended to apply more to the younger children in the cohort than the adolescents (who were often resisting parental involvement), and to children at risk in particular. Perhaps this is an indication of how far accommodation was being used as a form of family support, not simply rescue, for some of the most vulnerable children. An aspect of this can be seen in the small number of cases of planned respite care: 15 children were identified as receiving regular care on this basis (10% of the sample), all but one of them younger children, and over half of them children 'at risk'.

Leaving accommodation

The process of leaving accommodation is best illustrated by those in Group 1. A majority of exits were planned (two-thirds in all), and in a smaller majority (57%) that planning was formalised at a meeting (true to form, this was much more likely to be the case in Shiptown than in Clayport). A substantial minority (1 in 5) were expected but not planned: events had taken their course without an explicit decision being made. For 1 in 8, however, the exit from accommodation was neither planned nor expected: placements had collapsed and there had been no other vacancies, or the parents, young person, or both, had taken matters into their own hands and exercised their rights to terminate the placement. It came as no surprise that adolescents dominated this small, yet significant group. Triseliotis et al. (1995, p.109) note that: 'some young people moved house, changed carers or left school with only passing reference to a social worker'.

Outcomes

Linking the work done and the services offered with outcomes in terms of changes for the better or worse for the children and their families is not easy. The amount of evidence available varied according to the complexity of the case and whether or not it was still open. Comprehensive assessments at exit from care or at case closure were less evident than at the point of entry. Further, our follow-up study was undertaken at an arbitrary point when, for many cases, the work was still in progress and outcomes were uncertain.

Nevertheless, patterns did emerge. The clearest was the link between the four groups and the changes for the child and family that were recorded. For Groups 1 and 2, positive outcomes in parenting, parent–child relationships, material circumstances, risk factors, parental health, and the child's schooling, behaviour and health outweighed the negatives. For many, where some of these factors were not at issue at all, they remained the same.

By comparison, the family circumstances of those in Group 4 were more likely to have deteriorated (or to have remained the same, no better than when the child was admitted), whereas some improvements were noted in the child's behaviour, schooling and health. This seemed to support and justify the child's stay in long-term accommodation, offering a cautiously optimistic view of its beneficial effects.

In contrast, the comparatively poor state of the families of those in Group 3 was very evident. On almost every issue there were more cases of deterioration than improvement, and only the child's schooling appeared to have moved in a slightly more optimistic direction. This added yet more weight to the view that this group embraced some of the most difficult cases and/or some of the most unsuccessful interventions of the social services departments.

Differences between the two sample authorities are harder to define. The predominantly gloomy picture of the children in Group 3 and their families was evident in both Shiptown and Clayport, as was the more static picture of the families' circumstances in Group 4. Both authorities concurred in the generally more optimistic assessments of the cases in Group 2. Only among Group 1 cases was there a more marked divergence. Here, Shiptown presented a much gloomier picture of parenting, marital relationships, parental health and behaviour as well as the children's progress than Clayport. This reinforces the impression that family situations had to reach a more serious state of breakdown before an admission was arranged in Shiptown, compared with the less withholding practice in Clayport. This may also be linked to Shiptown's large proportion of Group 3 cases, where placement instabilities were particularly high, and estimates of outcome were generally pessimistic.

Finally, it is even more difficult to discern clear patterns linking these measures of outcome with case types. The focus for concern and intervention was somewhat different for each type, and the picture is confused. 'At risk' cases that entered long-term accommodation tended to show improvement for the child but deterioration for their families. Adolescents tended to experience the extremes of improvement or deterioration.

The 'others' are perhaps the most interesting group. On many criteria, features of family life or child welfare apparently neither improved nor grew worse. Indeed, for many of them, problems of parenting or risk or behaviour may not have been an issue, so they were the least problematic case type of the three. However, where changes in these features were recorded, problems usually got worse, or perhaps emerged for the first time. Some in this category may have been in the early stages of a path leading to risk or adolescent rebellion.

One more tangible outcome that applied to a small proportion of the cohort was a change to legal status. Fifteen children (10%) were on

Care Orders, and three had been adopted. Residence Orders had been applied to five more. Given the substantial number of 'at risk' cases now being accommodated, these proportions seem modest and may reflect the impact of the 'no order principle'. However, this does not give the full picture, and there were a few cases where such changes were being considered or set in motion but not yet come to fruition. Detailed scrutiny of some of these 'pending' cases raises concerns about delay.

A 4-year-old boy was admitted to accommodation on three separate occasions within six months, at times of crisis, when his mother and stepfather were unable to cope. Supports within the home and day care for the boy proved insufficient to sustain the situation, and by the time of the six-month follow-up he had been reunited with his father and the plan was for him to apply for a Residence Order. Within the following 20 months there were two further admissions, when the father and stepmother were also failing to manage him, and the plan had shifted to 'going for a Care Order'. Later still, the plan changed again. The boy was reasonably settled with his previous foster carer, but the father was in regular contact and was judged to have matured, and according to the Guardian ad Litem in the case, the child's attachment to his father was strong. The new plan was to return him to his father, but to maintain his foster carer as a permanent anchor-figure in his life. By then he was 7 years old.

Another 4-year-old boy had initially been admitted to give respite to his disabled parents, but also to assess whether he had been the victim of abuse. Six months later, he was still accommodated and his name was on the Child Protection Register. The plan at that stage was to continue to intensify support services, to improve his family's parenting skills and to maintain his 'accommodated' status. However, because of their concerns, the child protection meeting agreed that should the parents seek to remove him, a legal meeting would be convened to consider application for a Care Order. In this sense it was an example of 'enforced accommodation'. Fifteen months later, he and his mother had completed a period of attendance at a family centre for further assessment of the likelihood of his being able to return home. This had failed to reassure social services, and he returned to his foster family. Three months later – and two years after his initial admission – a permanency planning meeting agreed to long-term fostering in his current foster home, and to apply for a Care Order. He, too, was now 7 years old.

A toddler of 18 months had been accommodated when his mentally ill mother's health had deteriorated. After six months he was still in accommodation, as his mother remained very ill. At that stage the social services department was planning to apply for a Care Order with a view to adoption, but the putative father was maintaining an interest and was said to be asking for a Residence Order. In the event, it was decided to attempt rehabilitation with the father. Contact was gradually increased, supports were built in to give him assistance, and a phased return home was effected over several months. His foster mother remained in close touch, to provide continuity. Three months later – and well over two years after he was first accommodated – the arrangement broke down, he returned full-time to the same foster home, and the plan was for the foster carer to apply for a Residence Order.

These were not the only cases where the plans changed as events unfolded and where 'permanent' decisions were repeatedly delayed or altered as time passed. The reasons for this are complex. Certainly, the legal emphasis on parental responsibility and the significance of the wider family network to the child encourages social services departments to look for solutions that take these into account before they consider severance or permanent substitute care, and immense effort is expended on this. Sometimes, too, the slow-grinding nature of the machinery of joint decision-making – child protection conferences, legal planning meetings, the court processes themselves – can mean months and even years are spent in reaching a final order. But, in addition, a social services department's own planning on occasion seemed to depend too heavily on the key worker. More than one case was held in limbo for months because the social worker responsible was off sick and no one else could, or would, stand in to contribute to crucial decisions. It was fortunate that in these three cases the stability and sensitivity of a foster placement gave a measure of continuity to the child. Others might not have been so lucky.

Meeting the needs of the child

One final, summarising outcome measure attempted to judge whether the provision of accommodation, combined with any other support services that were offered, had met the child's needs. This was a question we had also addressed at the six-month follow-up stage, and for those in Group 1, who had experienced only one short episode of substitute care with little further intervention, the answers were likely to have remained the same; however, for those who had stayed in accommodation for longer periods or who had been readmitted, the picture might have changed.

In general, the analysis after two years was rather less optimistic than at six months. The child's needs were thought to have been fully met in only 44% of cases, compared with 58% at the six-month follow-up. More cautious estimates that needs had only been met in part were more prevalent at the two-year follow-up – 40%, compared with 34%. The perceived failure rate, where a child's needs were thought not to have been met at all, had also risen, from 7% at six months to 11% at two years. Outcomes for a small handful of children were unknown. It seemed, therefore, that the two-year follow-up revealed deterioration and 'failures' that were not apparent at six months, and some of the readmissions clearly demonstrated the decline. Assessments were at their gloomiest for those in Group 3, where only 37% were thought to have had their needs met fully, and 21% not at all. By contrast, 3 in 5 of those in Group 4 were thought to have had their needs met in full. Those in Groups 1 and 2 fell somewhere in between, with modest 'failure' rates and fully met needs in nearly half of the cases.

Thus, different intervention packages seemed to produce different results, but analysing our data in terms of the three different case types produced still greater contrasts. The needs of adolescents compared with those of the two groups of younger children were perceived as much harder to meet. 'Success' rates for the younger children – whether or not they were thought to be at risk – were almost identical. For 56% of those at risk and 54% of the 'others' there was confidence that their needs had been met, and for 37% of those at risk and 36% of the 'others' they were said to have been met in part. For the remaining few, outcomes were unknown. In no case was there believed to be outright failure to meet a child's needs.

In stark contrast, there were fully satisfactory estimates only for 29% of the adolescents, and although in 47% of the cases some benefits were acknowledged, in 22% it was estimated that their needs had not been met at all. It is evident that teenagers pose particular difficulties for the care system, and that its benefits are, at best, partial, and too often absent altogether, at least in the eyes of the social workers who arrange and supervise their care.

Finally, what of outcomes in the two sample authorities? Their estimates of failure to meet the child's needs in all respects were very similar –

10% in Clayport and 12% in Shiptown – but they diverged widely in their optimism about the benefits for the rest of the cohort. Clayport regarded half its accommodated children as having had their needs met in full, with a third classified as only partially successful. In Shiptown, this situation was reversed: a third were judged as entirely satisfactory, and a half as only partly so.

We have few independent measures that could confirm or negate these subjective evaluations. On average, Shiptown's youngsters did suffer rather more placement disruption, but on the other hand the range of support services and after-care facilities was high. Shiptown achieved a rather higher degree of 'shared care', it was also better organised in planning the young people's exits from the care system, and it was more decisive in closing cases – presumably because it was felt that improvements had been made. Small though the sample was, there was also evidence of a somewhat greater impetus towards permanence, and a speedier arrival at legal solutions.

More speculatively, the pessimistic view of what accommodation can offer that was evident from our first encounters with Shiptown and contributed to its strong resistance to admissions was consistent with its guarded appreciation of any benefits that might accrue. Similarly, Clayport's relatively greater readiness to use accommodation and to regard it as a positive service fits with its more generous assessment of the benefits which follow.

The effects of policies and processes on outcomes

We can now draw together our original data on policy and practice in the two sample authorities and attempt to relate this to the longer-term outcomes for the accommodated children and their families. To what extent were the differences of approach that were noted two years earlier sustained in the longer term; and if they were, to what extent might they account for any differences in the consequences for the children and families?

In our initial analysis, the two authorities diverged in several significant ways. Shiptown appeared to operate defensive gatekeeping, whereas Clayport was less resistant. Admission was viewed as a measure of 'last resort' by most Shiptown practitioners and managers, and this stance was reinforced by a strongly centralised and specialised management structure. 'Last-resortism', in turn, had an effect not only on the lower numbers of children admitted, but on the admission process itself. The majority of Shiptown's admissions were 'emergencies', effected within 24 hours of a decision being taken. This meant that planning meetings more frequently took place after an admission had been effected. Clayport's less defensive stance, on the other hand, led to half the numbers of emergencies and more advanced planning of admission to accommodation. But in Shiptown, once an admission had occurred, planning got into its stride and meetings became more frequent and purposeful than in Clayport.

A continuation of these different styles, and some of their consequences, can be detected in the follow-up data at the two-year stage. For example, over half Clayport's cases were open two years later, whereas in Shiptown the proportion was only 2 out of 5.

Taken at face value, and on the assumption that case closure generally denotes at least partial fulfilment of the child's needs, with no cause for continued support, Shiptown appears to be the more efficient agency. However, Shiptown was much more likely to reopen closed cases than Clayport: 9 of Shiptown's 26 open cases had been closed at least once in the intervening period, and 14 others had been reopened but were now closed. By comparison, Clayport had few cases of this kind.

Apparent differences between the two authorities in terms of outcome may therefore be, at least in part, differences of process. Shiptown appeared to continue in a more sharply focused but episodic style, steered by its generally negative views of the benefits of public care. In contrast, Clayport's somewhat more positive attitude to accommodation seemed to result in a more open-ended and perhaps lower-key approach to family support.

The disadvantages of Shiptown's attitude and style of working may be seen in its larger proportion of long-term readmissions, where placement disruption was at its highest and evaluations of outcomes were among the most depressing. The disadvantages of Clayport's stance may be delay and drift, with a much higher proportion of children in continuous accommodation, and a slightly lower proportion of children who had already achieved some form of 'permanence'.

Yet, despite these differences, most of our broad outcome measures were much the same for both authorities. The proportion of children who were in accommodation two years later was similar – just over a quarter in Clayport, just under a quarter in Shiptown. In both areas, half the children who had been accommodated were back with their original carers. Small numbers in each authority had progressed, or were on the way to Care Orders, Residence Orders or adoption, though the pace of change was slightly faster in Shiptown, and, as we have seen, in around 90% of all cases the child's needs were judged to have been met, at least in part.

In and out of care

The number of children readmitted during our extended follow-up period was striking and contrasts with estimates of readmission rates from the 1980s. In Rowe's extensive study (Rowe et al. 1989) she reveals that a quarter of her large cohort of children admitted to care had been readmitted at least once within two years. The Dartington Social Research Unit (DSRU) arrived at a similar figure (28%) in their own research cohort (Bullock et al. 1993). Our figure of 52% readmitted within the more elastic timescale of 19–27 months may be partly a product of our concentration on accommodation alone. Inclusion of admissions via the courts might alter the picture somewhat, as children entering care through the judicial system are likely to be the most vulnerable, and may either stay for much longer periods or be moved out of care and into 'permanence' through adoption, residence or other less formal arrangements.

However, the high rates of readmission may also point to changes in practice, encouraged by the Children Act, where accommodation is redefined as a positive support for families. Respite arrangements are a small-scale example of this, and the use of accommodation for needy families in recurrent crises may be another. A third possibility is that the requirements in the Guidance to the Act for more rigorous and regular planning for children in the system speeds up the return to their families, but does not necessarily prevent their readmission.

Retrospective examination of the children's care histories reveals an even greater degree of turbulence. By combining information about previous admissions with any readmissions they experienced during the follow-up period we can begin to build up a picture of the degree to which children may move to and fro between family and public care in the longer term. The extent of such movement – or 'oscillation' in DSRU terms – is striking. We know, for instance, that of the 153 children who entered accommodation during our eight-month study period,

62 (40%) had been in the care system at least once before. Full details of these earlier admissions were not available in every case, but we have information for 50. We know, for instance, that for 1 in 3 (11% of the whole cohort) there had been more than one previous admission, and for a similar proportion the time they had already spent in accommodation amounted to more than six months. In this sense they were very much 'old hands' by the time we first encountered them.

By following up the whole cohort for approximately two years we could also chart the comings and goings of these 'old hands' and compare them with the larger group of newcomers to the system. As we have seen, about half (78) of our original 153 accommodated children had experienced more than one admission during the two years, and 33 of these already had a history of care, but they had been joined by a larger group of 45 who were 'first-timers' when we originally encountered them but were becoming 'old hands' themselves. If we discount the 17 children in Group 4 who remained in accommodation throughout the study (another kind of 'old hand'), only 34 of the original 153 children (22%) had experienced a single, completed episode of public care which was now behind them. Had we continued to follow the fortunes of the children for longer, the number of genuine 'one-offs' might have shrunk still further.

Even when care histories are disregarded, the number of readmissions per child during the two years of the project is striking: 26% had been through two or more readmissions, and 15 of them were supported by regular respite schemes, so that in their case such readmissions were planned and meant return to a stable placement. But for the remaining 25 children, planning and placement stability were in question.

For the majority of children it seems that the care system is increasingly becoming a means of looking after children in need on an intermittent basis. 'Shared care' is literally that – with family (or friends and the community in the case of many adolescents) and social services taking responsibility in turn as crises erupt and subside, or more proactively as family stress is reduced or averted by regular respite.

The effects of the pattern of care are sometimes hard to judge from our evidence. In some respects the children who had a long care history appeared to fare no better or worse than those who did not. A similar proportion of 'old hands' and new entrants were back with their original carers or within the wider network of family or friends at the time of the two-year follow-up. On the other hand, we do know that readmissions of a longer-term nature produced the worst outcomes for both child and family, and most readmissions carried the risk of placement change. Where the child returns again and again to the same placement, accommodation takes the place of a familiar and reliable relative, and in these circumstances the social services department becomes a substitute for the extended family. But because respite schemes were rare and available for only 10% of all children, most of those readmitted experienced a change of placement: 4 out of 5 of the readmitted children had at least one change of placement within two years, and 48% of them had three or more different placements, with all the strain of negotiating new relationships that this implies. Add to that the fact that around half the readmissions were unplanned, and the potential for stress and disruption for the child is high.

Thus, if the proportion of 'oscillators' is growing, as our evidence suggests, evaluation of the effect of this upon the children concerned seems imperative. Application of the Department of Health's 'Assessment and Action' records to these children who move in and out of accommodation would be am important first step.

Summary

A first follow-up was conducted at six months, and a second approximately two years after the children and young people were admitted to accommodation (minimum period 19 months, maximum 27 months). The two-year follow–up is the main focus of this chapter.

A third had experienced only one episode of accommodation, which had been completed. Duration of such episodes varied from a few days to eighteen months. Ten per cent were still in accommodation or care, never having left the system. A quarter had experienced more than one short episode, with each episode lasting no more than a month. Just over a quarter had experienced repeat longer-term admissions lasting more than a month.

The readmission rate within the two-year span was over 50%: twice as high as that recorded in studies of the 1980s.

Time spent in accommodation varied from a few days to years. Over a quarter of children stayed for less than a month, and a quarter over a year.

Families whose children were accommodated nearly all received other forms of service before, during and after the care episode.

Three in five children experienced at least one placement change, and the average was 2.4 placements per child. Disruption was greatest for adolescents, and for those readmitted on a longer-term basis. Changes of placement within the residential sector were as frequent as those between foster homes. Shiptown had a higher rate of placement change than Clayport.

Changes of social worker were less numerous than changes of placement, but were particularly common for children at risk. Intake structures, policy, organisational change and staff turnover were all implicated.

Working to improve family relationships and/or effect behaviour change was widespread. Preparation for independence or permanence applied to Shiptown cases in particular. Material help to families and young people was more common in Clayport.

A range of after-care services was provided for all but a small group of families, whose children were accommodated for only one brief episode. A different mix of supports was evident in the two authorities, reflecting differences in the ranges of resources available.

Different degrees of 'shared care' operated in a substantial minority of cases, particularly where there were a series of admissions.

A majority of those leaving accommodation had a planned exit, but this was more often formalised through meetings in Shiptown than in Clayport. Adolescents were more likely to leave in an unplanned way than younger children.

Positive outcomes in terms of improved family and child functioning were greatest for those who went through a single admission or repeated short-term entries. Children who stayed in care continuously were likely to improve, but their families' functioning generally worsened. Both family and child behaviour and circumstances tended to worsen for those who experienced repeated long-term admissions. Differences between outcomes in the two authorities and among the different case types were less obvious.

Fifteen per cent of the children were on Care Orders, Residence Orders or had been adopted. Consideration had been given to these measures in some other cases, and in a few instances they were being pursued. There was some evidence of delays and drift in a few cases concerning young children.

In less that half of all cases were the child's needs regarded as having been met in full – a more pessimistic view than that taken at the six-month follow-up stage. For 1 in 8 the verdict was wholly negative. Adolescents, especially those who had been readmitted on a longer-term basis, had much the worst outcomes. Estimates of total failure to meet needs were similar in the two authorities.

The whereabouts and legal status of the children and young people at the second follow-up were broadly similar in both authorities, despite the differences in approach and process they demonstrated.

In both authorities, combining data on care histories with the follow-up material reveals that most children enter the care system more than once, some of them a number of times. The full effects of this pattern of 'oscillation' warrant further study.

Conclusions from the two-year follow-up

Our extended follow-up of children who entered accommodation soon after implementation of the Children Act 1989 tells us more about the accommodation experience itself and the processes by which it is mediated than it does about outcomes for the children and families involved. We lacked detailed measures of the children's well-being, such as those in the 'Looking After Children' project (Ward 1995), and depended on more impressionistic estimates drawn from social services files and discussions with social workers.

Thus, we have seen that 'accommodation' can take a variety of forms, depending on the nature of family problems and the policies of individual social services departments. At one extreme it can be a short-lived, 'one-off' child care service for a family in crisis which lacks supports from extended family or friends. For others, where difficulties are more complex or long-lasting, a longer stay combined with an array of other forms of support may be the 'package' on offer. For many – and the high rates of readmissions suggest that this is a growing trend which warrants further investigation – there may be several episodes, in response to recurrent crises. For a favoured few, a pattern of regular relief or 'respite' can support a family under strain in the longer term. Finally, for a small number accommodation will represent a long-term separation from their family which, sooner or later, may lead to 'permanence' within or outside the system, or to 'independence' for the young person who cannot, or will not, return home.

It is evident from our data that accommodation as a support service rarely stands alone. It is nearly always one of a number of services offered to families under stress, and not simply an alternative to them. It is also a service that is now provided for a much wider variety of children and young people than was the case under preceding legislation. The needs – and experiences – of adolescents in conflict with their parents or adults in general, and those of younger children who may or may not be at risk, are inevitably different. On the whole, it is the teenagers who pose the biggest problems for carers, and for whom a stable placement and successful outcome are most difficult to attain. Ensuring that substitute care does not perpetuate or even exaggerate the antisocial and self-destructive behaviour of young people in need is one of the biggest challenges that faces the new system.

Given the range of children and young people who are now accommodated and the different purposes and time-scales that apply, it is hardly surprising that its impact is equally varied. Stability of placements is affected by the length of stay, the number of admissions and the nature and degree of difficulties the children and young people present. Allowing for – and counteracting – some of these influences is a difficult task for providers of residential and foster care alike.

We found that 'shared care' as a manifestation of the Children Act's aims to work in partnership with parents of children in accommodation is taking root, but is not universally applied. In part, this is appropriate because the care episode is too short for parents to be much involved, or they may be too ill or incapacitated to play an active role. Indeed, for some, a period of relief from caring tasks, and even decisions, may be what they need. But in the longer term there must be scope for further development of shared tasks and genuinely shared decisions between social services departments and the families they serve. As a move in this direction, in the main study and at follow-up we saw a proliferation of formal planning meetings at which families were present, but we question the degree of genuine sharing in some we observed. Smaller-scale and more informal methods of collaboration may be less visible, but are potentially more effective.

Finally, we have examined the processes of decision-making and implementation in the two sample authorities. Contrasting styles of work and attitude to admission to accommodation have been seen to have an effect not only at the point of entry, but on the detail of the accommodation experience and its aftermath. Most notable are the different patterns of entry and exit, the different levels of placement change, and the speed and decisiveness of decision-making. Yet despite these different approaches, the broader picture at the two-year follow-up stage was remarkably similar in the two authorities. In each, only half of the children were back living with their original carers, and a quarter were in accommodation or care. The rest were scattered throughout the community with friends, relatives, living 'independently' or in custody.

Perhaps we should not be surprised at such findings. It would be naïve to expect that a modest, newly framed support service for families of children 'in need' – however interpreted or delivered – could override or compensate for the powerful and growing influences of poverty, family disruption and disintegrating communities from which most accommodated children come. To individual parents and their children, such differences of approach may be of great significance, but to poor and distressed families in general, their impact is inevitably small.

3 Processes and perspectives on the provision of accommodation

In Part Two we carried out a detailed examination of the nature of decisions to accommodate children, as revealed by our monitoring exercise, and looked at the wide range of family situations in which the newly framed service was being applied. We also made comparisons between practice in the two sample authorities, and looked at the accommodation experience and some of the consequences in the medium term. In this final part of the study we consider in more detail the perspectives involved in reaching those decisions, and the processes by which they are established.

First, in Chapter 11, we look at decision-making in the hurly-burly of the social services Area Office, and then, in Chapter 12, in the more formal area of the ubiquitous planning meeting. In Chapters 13 and 14 we go on to consider accommodation from the perspective of the consumers of the service, through interviews with some of the parents and children involved. Then, in Chapter 15, we attempt to draw together the main threads of the study as a whole.

11

Social workers' and carers' perspectives

The views of social workers about the provision of accommodation have already been described in earlier chapters, either as they applied to the cases in the extensive study (Chapters 5–8) or to the policies of the social services departments (Chapter 9). In this chapter we consider in more detail how the provision of accommodation fits into the everyday crises and working philosophies of area social workers, foster carers, and residential and day care staff.

We gathered qualitative data about the provision of accommodation from several sources. For the cases which formed the extensive dimension of the study, we discussed with social workers and carers how accommodation was used in particular cases. During our fieldwork we interviewed staff in positions where accommodation was routinely discussed and managed – the emergency duty staff, family centres and duty teams. Furthermore, we were often present in social work offices when children were accommodated, and were able to follow the unfolding events.

Discretion, crisis and shortages

In discussing the implementation of laws and policy in local authorities, there is a danger in assessing the actions of social workers in terms of a mechanistic application to actual cases. In Chapter 9 we saw how social workers identified with, but on occasion resisted, what they saw as departmental policy on accommodation. Theories of implementation (Whitmore 1984) or street-level bureaucracy (Lipsky 1980) have demonstrated that there are many more intervening variables than mere implementation. As Webb and Wistow (1987, p.125) note:

♦ All organisations, especially those employing professional staff, tend to evolve and adapt ways of working in such a manner that it is difficult to know how or where many changes in practice were agreed – or even if they were agreed. Many changes, and ways of working, simply 'emerge'.

Decision-making is thus a more uncertain process. Social workers weigh up situations using a variety of local working practices and rules of thumb. They must *interpret* situations in terms of what they see as 'policy' – does this set of circumstances equate with that policy guidance? Having decided what type of case they are dealing with and the appropriate intervention, ambitions may be compromised by lack of resources. Working at the interface between the organisation and the public, everyday problems are handled by exercising flexibility in deploying the law, procedures and resources. There is considerable discretion in making assessments and decisions, but there are also constraints of office practices, gatekeeping procedures and shortages (see Adler and Asquith (1982) and Giller and Morris (1981)). We will investigate such contextual influences on decisions by examining a typical incident in an Area Office that was observed by one of the authors.

A young woman had been running away from home for several weeks. The family had had contact with social services two years previously concerning other matters, but the case was now closed. The mother re-contacted the social services duty office, saying that the situation was becoming very serious and she wanted her daughter removed. They were having arguments, she was not going to school, and she was staying out for long periods. One argument had developed into a fight, and the daughter had been bruised on the forehead. At that stage the duty officer visited, and in consultation with his team leader decided not to hold a child protection conference, but to allocate a social worker. It was not considered a major problem, the dispute would probably blow over, although some risks were identified. It took a month to allocate a social worker.

Having heard nothing from social services for three weeks, the mother called the night duty officer and the police to report a burglary at her home, and that the house had been ransacked. She blamed her daughter and friends, and she wanted her accommodated immediately. The night duty officer did not accommodate the girl that night, but told the mother to contact the office the following day. The next day, the social worker met the family for the first time and persuaded the mother to let the daughter stay the night with a boyfriend, on the understanding that both mother and daughter would come to a planning meeting the next day. The mother was not happy about the boyfriend's family, which was known to social services. Before the meeting, the social worker thought the case had become more serious than a mere teenager–mother argument, since the daughter appeared to be out of the mother's control, and the mother was in danger of causing her daughter serious harm. He felt that an admission to accommodation was now inevitable and appropriate.

The social worker began to look for a placement before the meeting, but found that there were no foster placements for teenagers, and the local children's home was full. He looked outside the Area, and after several phone calls found a vacancy in a children's home in the next town. However, the children's home was reluctant to make the bed available since it would mean there were no vacancies for their own emergencies. The social worker had to get his Area Director to contact the Area Director of the neighbouring town to formally request the placement. He went into the planning meeting without this being resolved.

In the meeting, the mother listed a series of behaviour problems and disputes with her daughter over the previous months, saying that she now wanted a break from her. She was calm and had heard of the possibility of respite care from a previous social worker. She would not agree with her daughter staying with her boyfriend's family since she believed that they were part of the problem. The team manager checked whether there were other family members who might look after her for a while. The meeting discussed various options for working with the family, but accepted that the girl should be accommodated temporarily to allow them both a breathing space. The daughter was surprised that she could not stay with her boyfriend's family, and felt she was being blamed unfairly. She was particularly alarmed that she would have to go to a children's home in another town. The meeting ended with a promise to look for a placement nearer home and to start working with mother and daughter. Meanwhile, the search for a vacancy had continued, and a different children's home had been identified, also in another town. The social worker took the girl to the children's home that night.

What this episode shows is the way in which the assessment of the case and decision-making altered as events occurred and resources were sought. At the beginning, this could have been seen as a child protection case, a conference could have been called, and there might have been an immediate admission. Rather than allocating a social worker, the family could have been referred for family work. Allocating a social worker more quickly might have defused the intensity of feeling. The night duty officer could have admitted the girl to an emergency bed at the local children's home. Social services might have considered it more appropriate for the girl to stay with her friends (however unsuitable). Placement in residential care for a girl with no experience of care or history of disruption is contrary to departmental policy, and making placements in residential units in other areas is also against policy, so given the lack of a suitable vacancy, the meeting could have tried to persuade the mother to wait until a placement was available locally.

These uncertainties and contingencies are by no means unusual in admissions to accommodation. In other similar cases in our sample a child protection conference was called, parents were persuaded to wait for a more suitable placement, the family were offered family therapy, and a young person was allowed to stay with 'unsuitable' friends. At several stages the case could have taken a different course, either speeding up or avoiding the admission. The increasing sense of crisis interactd with local working practices, policy options and routes to resources.

This was typical of the sets of circumstances faced by social workers in our study. There was uncertainty about which aspect of policy guidance to deploy or which feature of 'good practice' to prioritise. In cases of more serious child abuse the sense of crisis was even more intense, as social workers struggled to make realistic assessments of risk and considered judgements. Such frantic decision-making in an atmosphere of crisis and concern could easily be influenced by rules of thumb, shortage of information or a lack of resources. This is not to suggest that such decision-making was haphazard or deficient, but to indicate that attempts to follow policy and guidance carefully could be compromised by the exigencies of the situation. The duty room was often a place of tension and drama. In such situations the ability of the duty team manager to remain calm and supportive and that of resource providers to remain flexible was crucial to whether these crises were handled well.

Working philosophies

Other influences on the immediate situation of the admission were the 'working philosophies' associated with accommodation. Hardiker (1977) has noted the distinction between social work ideologies and operational philosophies, the former being the practitioners' convictions about wider principles of need, harm or justice, and the latter the attempt to put such principles into practice. Cleaver and Freeman (1995, p.68) define 'operational perspectives' as the perceptions people use to make sense of everyday situations. In what sort of circumstances are admissions to accommodation appropriate and justifiable, and what is the nature of the services offered while the child is in accommodation? We noted in Chapter 5 that social workers reported that Section 20 admissions fulfilled a number of purposes – assessment, 'cooling-off' family relief, protection, and so on, and social workers had views on what the period in accommodation hoped to achieve. At the same time, they also regarded some admissions to accommodation as inappropriate, and thought they should have been avoided. Views on the voluntary admission of children to accommodation are complex and based on deeply held convictions of family responsibilities and state intervention. Fox, in her early essay on two value positions in child care (1982), noted the 'kinship defenders' versus 'child rescue' dichotomy inherent in debates about child care. The Children Act aims to balance the family support and family responsibility features of social services assessment and intervention, but it is also open to differences of emphasis and interpretation. To what extent should social services provide accommodation to support the family, or should it insist on the child remaining at home while the family is assisted in sorting out its problems?

Most social workers we interviewed were eclectic in their approach to families, recognising the need to respond in different ways. They appeared to balance both sides of these debates. However, in some cases particular lines of argument or preferences could be identified in the nature of the intervention: admission might be part of a plan to support the family, or intervention might confront family functioning. Having assessed parenting skills and risks to the child, intervention might move to separate the children or enable the parents to regain control. Thus, social workers' interpretations of the purpose of accommodation, and their strong views about its appropriateness could be identified as a working philosophy which shaped their actions. We interviewed a number of service providers – foster carers, residential workers and family centre staff – who offered particularly strong versions of these working philosophies. The social worker's choice of which service to involve might be influenced by a particular working philosophy about the nature of their role, and hence of the purpose of accommodation. These workers did not necessarily offer strict versions of these working philosophies, but some did.

Parental responsibility

A number of social workers approached a case by emphasising the parents' responsibility to look after their own children. This view was most clearly exemplified by a worker at a family resource centre. This centre had been set up in the mid-1980s as a part of a departmental policy to avoid admissions to care, and the same mandate was still emphasised. Families were referred from the local social services office when there were serious concerns about family functioning. The aim was to avoid an admission to accommodation, or to rehabilitate a child who had recently been accommodated. The centre offered a programme of family therapy and group work in order to untangle the family dynamics and re-establish the parents' control over their children. The parents were thus expected to look at their child's acting-out behaviour as a feature of family dynamics and dysfunctioning. The work concentrated on issues internal to the family – love and control, blame and attachment; it did not encourage the problem to be seen as a naughty child who should be removed to be dealt with separately from the family.

This view of how to approach family crises meant that this worker aimed to avoid admission to accommodation at all costs. The removal of a child from a family at a point of crisis because of his/her behaviour could only been seen by the child as rejection, undermining re-establishment of the parents' control and authority. The worker felt that a family should only be split up for very serious reasons. Therefore, the use of accommodation as a service the parents could 'request' was disputed, and the overriding principle of 'the best interests of the child' was invoked to avoid admissions to accommodation.

Whilst accepting that some short breaks might be necessary when family relations were under great stress (for example, during family therapy), the worker believed that accommodation should be reserved for those cases where there was serious risk to the child, or the beginning of a permanent separation. This was based on a strong version of the belief in restricting the role of the state to intervene in family affairs. This approach affirmed that, in general, families should sort out their own problems, although they could be helped to do this, so it questioned whether accommodation is a positive service to parents, since it takes away the family's ability and opportunity to sort out its problems.

An extreme version of this position has been described here, but it was prevalent in cases where social workers thought admission to accommodation meant the family avoided facing up to the 'real' problem.

'Prevention'

Another view also maintained that accommodation should be avoided, but here the intervention aimed to support the family, and thereby prevent admission. Families, especially those with younger children, were seen as facing intense financial and coping problems. By supporting the family with a wide range of interventions – day care, transport, counselling, teaching parenting skills, aid in cash and kind – the family unit could be maintained and admission to accommodation could be avoided. Such a view was based on the 'diminishing the need for care' mandate of earlier legislation.

As well as being a feature of much of the traditional casework support of social workers and the use of Section 17 monies, this version of 'prevention' was associated with family centres. ('Prevention' has been supplanted by 'family support', but Hargreaves and Hadlow (1995) consider that it persists in practice under the Children Act 1989.) Family centres in both the local authorities had often developed from the social services day nursery of the past. They had moved away from offering day care to children to a programme involving parents and their children attending the centre together. In this way the parents could be observed handling and interacting with their children. They were given guidance in parenting skills, and encouraged to talk about their concerns with other parents and staff. Parents whose children had particular developmental difficulties were encouraged to use a range of techniques of behaviour modification or play therapy. Isolated parents were able to support one another and receive advice from staff on a wide range of social and personal problems. The children were also provided with opportunities to play with other children, their particular behaviour or relationship problems were observed, and coping strategies were worked out with their parents. Parents at such a centre told us that they faced a wide range of differing problems of isolation and child rearing. Many were unlikely to contemplate asking for their children to be accommodated, and were referred by health visitors rather than social services. However, such services to help parents overcome their isolation and help with child care were seen by social workers as a vital resource in preventing admissions to accommodation, and might form the basis of a 'preventive package' offered to families.

The view that other forms of help should be tried before offering accommodation remains prevalent, and can be supported by the duty to 'promote the upbringing of [such] children by their families' (Section

17(1)(6)). If parents of younger children approached social services asking for accommodation, but were less vehement in their request than others, they might be referred to family centres. Offering support services in order to avoid accommodation is based on the view that a child's developmental problems or a parent's isolation or lack of skills might endanger the normal functioning of the family. As with the working philosophy based on parental responsibility, accommodation can be avoided by 'prevention'.

'Cooling-off'

The converse of the working philosophies described above is the view that it is legitimate for children and young people to be admitted to accommodation for short periods in order to let a family crisis cool down. This version suggests that in the extreme tensions of a family dispute, intense and destructive feelings are ventilated. In such circumstances, removing children to let the parents and children calm down may allow the crisis to subside. After a short break from one another, they can begin to move towards reconciliation, and a rapid return home is envisaged, perhaps within a few days. The return might be associated with family counselling, or at least negotiating contracts about, for example, behaviour or time-keeping. This appears to be less a philosophy about the relationship between the family and the state and more a pragmatic response to handling crisis situations and the intense demands of distraught parents and 'wild' children. Although there is a link to 'accommodation as family support' (see below), it seems less a principled position and more a reactive response. However, parents felt that 'cooling-off' was an appropriate motive for the state to intervene in the case of difficult children (see Chapter 13).

One residential social worker told us of how young people came into a children's home relieved to be away from a family crisis, and sometimes with a sneaking excitement about the comparative freedom of such an establishment. However, they soon realised that there were house rules at the placement which were as restrictive as those at home. They could no longer wander down to the kitchen at any time to make a snack, nor could they control the television. Home comforts which they previously took for granted became noticeable by their absence. Most young people returned home quickly once reality had set in, and communication was established with their parents, often facilitated by residential staff.

A foster mother who specialised in taking in teenagers in emergencies (up to three at a time) offered a (flexible) three-week stay in which to sort out the crisis. Many arrived at night, when they were greeted with 'a cup of tea, a biscuit, ten minutes' chat and then turn in and get sorted out in the morning'. Parents quickly became involved, many meetings were held in the front room, and for some, if not all, the breathing-space enabled tempers to cool and rules and relationships to be renegotiated.

Whilst this is not a clearly developed philosophy about family relations and the role of the state, if social workers acknowledged the benefits of 'cooling-off' periods they would probably be less inclined to resist the sometimes intense pressures for accommodation from parents and young people. The strategy enjoyed strong support among parents and carers, who felt that such a breathing-space was legitimate and promoted positive family relationships in the long term.

Accommodation as family support

We have already noted how the Children Act 1989 promotes accommodation as a family support service (see Chapters 1 and 8). As a working philosophy, admission is justified since a long-term family breakdown can be avoided by providing accommodation for parental support and relief. Such an approach had been developed for some time in both County and Shire as a service for parents with disabled children. In these schemes parents were offered temporary respite care for their children in a non-stigmatising way by promoting the relationship between the carer and the parent, and allowing considerable freedom regarding when and for how long such stays would take place. Whilst such parental control of admissions to accommodation was rarely offered in the case of non-disabled children, elements of the principle of parental control of resources were hinted at in some respite care arrangements (see Aldgate 1992; forthcoming).

In this working philosophy social services acknowledge that parents are aware of their own need for a service, and see these as realistic demands. As with the 'prevention' working philosophy, social services are seen as filling gaps in family and community support. In some cases, social services offered respite care as a form of 'sharing the care' of the children, in partnership with the parent. On occasion such a service would be made available on a long-term basis to enable parents to remain the primary carers of their children.

A foster carer told the authors of a case in which she had been offering respite care for one weekend a month to a 5-year-old child exhibiting severe behavioural difficulties. The aim of the programme was to give the mother a break from the intense demands of caring for and controlling the boy, and to allow her more time with her other child. The mother was a lone parent, and received limited help with the child from her family. In this instance, respite care was therefore seen as providing relief for the parent, and it was offered in partnership with the mother, since she had recognised the need for the service herself, and was involved in devising the programme – how often, for how long, arranging transport, and so on. There were other benefits. The mother was able to share her concerns with the foster carer, and together they devised ways of working with the child, to which they both adhered. The mother thus saw the period in accommodation as supporting her efforts with the child, and the child was able to benefit from a wider set of social experiences and relationships during the stay with the foster carer. It was a socially enriching experience, although the main justification had been to support the mother.

In this approach to accommodation, the parents are treated as partners in identifying and devising a service which aims to support them in caring for their children. In this way, as with the 'preventive' working philosophy, social services recognise the need for sharing in the care of children who place intense demands on parents. However, unlike the 'preventive' approach, which denies parents the option of accommodation, the 'respite care' approach sees periods away from home as supporting rather than undermining the family unit. By allowing parental control over the extent of respite care, parents were able to see the service as non-stigmatising, supporting their efforts with the child.

Accommodation to enable investigation and assessment

In some situations, accommodation was provided where social services had serious concerns about the parents' care of their children. There was proof or suspicion that the parents had abused or neglected their children, and accommodation was an initial response to protect the child. Sometimes the children were accommodated as part of the investigation process. (In a study of child protection, Thoburn et al. (1996, p.225) found that 68 of their sample of 105 children 'where protective action was taken' left home during the 12 months of the study. Of these, 26 were accommodated under Section 20, 14 as an alternative to court action.) Assessment of the parents' abilities and risk factors determined whether the children would return home. In such protective strategies, the foster carers would be expected to offer a range of opportunities to enable the parents to care for and interact with their children: regular access to their home for the parents, and including them in the daily care tasks. Their observations might contribute to an assessment of the parents' skills and the possibility for change.

A foster carer told us about a baby who had been accommodated following a child protection investigation. The baby had been neglected and was in a poor state of health since her mother was involved in drugs and a violent relationship. The initial rehabilitation plan did not work, and there followed an assessment of the mother's parenting skills and caring capacities. She had various psychiatric and addiction assessments, as well as attending the foster carer's home every day in order to be involved in the child's routine care. Part of the aim of the link with the foster carer was to teach the mother the basic skills necessary to care for her baby, and to enable her to experience positive and protected interactions with the child, and it was hoped she might also build up a supportive relationship with the foster carer. The extent of the mother's involvement at the foster carer's home was negotiated between the mother and foster carer, and her commitment and reliability were used as indicators of her co-operation with the rehabilitation plan. In this case, however, the mother was unhappy that the child was accommodated, and did not co-operate fully with the programme. After a long assessment the baby returned home, only to be accommodated again, and eventually placed for adoption.

In circumstances like these there is a concern that the parents may be unwilling partners in the protection plan, so they may not agree with the admission to accommodation. The partnership is thus a 'sham', since the parents are being forced to accept that their child should be accommodated and their needs and skills assessed. Technically, of course, without a court order, parents can remove their children from accommodation at any time if they wish. However, when child protection concerns are uppermost, an admission to accommodation is sometimes 'enforced', with the threat of taking out an Emergency Protection Order if parents do not comply (see Chapter 7). This threat may be explicit or implicit. Such an approach, which uses Section 20 accommodation instead of an Emergency Protection Order, can be justified under the Act on the basis of working with parents to avoid court until all voluntary options have been tried (the 'no order principle'). As in the case above, at the child protection conference social services' concern for the safety of the child was made clear to the mother, and the mother indicated that she was not in agreement, but was prepared to co-operate. Each party knew where the other stood. Thoburn et al. (1996, p.237) found that an element of 'coercion' was present in nearly half the out-of-home placements of children at risk, although in two placements there was no clear explanation of the alternatives given. Most parents concluded that in such cases it was the 'lesser of two evils'. Such an approach to accommodation is against the spirit of Section 20, but can be defended as a way of working with parents through an assessment of children's and parents' needs, and thereby keeping options open until the major decisions are made.

Team cultures

The working philosophies discussed above are suggested as individual responses to the use and justification of Section 20 accommodation, or its avoidance. There was some flexibility for social workers to invoke them in different situations in order to make a case for or against admission to accommodation. We are not suggesting that social workers held such working philosophies rigidly, although some may have done so. We gained an impression that certain Area Teams might have developed particular ways of analysing and justifying cases which favoured one philosophy rather than another. Some respondents told us that the personalities and opinions of the team or duty manager were significant. The intense working relations and tensions in Area Teams are likely to produce local idiosyncrasies and more uniform working practices. Workers in one Area Office in County explicitly described themselves as subscribing more to the 'preventive' working philosophy, as did all three Shire Area Teams, but it is difficult to pinpoint the extent to which local cultures were based on more than hearsay and gossip. In Shire, one Area Team consistently admitted more children to accommodation, and it was sometimes suggested that they were less diligent in preventing admissions. However, although smaller than other Areas, this Area had a much higher level of poor housing, bed and breakfast accommodation and migration. It is hard to tell the extent to which local policies or local socio-economic factors explain such differences. The influence of the local Area Office culture is difficult to demonstrate without detailed comparison of how different teams would handle the same circumstances.

Summary

This chapter has suggested that the decision to admit children to accommodation can be influenced by a wide range of factors in negotiations between social workers and families. Whilst there are features of the families' circumstances, departmental policy and the law that are not reliant on professional interpretation, they are all brought together in the encounter at the Area Office. Once in the professional arena, parents' demands, children's needs, policy and the law are juxtaposed by professionals who bring to the situation their own interpretations of events and appropriate action. We have suggested that interpretation and action can be influenced by the exigencies of such occasions, the availability of resources, working philosophies and, possibly, local cultures.

This discussion of working philosophies suggests that there are a number of positions in relation to admitting children and young people to accommodation that are legitimate under the Children Act. The voluntary and service nature of the provision of accommodation under Section 20 can be overridden by assessments of the 'best interests of the children' and 'significant harm'. Each of these working philosophies draws on deeply held convictions about the respective responsibilities of families and the state in caring for and protecting children. We have suggested that all these working philosophies were hinted at by most social workers in their assessments of need and strategies of action. We do not suggest that social workers had the discretion to choose to implement one working philosophy rather than another consistently, since family circumstances or crisis situations contain elements which constrain interpretation and action. Even so, some working philosophies might have been favoured by some social workers, managers, teams or social services departments.

12 Meetings

In this chapter we consider the meetings between families, social services and other professionals, since they offer an opportunity to observe the process of working in partnership and negotiating the provision of family support under Part III of the Children Act 1989. Twenty-nine meetings were observed, the majority of them in Shiptown, and detailed recordings were made of the process and content. The authors' field notes tried to record the gist of every contribution, and where possible, the actual words used. Two meetings were tape-recorded with the permission of all participants. The meetings selected for observation were those which involved consideration of accommodation, and where the social workers felt families would agree to our presence. They were evenly distributed in terms of their purpose: preventing admission to accommodation, agreeing to admit, planning after an admission, or reviewing rehabilitation plans. Most were planning meetings, but three were child protection reviews, and one was an initial child protection conference.

Meetings between families, social services and other professionals to consider the needs of children and to review services in relation to looking after children or child protection are subject to regulation; however, more informal planning meetings have become an important element in the provision and review of Part III services in many local authorities. (There has been substantial research into statutory reviews (for example, Gardner 1985; McDonnell and Aldgate 1984; Sinclair 1984) and child protection conferences (for example, Farmer and Owen 1995; Thoburn et al. 1996), but the only work to date on more informal meetings is Owen (1992) on pre-admission meetings.) Planning meetings have similar features to child protection conferences, but there are also important differences. Planning meetings aim to gather information and discuss concerns with families and professionals, with a view to providing a package of services to meet those concerns. In child protection conferences, particularly the initial conference, there has been an emphasis on considering evidence, with less concentration on developing 'protection plans' (Farmer and Owen 1995, p.179). Lewis (1994, p.104) describes them as a 'pseudo court'. The promotion of partnership here is linked to a 'citizen's right' to hear such evidence and contribute to decisions on appropriate action (DoH/Social Services Inspectorate 1995, p.10). In planning meetings and child protection reviews, on the other hand, the 'facts' are generally already known to most participants, and the discussion aims to establish agreement about need and to identify appropriate services, so it might be expected that interaction with parents would be less investigative, not accusatory and offer more opportunities for participation than child protection conferences.

The structure of the meetings

There was a similar structure to most of the meetings, but with significant exceptions (for example, there were important differences in structure, the use of evidence and formality compared with the child protection conferences described by Thoburn et al. (1993, Appendix 3)). They were chaired by a team manager or senior practitioner, usually with the social worker, parents, teenagers, other professionals and a minute-taker present. On average, meetings involved 10 people in Shiptown, compared to 6 in Clayport, but on one occasion in Shiptown there were 19. In Clayport there were few other professionals at the planning meetings observed, but since only six meetings were observed in Clayport, we cannot assume that this was normal practice. However, as discussed in Chapter 9, County's guidance, in contrast to Shire, hints that planning meetings are held primarily to allow families and social services to meet.

Participants were invited to introduce themselves, giving their name and organisation, but usually without explaining what their job entailed or why they were at the meeting. The appropriate social worker summarised the most recent events and the purpose of the meeting, sometimes with a written briefing sheet or case summary. The parents were then asked if they wished to comment on the report or indicate mistakes.

Next, other professionals were invited to make their contribution. Some professionals regularly attended meetings, others only occasionally. The most frequent contributors were teachers, health visitors, family centre workers, foster parents, residential staff and education welfare officers, with less regular contributions from therapists, GPs, psychiatrists, nursing staff, housing representatives and solicitors. In the meetings observed, the number of professionals present varied from two (the social worker and team leader) to 11.

The professionals could contribute in one of three ways. First, those already known to or providing a service to the family were invited to make the initial contributions, especially teachers, foster parents, residential staff, health visitors and family centre staff. These professionals often had a specific point of view on the case which they wished the meeting to hear, and they might have requested that a meeting be convened. Second, some professionals – particularly health visitors and education welfare officers – offered a view of the child and family from the perspectives of their organisations, whether or not they knew the family well. Sometimes this gave rise to complaints from the parents, since such representatives were unknown to the family yet still made a contribution. Third, some contributors were unknown to the family but were invited because of their expertise or because they might offer a service to the family – for example, family placement social workers, family centre staff. The precise membership of each meeting was important, for although some members would be expected to be invited, omitting to invite certain professionals or inviting others could make a difference to the discussion.

After each contribution the parents were usually invited to comment. The other professionals rarely spoke at this stage, saving their comments for their turn. When all the professionals had spoken, the parents and/or children were offered the chance to make a general contribution, with the chair usually inviting comment on concerns raised by the professionals. There then followed a period of open discussion, during which the parents, children and professionals were able to contribute. Contributions were usually made via the chair, with the professionals volunteering comments or points of view, as well as being invited to do so. In this task of asking questions in order to direct the discussion, the chair was sometimes supported by the social worker, eager to ensure that particular contentious areas were covered.

The discussion merged into a decision-making period, without a sharp break. It was hard to pinpoint when decisions were made, but they might be identified as 'decisions' when the chair began to close down discussion and summarise where the meeting had got to. In child protection conferences, the decision to place the child's name on the Child Protection Register or remove it was specifically put to the 'core team'. Unlike a panel involved in gatekeeping of resources, participants were not asked to endorse a decision to allocate a specific resource or set out a strategy of intervention. However, it was generally assumed that unless there were specific objections, all present would go along with the 'decisions' as summarised by the chair and reported in the minutes. Particular efforts were made to set target dates for services to be made available or for parents to make their position clear. The minutes recorded the decisions made and the targets set, rather than the detailed discussion, and were an important part of the meeting, since they served to transform discussion into decisions, commitments and hence action. They were circulated to all present, and would form the starting point for the next meeting.

Most planning meetings followed this pattern, and in general there was a formal approach, with contributions and discussion directed through the chair. However, other structures were possible. Some meetings moved through the 'information' quickly, and spent more time on discussion, particularly if there were fewer professional contributions or where the 'facts' were well known. In these smaller meetings there was more of a dialogue between social services and the family. Other meetings reversed the roles completely, with the family members providing the information and outlining the problem to be solved.

Parents' participation in meetings

A simple typology would neither do justice to the complexity of the meetings observed nor make it easier to evaluate decision-making. We will consider the meetings in terms of the nature of the interaction between the parents and professionals. We will not discuss the participation of young people in these meetings, since they were present in only eight. However, it can be noted that they generally appeared to be supported in such meetings. They appeared to play a cautious role, criticising neither their parents nor their placements. (See Chapter 14.) Parental participation in all aspects of decision-making has been emphasised in the Guidance on the planning process (DoH 1991b, para.2.49). Research has supported the importance of parental participation in child protection conferences (Lewis 1992). The DoH/Social Services Inspectorate (1995) practice guide outlines different levels of partnership – information-giving, involvement, participation and partnership – offering a useful way of approaching these meetings.

Some parents say little

In about a quarter of the meetings observed the parents contributed little. They only spoke when invited to do so, and their contributions were short replies to specific questions. As mentioned above, parents were usually invited to respond to the professionals' contributions, especially the opening remarks of the social worker.

MEETING 1

[*The meeting has had the opportunity to read three reports.*]

Chair [*to mother*]: Have you anything to say about the reports?

Mother: I've not much to say, really.

Chair: Are they unfair at all?

Mother: Fair-ish. It doesn't say that I am still seeking help.

[*The social worker is asked to explain the first contact and request for accommodation.*]

Chair [to father]: Do you want to say anything about the reports?

Father: No.

Chair: Are they fair?

Father: It depends on your perspective. They are factual.

These parents had little previous contact with social services, and appeared overwhelmed by the occasion and the information made available to the meeting. In this extract the mother offered a defence of herself by mentioning that her seeking help had not been noted, and the father hinted at the difference between facts and interpretation. Throughout the rest of the meeting the parents contributed little, and their position in relation to the accommodation of the child was only made clear towards the end of the conference with the help of their respective solicitors. This was a child protection review, and of the 115 separate contributions in the meeting that were noted, only 11 were by the parents. At a planning meeting on the same case a few weeks later the mother similarly said little, making 10 contributions out of 97.

At a planning meeting, concern had been expressed about the children's hygiene, both by their teachers and an outreach programme at a children's home, where they 'always had a bath'. The mother had blamed the children and defended her efforts to get them to look after themselves. Later, however, her defence was challenged:

MEETING 2

Social worker: There is one issue I want to bring up. All the animals in the home: it means the dogs are kept in the bathroom when you go out.

Mother: It's not like that. Only one, because he runs away.

Teacher: I remember that. The boys mentioned that.

Chair: You need to look at that.

Young person: There is a field nearby.

Chair: It is important.

The hygiene issue was directed away from the children and aimed at the mother, being substantiated by the teacher and the young person quoted above. The intervention humiliated the mother and challenged her presentation as the innocent party, locating her as a prime source of the problem. It seems that this outcome was intended by the social worker, in order to highlight particular concerns, but also to establish the mother's culpability. Her silence was not enough to defend herself. The mother made 8 contributions out of 41.

Faced with such criticism, some parents attempted to defend themselves by contesting the information. Conflict often arose when professionals attempted to make a general comment on a parent's care, but the parent contested the specific evidence used for the assessment.

A social worker had been asked by the chair at a child protection review to comment on the mother's physical care of the children. She talked about food and clothing at length, painting a picture of poor but not negligent parenting:

MEETING 3

> *Social worker:* My concern is that when I do visit, I do see the children eating a lot of sweets and other things, crisps, and I'm very conscious of that. Now obviously, when I visit that's just a snippet of the day, but I do observe that. Maybe other people can comment from what they've observed about the diet, but I still feel concerned about the children's diet, and I know that there has been some concerns about Ellen and her weight gain . . .

The social worker went on to describe the poor housing conditions, and then brought up concerns about the children's clothing. The mother defended herself in detail:

> *Mother:* About the socks and things. I mean, I try to get her socks on and she just walks out of the front door without them, and I think, 'Well, it's up to you if you want to be cold, then' . . . They are all laid out for her to wear . . . They do have a cooked meal at home, and then I just sort of make sandwiches for their tea, but if they're hungry when they come home from school then sometimes I will give them a cooked dinner again, but I've got to cut down on Ellen. But I don't think it's fair for Terry to have a cooked dinner and not Ellen.

We can see how detailed criticisms were made of the mother's care of her children in the course of a general assessment of adequacy, but the mother challenges the specific allegations. Later, the mother's motivation to be helped was challenged when a report was given of the failure of a home economist to make an appointment. Again, the mother's response was to challenge the specifics – she had not received letters. The importance of a lack of co-operation was recognised by all participants, and precipitated the first involvement of the social services department's solicitor:

> *Solicitor:* What was she saying? Sorry, you might be able to tell me, what were the reasons for you not wanting to attend?
>
> *Mother:* The last two weeks was because Neil, I had to bring Neil home from school dinners, and I was actually staying in the school dinner hall and then coming out. By the time I got Terry home, given him his dinner and got back to school and all his sleep, I just didn't have the time . . .

The mother did not answer the question, 'Why did you not want to attend?', but rather, 'Why could you not attend?' More important, this extract demonstrates the uncertain position of the mother in the meeting, since the solicitor's question was initially directed to the chair, but then redirected to the mother. Is it appropriate to challenge the mother directly, or to seek the professionals' view of the mother's motivation? Is she at the meeting as a participant or an observer, to be talked about or spoken to? Most contributors used the formal mode of address, telling the chair what the mother was like, usually with no eye contact, reference to or acknowledgement from the mother (compare this with Thoburn et al. 1993, p.340).

This meeting was tape-recorded, so a more detailed count of the contributions is possible. There were 394 contributions, of which 69 were by the parent. However, 19 of these were procedural (acknowledging introductions or information), and 30 were no more than a few words. The mother contributed when she was engaged in a dialogue with the chair or, as above, when specific accusations were contested. For long periods she did not speak – not only when the professionals were making their contribution, but also during the discussion phase.

Other parents spoke little, but used their contribution to make their position clear:

MEETING 4

[*The mother is invited to respond to the briefing sheet.*]

Mother: There are one or two alterations. Point 4: [daughter] does not look after the younger children. And she visits every Sunday. I am very worried about the running away, and where she goes to if she wanders further. I am in regular contact with [foster parent]. She is usually OK on the Sunday visits, but can be hyperactive. As she has grown up more, there is more of a bond, and she talks more. But I am worried about the temper tantrums, though she has less at home. There is a good possibility of her coming home more often, but not at the moment.

The mother added three more contributions throughout the rest of a meeting which concentrated on the problems faced by the foster carer. By stating her position at an early stage of the meeting, the mother had effectively excluded herself from the discussion. The position she affirmed was difficult to counter – things were getting better, but not enough to increase the level of contact.

The nature of parents' contact with their children in accommodation was frequently used as an initial invitation to parents to talk. However, it was often interpreted as indicating lack of commitment on their part, and provoked a defensive response:

MEETING 5

Chair: Have you seen [daughter] since she was admitted to [foster parents]?

Mother 1: It's hard to get up there, because of money and the younger kids. I've not seen her for two weeks. I did not know about this weekend [at home] until last night, but it's no problem.

MEETING 6

Chair: Have you had any contact with [daughter]?

Mother 2: None.

Chair: Is that through choice?

Mother 2: It's mutual.

These two extracts from meetings about different cases were the first exchanges with each mother, and they preceded rather different dialogues between the mothers and the professionals. In Meeting 5, mother 1 only spoke when invited, and her approach was defensive. In Meeting 6, however, mother 2 was seated (angrily) outside the circle of speakers, and spent most of the time looking out of the window. She continued to respond in short replies, and the focus of the meeting switched to the private foster carer. However, towards the end of the meeting her uneasy silence ended:

> *Social worker:* Would you feel happier if it was assessed?
> *Mother 2:* I'm just sat here listening. Do what you want, I'm not a part of making any decisions. [*Turns away and starts to cry.*]
> *Chair:* Do you have any alternative to offer?
> *Mother 2:* [Daughter] can just please herself, which is what she does anyway.
> *Chair:* We want you to be a part of the process.
> *Mother 2:* Well, I'm not. She should be at home. I want her to come home.

The social worker had said earlier in the meeting that she was aware that the mother was not happy with the arrangement of her daughter living with a family friend, but attempts to get her to state her point of view had been unsuccessful. When the mother eventually began to speak, the meeting supported her view that 'young people should be with their families', and a programme of family work was instigated.

In summary, parents made limited contributions for different reasons. For some, their silence was a defence against criticism: their parenting was under scrutiny and subject to accusations. As one parent said: 'I was on trial.' A number of parents commented to the authors that they found meetings humiliating, and hence said little (see Chapter 13). They could only respond by means of defensive rebuttals, thereby closing off debate or dialogue while the professional debate carried on around them. Other parents excluded themselves, or felt excluded, from what was being discussed. Their silence was unwelcome, but when they did speak their contribution was welcomed and supported.

The fact that parents make so few contributions questions the point of meetings – is merely listening to professionals talk a justifiable purpose, if the parents are unable to explain themselves, contest the professionals or seek clarification? As the DoH/Social Services Inspectorate guide (1995, p.11) notes, this is 'involvement', not 'participation'. In some meetings it seemed that the parents were merely observers of inter-professional negotiation, as social services, for example, sought the support of other professionals, or a commitment to provide services.

Discussion of information that may be considered critical and humiliating might be expected at a child protection conference where evidence is being assessed. However, most of the meetings considered here were planning meetings, often concerning well-known cases. The professionals appeared frustrated at the lack of progress in achieving change in the families, and used the meetings to reinforce their strategy. Not only does this fail to encourage parental involvement, but such meetings serve as an occasion for calling the parents to account in a public arena, often in the presence of teachers, doctors or health visitors whom the family see daily in other contexts.

Supportive dialogues

In some meetings the parents were approached as needing the support of professionals, rather than their criticism. This was especially true of newer cases where the family problems were less well known, and a dialogue was developed to understand how the family could be helped. It was also typical of those situations where a package of services was being offered to families in order to prevent the children being accommodated. In meetings which stressed the helping role of social services, the chair could be observed diverting or defusing any angry exchanges.

In two meetings the social worker was trying to take a tougher line with parents, voicing serious concerns about risk and the adequacy of parental care. These accusations provoked angry denials from the parents, which in turn ignited some heated exchanges between family members. Both were swiftly dampened down by interventions from the chair: 'Now, this is not a child protection meeting.'

At a review meeting, a mother of four was blaming herself for the behaviour difficulties of her young children:

MEETING 7

> *Mother:* I've not given the children stability.
> *Chair:* There's no point in blaming yourself. You have an understandably hard task. The important thing is how we can help now.

In another meeting, the mother of two toddlers was clearly depressed, and wept throughout. She was requesting that they both be accommodated together:

MEETING 8

> *Mother:* I can't look after them. I've told [daughter] I'm poorly – always crying and shouting. I'd like to cope, but I don't know. I can't read the future.

The chair's response was to indicate the voluntary basis of accommodation, with 'its lack of strings', and to suggest that time should be taken to find the 'right' foster home. The admission to accommodation should be open-ended, 'until Mum feels able to cope'. Only after the meeting, when the parents had left, was there speculation about the possibility of irrationality and manipulation on the parents' part. The social worker felt she could not have tackled the family problems in the meeting: 'It would be like kicking the girl when she's down.'

A number of meetings were convened when families were experiencing problems but had made arrangements for the children to be looked after by friends or family. Accommodation was thus avoided, and the meetings tried to support such arrangements. In one meeting, emphasis on the parents' mental health problems was redirected by the chair towards the children's needs and support for the family:

MEETING 9

Chair: This is obviously a new situation for everyone. The purpose of this meeting is to focus on the children. What help can be offered in the children's best interests? What plans do the family have? Where do we go from here?

[*There is a long discussion, and there are offers of help, mainly from family and friends.*]

Chair: I think this is an excellent package. It is important that the children are safe and that our ongoing concerns are met. You have met the social worker, [name], who will become involved, offer support and liaise with the other professionals . . .

The concerns of the social workers for the children's safety and 'their best interests' were affirmed, and ensuring adequate support for the family was posited as crucial to allaying such concerns. Early exchanges during the meeting were interpreted by the parents as critical, and in response they mounted a strong defence. With the change to a supportive dialogue, mainly through encouraging offers of help from relatives and friends, the parents became more co-operative. Of the 55 turns of speech during the meeting, 12 were by the parents and 12 by friends or relatives.

In another meeting the professionals each made their usual initial reports, but most of the meeting involved exploring the issues raised through asking the mother what services could be offered. The family centre worker and the chair of the meeting jointly questioned her. For example, immediately after the teacher had finished speaking, the mother was introduced in a supportive and inquiring manner:

MEETING 10

Family centre worker: [Mother], are you on your own?

Mother: Yes.

Family centre worker: Does he see his father?

Mother: [Child] sees his father, but he thinks there are no problems . . .

[*Later.*]

Chair: How are we going to resolve this? Given no support, what can we all offer?

[*Later, there is discussion of the possibility of residential assessment for the whole family.*]

Social worker: . . . [Mother] has been reluctant to consider this in the past.

Mother: No, I'm not happy about that.

Chair: Why's that?

Mother: It means leaving home.

Chair: Perhaps we need to explain further, but if it would improve the quality of parenting. We could take him into foster care.

Mother: I don't want that.

Chair: It would alleviate things for a few days, but the problem would not go away.

Mother: I don't know.

[*The chair goes on to discuss day assessment.*]

This meeting focused on what support could be offered to the mother, and attempted to base services on her view of the problems: her support systems were explored, a wide variety of suggestions were made, and the options explained. Of particular interest for this study is the failure to offer accommodation as a service in a positive way: it was offered as 'foster care' and in contrast to residential assessment. It was neither explained nor posited as a positive option, and was lost in the discussion of assessment. Thus, despite the fact that the meeting appeared to be an open exchange of views and possible solutions, social services' view of preferred solutions was the hidden agenda behind the exchanges. However, the mother was to able to contribute to the meeting, even though an element of persuasion was in operation. Of the 68 turns of speech in the meeting, 22 were by the mother and 3 by her friend.

(This was the only meeting where there was a friend who supported the parents. In another there was a volunteer who acted in a supportive capacity. Compare this with Thoburn et al. (1993, p.335).)

In another meeting the mother was treated in a supportive manner, and accommodation was made available to the family. The 'decision' to accommodate had already been accepted as inevitable, thus the meeting explored issues in the case in a manner that supported the mother and criticised the daughter. There were 77 turns of speech, 14 by the mother and 13 by the daughter. The mother felt able to interrupt to explain events, and gave a long description of her position, as well as indicating how the period of accommodation should be used:

MEETING 11

> *Mother:* I don't want her away for long, but we both need a break from one another.
>
> [*Later.*]
>
> *Chair:* What we are saying is that there is so much anger between you that there is a risk to you both. There is not enough from [daughter]. You need to get together, but it is too early today. We will look for accommodation as near as possible, and get back when the time is right.

The meeting also discussed what work was necessary to 'build a bridge' between mother and daughter, but the details of how this might be carried out were left to later, given the need to find the child a bed for the night.

In summary, some meetings where the parents made a greater contribution were characterised by a supportive dialogue between parents and professionals. These parents were supported in their efforts to carry on caring for their children at home, or accommodation was offered as short-term relief. There was general agreement between the parents and the professionals about what was the best way forward, and any criticism of the parents' care was kept out of the discussion.

Argumentative encounters

Some meetings were argumentative from the outset. Unlike the critical stance of the meetings where the parents were silenced, in these meetings the parents challenged and contested both the information and suggestions for action.

Before one meeting, the chair saw the aim as reviewing a long-running respite care arrangement for two brothers. The mother had taken on the care of her troublesome niece, and the chair wondered why the family still needed respite care. The mother and her sister (the mother of the niece) quickly realised the position, and were immediately defensive:

MEETING 12

Chair: I am concerned about [niece moving in with mother].

Mother: I had no choice, before you moan . . .

Sister: That [social worker at another Area] said I would have to beat her up before they would take her into care.

Mother: I wouldn't want her sleeping on the street. [Sister] was begging for help since [niece] was 5.

Chair: And what effect has it had on [son]?

Mother: They don't get on, and he goes to his grandparents. We will slag [niece] off rotten here, and she has done some evil things. But [sister] asked for help, and social services passed the buck. She really needed help, and it's social services' fault.

This exchange took place early in the meeting, before the professionals had spoken – the social worker did not make a report, and the head-teacher arrived late. The meeting was immediately argumentative, with each side attempting to blame the other for the problems and offering different versions of what should be done. A combative mood prevailed throughout the meeting, and eventually the mother was persuaded that she needed help with her niece, and a plan for a period in accommodation was agreed. The mother's reaction to the decision was: 'I don't have any choice. I don't like it at all.' Of the 57 turns of speech recorded, 25 were by the mother or her sister, and apart from a short report by the headteacher, the meeting was an acrimonious exchange between the mother and team leader. In a meeting such as this, where the two sides disagree strongly on almost all aspects, it is difficult to see how any degree of agreement could be achieved. Accommodation as a resource for the family appeared to be offered or withdrawn in accordance with social services' view of the preferred family set-up.

Disagreement about how a problem was viewed by the mother and social services produced a combative dialogue throughout another meeting. At a review meeting the mother had at the last minute refused to have her son home for the weekend, and she withdrew support for a programme of rehabilitation based on regular weekend visits home. This threat to the care plan was a source of dispute throughout the meeting, and was still unresolved at the end:

MEETING 13

> *Chair:* But what about the future?
>
> *Mother:* I am happy with just the teas [a weekly visit home for tea] until he comes home.
>
> *Social worker:* But that is not logical, if you want him home but not for weekends.
>
> *Mother:* I have said I'll have him, haven't I? I have had enough of all this. I don't need this. I don't have to come here.
>
> *Social worker:* But he's your son, he's your responsibility.
>
> *Chair:* OK. Let's not carry on. What is the date of his return home . . .?

The rehabilitation aim remained intact, but the method of achieving it was disputed. The mother dug her heels in, and was not persuaded by social services' attempts to undermine her position. The social worker used a strong counter-argument – her position was described as 'not logical', and her parental responsibility was invoked – but the chair was forced to back down whilst reaffirming the rehabilitation goal. In this short meeting there were 19 turns of speech, 7 of them by the mother.

In another meeting the parents were voicing concerns about the speed of rehabilitation. Most of the meeting consisted of exchanges in which the parents raised problems, the professionals offered solutions, and the parents raised further problems. For example:

MEETING 14

> *Mother:* As I said, I can't cope with him for more than two or three days [at home]. What can I do?
>
> *Health visitor:* Proceed with the referral to family therapy.
>
> *Mother:* But until then I'm at my wits' end. I need someone to phone when I need help. [*To the family placement social worker*] How often do you visit [the foster carer]? We need a social worker to visit us. Someone we can call.
>
> *Social worker:* There is always night duty.
>
> *Father:* No. Someone who knows him to come round when needed, not an appointment in a month's time.

In this meeting there were 97 turns of speech, of which 38 were by the parents. Dispute centred on whether the child's behaviour was normal for his age, or abnormal and in need of treatment. The parents raised problems which the professionals countered. A wide range of support services and flexible responses were offered to the family to allay their fears, but none was accepted as a solution. Only after the meeting was over did the social worker question the mother's commitment to the rehabilitation, to which she replied: 'I've said I'll take him, haven't I?'

In the last two cases the rehabilitation ultimately failed. It is easy to state the obvious after the event, but perhaps both meetings display the likelihood of failure in the presence of such a degree of disagreement and lack of flexibility, even though the long-term goal was apparently supported. Confronting uncertainties rather than discussing them away might have produced a more honest exchange, and plans to which the parents were more committed. Much of the debate around continuing accommodation is that 'drift' should be avoided by decisive planning. However, Section 20 accommodation raises and promotes a wider range of possibilities between permanence and rehabilitation, and moreover suggests that parents should have a major role in selecting such options and deciding how quickly to proceed.

In the meetings discussed above, opposing views of events remained throughout: both sides had strong positions, and no resolution was possible. In other meetings there were disagreements, but eventually some degree of compromise was reached. At a typical meeting the parents requested admission to accommodation, but social services resisted by offering alternatives. (This model resembles the pre-placement panel with a specific gatekeeping function (see Owen 1992, Chapter 11).) Aspects of such an exchange occurred in a number of meetings. Often the outcome had been anticipated, and the meeting merely went through the motions.

In one meeting there was a detailed examination of all aspects of the situation, during which the parents were forced to defend their position at length. For example:

MEETING 15

> *Chair:* You have had a lot of help in the past, and [boy] wants to stay at home. What shall we do?

Mother: I don't want him.

Chair: There are lots of other remedies.

Mother: We have tried them all.

Chair: [Family centre] have said they can do what they can.

Mother: It's like having ten children.

Family centre worker: There is not the motivation. He knew what to do, but it needed something more than just behaving differently.

Chair: So you want out.

Mother: I can't cope. I can't handle him. I don't want him. [*She begins to cry.*]

Chair [*to father, who lives elsewhere*]: Can you help more?

Father: I only have alternate weekends, depending on the job. I am worried by the phone calls from [mother]. It will cause her a nervous breakdown.

Chair: Can we look at respite again?

Family placement social worker: There are no possibilities at the moment.

Mother: Weekends are not enough. I've had enough. I want him out. He is making my life hell. He tried to burn my little girl, and he has displayed sexual behaviour to her.

Chair: I have to ask this: are there any family members who might take him?

This extract comes from the end of a meeting which had started with the mother stating that she had had enough. After negative contributions from the school, housing and the family centre and a report from the police, this exchange appeared to push the mother into making extreme statements to establish the hopelessness of her position – 'like having ten children', 'can't cope', 'don't want him', and finally crying. She was forced to move from 'very concerned' (in her first comment to the meeting) to an active rejection at the end. The comment by the chair, 'I have to ask this', suggests that there was an implicit ticking off of alternatives to accommodation, and hence a defence against future criticism that not all options had been considered. However, in this case such a process provoked the mother to an extreme position to which she might not otherwise have resorted, and which confirmed her status as a 'rejecting mother'. Accommodation was thus offered in a situation where all else had been tried and where the parents were pushed to reject the child. It was not raised within a debate concerning offering support to a family whose integrity and stability were being promoted.

In one meeting the father had been describing at length his son's difficult behaviour, and explaining why he was not prepared to have him back home. Towards the end of the meeting the chair attempted to salvage at least some concessions about the future direction:

MEETING 16

Chair: How long is this going on [not seeing his son]?

Father: We have said he can write a letter, we can sit down and think about it, we don't know how he feels.

Chair: He is here. What about after the meeting?

Father: That wouldn't be wise. I've got to get back to work.

Social worker: Contact is very important: he's feeling very isolated.

Chair: Are you on the phone? Why not phone him?

Father: I'm not sure.

Chair: I'm pushing you: he needs to know what is going on.

Father: He's got enough. He is in the right place, having his needs met.

Family placement social worker: He needs contact with his father. It would give him a new lease of life.

Father: He would be better off with me. He must realise that, then he can come back.

Family placement social worker: You don't need to look at all sides of the problem. Just the tiniest contact. Just talk about little things.

Chair: Just pop your head around the door. Say 'hello'. Acknowledge he is there.

Father: OK.

Social worker: He would appreciate it.

Headteacher: When he came, he made a beeline straight for the door, he knew you were here.

Social worker: His eyes lit up.

[*The chair begins to summarise the meeting.*]

This extract displays a number of features in the interplay of professionals with families in meetings. First, the case-holding social worker and other social services staff (the family placement service worker) supported one another in persuading the father to go along with their strategy. It was probably not planned in advance, but several professionals rose to support the strategy of conciliation. Second, such contributions established assessments of the child's predicament ('he's feeling very isolated'), pointing to evidence for such needs ('His eyes lit up') and giving precise instructions ('Just talk about little things'). This type of discussion, which concentrated on achieving objectives by negotiating specific 'small-scale' interaction, was rare in our data, but here it can be seen to both extract a positive statement of future hopes from the father ('He would be better off with me') and project progress for the therapeutic enterprise in small steps.

These 'argumentative' meetings were characterised by acrimony. Sometimes this resulted in a lack of agreement about the appropriate way forward, and perpetuated begrudging reactions. The parents' participation was forceful, but their position was ultimately untenable since the meeting pushed them to extreme responses. In other cases parents were persuaded to support the therapeutic enterprise.

Whilst disagreement and bitterness may be an inevitable feature of some situations where accommodation is being considered, the question is whether a meeting can resolve or perpetuate such problems. It is interesting that in all five meetings considered under the heading 'Argumentative encounters', the issue in dispute was the provision, nature and duration of accommodation which all the parents wanted. However, social services were worried that they might abandon their parental responsibility altogether, so they felt that the provision of accommodation should be withdrawn or avoided.

Family decisions

In three meetings most of the discussion was directed by the family. Whilst these meetings had not been set up specifically to allow the families to draw up the plan, it became clear that key decisions could not be made by the professionals, but depended on what solutions the families themselves provided.

In one meeting the family members outnumbered the professionals and dominated the discussion, even telling the opening 'scene-setting' story. The problem in this case was which family member should look after a 15-year-old whose mother was terminally ill. The role of social services was to facilitate the discussion and offer whatever resources would support the plan. The girl was offered accommodation until one brother could transfer to a larger flat. In this case social services appeared happy to provide accommodation, which the family saw as unstigmatising and helpful.

Respect for a family's autonomy and right to choose was a theme in these three meetings. One meeting, in the case of a teenage girl who had been living in private foster care because of disputes with her father, took the form of a large family gathering. The social worker was clearly anxious about her wish to return home. His opening summary stressed the improvement in her physical health, and he believed she was happy in her placement. He hoped she would remain there. But the girl wept and said that, although she had enjoyed being with her foster mother, she wanted to go home:

MEETING 17

> *Girl:* I want to stay with Dad – it's my dad, isn't it?
>
> [*The father, in turn, defends himself.*]
>
> *Father:* I've reacted perhaps in a way I shouldn't . . . I'm not a perfect parent . . . perhaps a little too strict . . . but we are getting on a lot better now.
>
> [*The chair steers the meeting towards what seems to be the inevitable outcome.*]
>
> *Chair:* We'd want to support [girl] in the new situation of her choice.

The chair went on to stress the ways in which support might be provided for the girl and her welfare safeguarded while contacts with other members of the family were maintained.

In another meeting the forthcoming divorce hearing and subsequent custody arrangements would determine the fate of the children, so the meeting could not make any comment on what should happen next. The situation was unusual, in that the meeting consisted of the mother and father carefully rehearsing their likely position at court and the social services avoiding becoming involved, therefore the parents implicitly enlisted social services' approval, whereas social services remained non-committal about the preferred outcomes or potential problems:

MEETING 18

> *Chair* [*to mother*]: So, do you need support from social services?
>
> *Mother:* I want help.
>
> *Chair:* Like parenting skills or support?
>
> *Mother:* Everything. Someone to come round and see how I'm getting on . . .

Social work support was viewed as potentially crucial in achieving the mother's aim of getting her children back, which meant that social services' endorsement took on positive connotations: unlike the argumentative or critical meetings, where social services support was resisted, here it was viewed as legitimising the family unit.

It is worth considering how in other more contentious cases social work intervention can be seen as empowerment rather than interference. What is needed is to change the role of social workers so their involvement is welcomed as supporting and thereby endorsing the family unit, rather than threatening it.

Professionals' contributions

One important function of meetings is to promote and display inter-agency co-operation. There appeared to be unspoken rules governing conduct in meetings. First, there was little overt disagreement among the professionals (see Lewis 1994, p.109; Marks 1992, p.7). Second, these were social services' meetings: when other professionals were invited, they were to act in a supporting role. However, within these parameters, professionals could attempt to impose their versions of the problems and the solutions on the discussions. How did they do this? We will concentrate on those professionals who regularly attend meetings: social workers, teachers, health visitors and family centre workers.

Some professionals say little

Some professionals made limited contributions to the meeting, remaining within their professional remit. Some teachers only discussed the child's educational attainment, and some health visitors only discussed issues of health and development:

MEETING 19

Teacher: [Young person] has been in my tutor group since September. She knew some other children from [other school] and has made good friends. She is a model pupil, hard-working and conscientious. I have a recent report from all the staff which is very good.

Foster parent: Getting her to do her homework is no problem.

Teacher: I think she is quite bright.

Chair: Have you been able to tell Mum?

Teacher: Not yet: there is a parents' evening next month.

Chair: Does she confide in anyone?

Teacher: With her friends. Like the foster parents, I have offered her the opportunity to talk to me in confidence, but she seems fine.

Chair [*to young person*]: A lot of nice things . . .

Questions from the chair about the pastoral aspect of the teacher's role were not developed in this meeting, and the teacher's contribution had the effect of establishing that school was one area which did not cause concern. It was not raised again in the meeting, although the teacher remained in attendance.

Similarly, some health visitors restricted their role to health and under-5s issues:

MEETING 20

Chair [*to health visitor*]: Do you want to say anything?

Health visitor: I have only just met the family and having nothing to say at this point. I do not have any concerns about the younger children.

However, such a restricted role in a meeting was not countered by any suggestion that it was inappropriate for the health visitor to be present. But short contributions by health visitors or teachers were not the norm.

Setting the agenda/capturing the debate

The discussion of a family's problems and concerns about children could encompass a wide range of topics, and it was up to the chair to decide which issues should be addressed. How did contributors make a bid to set the agenda of the discussion? Whilst the chair was able to pursue certain lines of discussion, s/he depended on the other professionals to raise topics and express concerns. Particular professionals might make contributions which not only summarised their concerns but also laid out the appropriate solution, thereby attempting to capture the debate. Most meetings went according to plan, as far as social services were concerned: the problems were raised in such a way that they could take the lead role. However, there was always the possibility that a strong opinion which had not been anticipated might develop in the meeting.

The agenda of the meeting could be set at the beginning by the case-holding social worker, who summarised the situation in a way that structured the discussion. For example, the briefing sheet distributed at the beginning of the meeting did not merely relate the 'facts' of the case. Here is an extract from a briefing sheet:

♦ [Stepmother] has told me she feels she needs a safety net, and if things are not going well she can return [child] to [foster parents]. We discussed the difficulties behind this, i.e.:

1 [Child] needs to know whether he is going or staying. He wants to be at home with Mum and Dad.

2 [Foster parent] needs to know so she can arrange her week.

3 [Foster unit] need to know as they will be waiting to use [foster parents] for other children.

Such a report is clearly more than a neutral account of events; it is a statement of the social worker's view of the problem the meeting must address, and his/her position in relation to it. It reports a conversation between the stepmother and social worker, which contrasts her need for a 'safety net' with the child's wish to return home. Her need for a 'safety net' is less important than the child's future security, the foster parents' time and the use of the placement. The stepmother's concerns are being noted but undermined, and the scene is set for the meeting to oppose any obstruction she may offer. In this way, briefing sheets or reports could set the agenda for the meeting.

Professionals could also influence meetings by describing their professional contact with the family or child, and reporting that certain problems were evident. Some teachers described behaviour in class which pointed to problems in a way that implied that something should be done (compare this with Farmer and Owen 1995, p.134):

MEETING 21

Teacher: When it first blew up they were very distressed. They went to the foster parents and it changed very quickly, it was unbelievable. They missed Mum, but they were happy. They seemed to reverse roles: K became quieter and M is more boisterous, it was nice to see. Since they have gone back home, they have gone downhill. K is very detached, and M has started taking things. I don't know where to go. I have asked about outreach. They have few friends, they are loners. I told them I was coming here, and did they want me to say anything? K said that he missed his dad, but that he was a witch and had powers. M missed Dad, but was frightened when he was drunk.

Social worker: I have tried to contact Dad. The other thing is that the aim of the outreach is to give attention to them.

Chair: Are there any other problems?

Teacher: Not with attendance.

Chair: Are they appropriately placed?

Teacher: Yes, but I am concerned about their behaviour and their being ostracised because of their hygiene problems.

Chair: That is related to home.

Teacher: Yes.

One implication from the teacher's contribution was that the children would be better off away from home. This was not developed further, but the chair was able to use it to identify that the problem was at home, hence this was where the work should focus.

A tide of opinion was developing in one meeting which suggested that social services should consider care proceedings. A child guidance centre worker commented that they were 'very concerned about the lack of change'. This was followed by the family centre worker, who used her long contribution to report that a series of interventions with the family had not worked. She finished as follows:

MEETING 22

> *Family centre worker:* . . . I would say that I have been concerned since Christmas, and this has been shared with [social worker], that I do not see her being very motivated as to interacting with [children], and in actual fact I actually question the actual overall feeling of [mother] herself about how she was feeling and her care for her own personal self, so I'd say that I have concerns and I'm really hoping that the house move will actually help because I feel that we've tried everything we possibly can in the family centre.

By depicting the family centre as running out of options, and transferring concern to the mother's self-image, this contribution pushed the debate to a more serious level. The scene was set for care proceedings as the next obvious step. It was only the intervention of the solicitor, who stated that more information was needed before going to court, that stopped an immediate move to care proceedings.

In summary, professionals made contributions which used their work with the family to present the problem, point out where things were going wrong and hint at what should be done. Where there was no overt disagreement, the contributions made and the positions taken by professionals could be decisive in controlling the agenda and capturing the debate.

The chair's influence

It is not easy to identify the chair's influence on a meeting. The chair can structure the meeting by inviting contributions and picking out the main issues to be addressed and highlighted. However, in our study, chairs relied on others to raise the issues and, on occasion, had to handle the tide of opinion moving in a way of which they disapproved. Lewis (1994, p.100) notes the unpredictability of child protection conferences.

Setting parameters

We have seen already how some chairs appeared to have firm opinions regarding what it was appropriate to discuss in a meeting and what was not. In the supportive meetings discussed in this chapter, we saw how the chair quashed criticism of the family, ruling that planning meetings, unlike child protection meetings, were forums for supporting parents, not criticising them. Chairs in other cases considered that certain matters should be resolved outside the meeting. In Meeting 13, we saw how the chair stopped an increasingly bitter exchange from developing by closing down the debate but re-emphasising the overall plan. One chair told one of the authors that meetings should not take place 'when the casework had not been done': the meeting should review the social work intervention, rather than being an occasion to carry it out. Agreements and positions should be developed between the social worker and family, not established in meetings.

It was clear that not all chairs viewed the meetings in this way, since the nature of the social work intervention was frequently established or re-established at the meeting. In Meeting 9, the social worker was introduced as the professional charged with the responsibility of carrying out the meeting's suggestions. We also saw how meetings could be used to challenge the family's position and re-establish social services' authority over how family relations should be conducted. In Meeting 2, for example, it seemed that the meeting was used to highlight concerns in a public arena, in order to define expectations of the mother. Social workers often wanted to use the meetings to challenge parents, and thereby gain support for intervention. Chairs therefore had to manage pressures to use and direct meetings in various ways.

Countering the tide

We saw in Meeting 22 that a tide of opinion was developing which contradicted the agenda set by social services and had to be countered. In another meeting, opinion appeared to be drifting in the other direction, in favour of a less extreme intervention, as the mother depicted herself as co-operating with seeking help. The chair was able to undermine this view by calling on the duty social worker to reaffirm the graver view of the situation at the time of the initial intervention:

MEETING 23

Chair [*to duty social worker*]: So, how do you see things generally now?

Duty social worker: The picture is that [mother] is very depressed. There has been an improvement, but my concern is when she can't cope. If [child] returns home, it can turn round in 36 hours. A phone call from [child's father] and everything is swept away.

Health visitor: I support those concerns. And [mother] is reluctant to receive support from her parents.

[*The father and mother are given the chance to outline the present position with regard to their relationship.*]

Duty social worker: The GP is also concerned that [mother] does not accept the problem of her drinking. She has a superficial relationship with the agencies, works with one for a while and then moves on to another. There is no meaningful relationship established, and then she moves on to the next. There is concern that [present referral] will be more of the same.

This summary of the situation re-emphasised the high level of concern at the time of the admission, despite an apparent improvement in the mother's functioning since then. It served to counteract any tendency towards a less extreme intervention by highlighting the fragility of the situation, and hence the danger of deterioration. When the social worker's stance was supported by the health visitor, this undermined any attempt by the mother to depict herself as having changed. A few minutes later, the duty social worker developed this position further by commenting that although the mother appeared to be strengthening her case by seeking help, such behaviour was a further illustration of her co-operation being merely superficial. We cannot tell whether the chair deliberately introduced the duty social worker at this point in order to alter the tide of opinion, but that was the effect it had.

Summarising the meeting

Another way chairs could control meetings was by summarising the tasks set at the end of the meeting and drawing up the minutes. Moving from discussion to task-setting appeared to be a way of avoiding the uncertainties that might have arisen in a meeting, and proposing a clear way forward. Since the minutes of the meetings concentrated on the agreements made and tasks set, they had the effect of simplifying and neutralising any disagreement in a meeting.

In one meeting a headteacher voiced a strong opinion that the family should be offered respite care:

MEETING 24

> *Headteacher:* I am trying not to exclude him. [Educational Welfare Officer] sees him a lot, and we both think that Mother needs respite care for [brother] so she can spend time with him. I am concerned that this may become a real problem. He is a very unhappy boy.

Such a strong statement of opinion about what another professional should do was rare. Although the headteacher's concern was mentioned in the minutes, his suggestion of respite care was not. (Farmer and Owen (1993, p.99) also found evidence of the careful editing of minutes.) In this way, the chair was able to establish apparent agreement. Similar methods were used to set out tasks for other professionals.

In summary, chairs were key figures in the meetings, and had a number of opportunities to establish parameters for the conduct of the meetings, to counter particular positions and to establish apparent agreement in the summaries and minutes.

Summary

This chapter has considered in detail the process and content of meetings associated with admission to accommodation. It should be emphasised that whilst all these meetings handled sensitive issues regarding concern and risk in relation to children, only four were a formal part of the child protection process.

One fundamental question should be asked: are such meetings the appropriate forums for negotiating and managing the provision of accommodation? Our evidence is that planning meetings served as the primary forums for deciding whether or not to provide accommodation. In Shiptown, this function seemed to be associated with the history of gatekeeping admissions to care in that local authority. There are good reasons for such an approach: it fulfils the inter-agency function of including other professionals in decision-making; it provides a stage for families to hear what professionals have to say and to present their own point of view to all the agencies; and it also means that decision-making is subjected to management scrutiny. Supportive meetings could offer reassurance to families by acknowledging that they were facing insurmountable problems and that the professionals were there to help. The parents' efforts in caring for their children, often in difficult circumstances, were acknowledged, and their family unit legitimised. In such meetings participation and partnership were being achieved through joint assessment, sharing concerns and by providing supportive services.

We suggested at the beginning of this chapter that these meetings might be less formal than child protection conferences, with more opportunity for participation and establishing agreement with families. The fact that some families did not contribute to the meetings, and experienced them as humiliating and undermining, suggests that their extensive use should be questioned.

The authors found that observing meetings was sometimes an uncomfortable experience. The discussion of intimate family matters by articulate professionals in front of embarrassed and silent families appeared to be the antithesis of family support. The problem was more than a mere lack of 'involvement', or exclusion from decision-making, but the experience of public criticism and humiliation. The comments of parents and children in the next two chapters support this observation.

This chapter has identified parents' contributions to meetings in four ways and made suggestions about how some meetings appear to promote partnership. The nature of families' requests for help and professionals' concerns about care and risk inevitably produce different levels of agreement, but should meetings serve as the forums for negotiating agreement, requiring families to defend themselves in front of several professionals?

The 'critical' meetings which effectively silenced the parents were of most concern. Failing to address the parents, talking about them as if they were not there and conducting sometimes long debates from which they were excluded hardly encourages participation. The parallels with a court case are clear: the 'defendants' were being accused of poor parenting, but without the opportunity to cross-examine, and without defence lawyers. Some professionals appeared to use meetings to 'have a go', highlighting family failures or lack of co-operation, and thereby seeking endorsement for their work. Such meetings were punitive in nature.

Child protection conferences, which are primarily concerned with accusations, apportioning blame and setting out expectations, have been encouraged to be more careful in handling the preparation of parents, providing explanations to them, and presenting evidence (Lewis 1994, DoH/Social Services Inspectorate 1995). Thoburn et al. (1993, p.338) highlight sensitivity to 'speculation' and 'soft evidence' in child protection conferences. Planning meetings, which are considered to be a more informal exchange of views, seem to lack such safeguards about the status of evidence and opinion, yet they can be equally challenging.

Could conducting meetings in these ways be avoided, or could measures be introduced to reduce the humiliation but still allow the concerns to be explored? One option would be to provide a parents' advocate at meetings, to question the professionals' evaluations and help the parents construct a defence: someone who is aware of social services' procedures, services and assessments, but who is on the parents' 'side'. Another might be for the professionals to discuss their concerns with the parents beforehand, so the meeting might be less of a 'trial' and more a joint report and review of how the concerns were being addressed. Thoburn et al. (1993, p.338) describe some methods used in child protection conferences to seek parents' views, including asking them to complete a short questionnaire or write a letter. The recent development of family group conferences also appears to offer an opportunity for family problems to be addressed in a way which does not entail humiliation and criticism (Lupton et al. 1995).

13 *Parents' views*

An important and illuminating feature of this study was the set of interviews we conducted with children who were accommodated and their parents. We have quoted from these interviews in earlier chapters, but in this chapter and the next we will consider them in greater depth. We interviewed 23 parents – 18 mothers and 5 fathers – concerning 24 children who were or had been in accommodation. The cases were selected to reflect a range of experiences of accommodation. We discussed the appropriateness of conducting each interview with the social worker. A number of families were approached after the authors had attended a planning meeting regarding their case. Five families either declined to be interviewed or did not make themselves available. We cannot claim that this sample was representative, but there are a number of similar characteristics to the larger cohort of accommodated children. Six of the children were teenagers, and five were under 5 years of age. Seven children had been the subject of child protection conferences, and seven had exhibited disruptive or delinquent behaviour. The sample included examples of the different uses of accommodation – respite care, short-term stay, longer-term stay and continuous accommodation.

The Guidance to the Children Act indicates a change of emphasis in the provision of accommodation: it is to serve as a 'positive support to a child and his family' and is to be arranged 'in partnership with parents' (DoH 1991a, paras 2.13 and 2.14). These interviews therefore offer an important opportunity to assess whether parents saw themselves as partners, and whether the children considered they were consulted. The parents and children were able to express their opinions and recount their experiences in a clear and eloquent manner, sometimes providing versions of events which were at odds with social services' view. The interviews with the parents were more fruitful, often lasting over an hour. They seemed eager to tell their 'story' to someone independent of social services, and did not appear inhibited in complimenting or criticising social services or others about what had happened. Most of the interviews were tape-recorded.

Some general features of the parents' accounts

The parents' views and explanations were complex and wide-ranging. We will discuss them in terms of topics surrounding the admission to accommodation, but we should emphasise that their overall description of what happened to their family was highly personal, recounted at different stages of their contact with social services, and many factors affected their presentation. They were not merely describing what had happened to them, but attempting to provide a justifiable and morally adequate version of themselves and their circumstances. In particular, the parents resisted being categorised by social services, and emphasised their unique circumstances:

> *Mother:* See, with social services, I just think to myself sometimes they think you're a bit stupid, they talk down to you. I mean, I suppose they deal with lots of different people and they don't look at everybody the way the person is, or maybe they don't want to know.

They resisted being seen as 'inadequate parents' or to be blamed for neglect or abuse. One mother whose child had been accommodated and placed on the Child Protection Register for neglect explained her attempts to convince social services (and the interviewer) of her integrity:

> *Mother:* Now, I did nothing wrong to my son, and that's what I can't understand. I didn't intentionally do anything wrong. It makes me feel bad now. It makes me feel worse and worse that he's kept away from me for so long and I never did anything wrong. I mean, I'd understand it if I'd coshed him on the head, like the neighbour complained. I mean, if a baby cries, you can't help a baby crying. I mean, you don't intentionally leave a baby on the floor crying, and it's like even the professional people I've seen now have said to me, 'If a baby cries it will cry, y'know, when it's thirsty,' and I said, 'Yes, I know that.' Unfortunately, people thought I wasn't tending to him properly.

This mother emphasised that her action was not intentional and contrasted it with those who hit their children. She also points to the conflicting views of professionals – is a baby crying normal, or a sign of poor parenting? In this way, parents attempted to show that they had been misunderstood and misrepresented. Such resistance to blame was a common theme in many of these accounts (see also Farmer and Owen 1995, p.73).

Some families explained their contact with social services in terms that were generally critical or appreciative, and this line was maintained throughout the interview:

> *Mother:* Y'know you can't impress me with social services in any way 'cos I've had bad experiences with them, so, I mean, nothing what anybody says will change my mind about how I feel.

> *Mother:* I stated what I wanted, and they were very accommodating indeed. I was very surprised it was so easy . . . I don't know why everyone criticises social workers so much. I'd advise anyone to go to social services.

Others were especially aware of the 'shades of grey' in situations, emphasising the complexity of their circumstances and their ambivalence about social services' involvement:

> *Mother:* . . . so I'm not very keen on social services. Well, I am and I'm not, y'know.

This mother had been in long-term contact with social services, and some of their interventions were seen as helpful. However, she also described how social services had on occasion acted against her wishes, and now she was unsure of how to respond:

> *Mother:* . . . when you say to social services [daughter's] done this or that, OK, but you don't know what's going to happen. If you can't cope with her she'll end up in care, and I thought . . . they don't help you when you are trying to manage on your own, y'know . . . I try to avoid them as much as possible now, and only go when I really need help.

Thus, even long-term involvement with social services does not necessarily result in developing a sense of trust and working in partnership. Like other parents, this mother admitted that she was having difficulties bringing up her family, but felt that as a single parent she was doing the best she could in the circumstances.

Some parents' accounts revealed a long-term view of their family problems and attempts to solve them. Their problems had pre-dated social services contact, and various solutions had been attempted before social services were called in. Others were able to recount various previous interventions by other professionals, so the present social worker was merely the latest in a long line (see Fisher et al. 1986, p.33):

> *Interviewer:* This was a problem going back over a year?
> *Mother:* That's only a tenth of it. It goes back much further than that . . .

There followed a long history of marital problems, disputes over who should look after her child, and social services' involvement, which the mother was able to assess and put into perspective. Whilst Fisher et al. (1986) described long-term contact with social services, in our interviews there was more intermittent contact as a case was opened, then closed, and services were offered and withdrawn. The parents were usually the only long-standing party in these interventions.

In general, then, these parents' accounts were detailed and complex, encompassing a long history. They depicted themselves as competent, caring parents, and resisted being categorised as 'not coping' or neglecting their children. They described problems with their children's behaviour, difficult personal circumstances, and in the light of this had succeeded against the odds. Some showed remarkable even-handedness and appreciation of the efforts of social services.

The admission process

Now we will look at parents' views on particular aspects of the admission to accommodation. The interviews were structured chronologically, in terms of the circumstances before, during and after the admission to accommodation.

Referral

Some families had been in contact with social services for some time – since their own childhood in some cases. For others, social services intervention was a new and uncertain experience. Most, however, had some form of previous contact, but not necessarily continuous. Referral was not a straightforward process, and few cases came to the attention of social services through a professional simply pointing a parent in the appropriate direction. Where this did happen, one mother was initially very reluctant to make the first approach:

> *Mother:* I was advised to [go] for quite a long time by my GP and by [child guidance centre]. I'd been going there for help with behavioural problems I'd been having with [child] . . . I mean, at first I wouldn't take anything up on it 'cos, I mean, I have always looked after the children myself, but it got to the stage where I ended up having a nervous breakdown and I went down to about six stone, you know the scenario . . .

For others, social services intervention was triggered by others expressing concern:

> *Mother:* Somebody was phoning up and saying that I was leaving [son] with the kids, and I wasn't. That's how I got in touch with them.

Another mother contacted social services as a result of reading a booklet about the help that could be offered, but they had already been alerted by relatives and neighbours.

Referral did not involve a process of recognising a problem and asking for help. Rather, it was a result of being overwhelmed by problems, or others expressing concerns. In all cases, parents were keen to point out that there was no other option and they had little choice in the matter.

Previous experiences of care or accommodation

Most families had previous experience of care and accommodation. Some had experienced at first hand the changes of policy from Care Orders and permanence to family support. The eldest child of one mother had been taken into care and subsequently adopted. Whilst still resentful about this, she was confident that social services' approach had now changed, and was happy for her children to have periods of respite care:

> *Mother:* It's different now. They tend to keep the kids with the parents. They tend to help you with them. Like, they don't like to take the kids in unless it's really necessary . . .

A large proportion of the children had been in care or accommodation on previous occasions (about 40% of our cohort of 153 children). Some of the teenagers had undergone periods in accommodation as young children, under rather different circumstances and with different social services responses. One mother had her two children 'received into care' when they were small, during a period in which she felt she was not coping:

> *Mother:* There was one time where they went for a week with short-term foster parents, supposedly to give me a break. It was good in a sense, because they hated the woman they stayed with, so they were glad to get back to me.

These services had been offered at different times and in different circumstances to the admission of her teenage daughter, so there was little sense of being offered the same service again. The negative aspects of this first experience had discouraged a further request for admission, and the next time this mother had similar problems she sought help elsewhere. We did not find instances of parents making repeated requests for their children to be taken off their hands.

Some children had been accommodated on a number of occasions, but with rather different outcomes. We have described in Chapter 9 how respite care and 'cooling-off' were offered to some families during a family crisis, and some were appreciative. Other families, however, saw respite or short stays in accommodation as only delaying an inevitable long-term stay. One mother was increasingly unhappy with the respite care offered, and shortly after the interview the child was placed in longer-term accommodation:

> *Mother:* They keep narrowing it down, and now they only give us one day a week [with foster carer]. That is no help at all.

Another mother described how a series of admissions to residential care only made matters worse, her son's behaviour in the children's home being more disruptive than at home until he was placed with foster carers. It seemed that for some children, periods of respite care or 'time out' only postponed a longer stay in accommodation, and in the process, the delay appeared to cause further damage to relations between the children, families and social services.

Requesting help: the offer of 'preventive' services

Families' initial negotiations to have their children accommodated were sometimes very difficult. Social workers often appeared reluctant to accommodate the children, and particularly in Shiptown, preventive interventions were offered first. Some parents felt that their concerns were being played down and the problems were treated as merely 'normal' adolescent behaviour (see also Fisher et al. 1986, p.34; Triseliotis et al. 1995, p.75):

> *Interviewer:* Do you feel that they listened to your point of view?
> *Mother:* In the beginning I had a job to sort of get them to listen, that, y'know, I couldn't cope any more, and if they didn't do something I'd end up doing something stupid. But they came round eventually.

A common complaint was that parents felt that social workers saw the problem as one of family relations, and not a child's behaviour:

Mother: [Social worker] gave me the impression, she never said it, that it was us not him that was the problem, and we tried to explain to her that it was him . . .

Mother: We went to [family therapy]. Everything was directed at me. He was just drawing pictures. It was a waste of time. I had better things to do.

There were mixed feelings about the interventions offered or withheld. Those who received counselling or family work were disappointed; those not offered them felt they might have helped. One father talked about how his daughter had been receiving counselling:

Father: She was telling all sorts of lies about our family, which we found out later, basically because she didn't want to tell them she was still being sexually abused by her brother, and she was making up all sorts of silly stories and repeating things out of context, and they all came round and, 'If you did this you are not a fit parent,' and I was getting scared to go out. Things calmed down when [new social worker] took over.

This family were very disdainful about what they saw as the 'new' approach of listening to the child. Other parents felt that some sort of counselling might have dealt with the deteriorating family relations and prevented the admission, but it was not offered:

Mother: Perhaps if we had had [family therapy] at the time it would have been sorted out earlier.
Interviewer: What would you like to happen now?

Mother: Me and her go to a counsellor together, both of us, and just say how we feel about each other in front of someone else, then they can see what I mean. She's got a barrier up against me, and they think it's funny.

In summary, for these families, preventive interventions which were offered when it was too late or in an effort to persuade the family not to demand accommodation were resented. We were unable to talk to parents who were offered preventive interventions where an admission to accommodation was avoided altogether.

Requests for accommodation

Some parents considered that they had requested the admission to accommodation. They felt in control of the admission, and were consequently more appreciative. Such comments were most in evidence where temporary care had been offered in a crisis, or where respite care had been arranged. One mother had felt her own mental breakdown coming, and turned to social services for help for the first time. Admission to accommodation was organised the same day:

> *Mother:* I was really depressed, and didn't have any family that would take them on. My sister had them for a fortnight, but she lives [90 miles away]. I was going into hospital, and likely to be there longer than a few weeks – it's a long time to be away. My husband didn't want to take any more time off work. I didn't know how long I'd be before I was well again. I needed a placement nearby, where we could keep in touch.

She thought social services had been 'really helpful', and was particularly appreciative that the children continued to attend the same school – 'the best thing about it'.

Another mother was in a state of distress when accommodation was offered, and was unequivocal in her praise for social services. She had recently moved into the area, and all her previous support services were crumbling:

> *Mother:* When I got in touch [with social services] I was in desperation, phoning up and asking Directory Enquiries for the local social services. [Social worker] came round. Talk about landing it on her lap! 'I don't want [daughter] moved from school. My marriage has just broken up, blah, blah' – this, that and the other. And she goes, 'Oh dear.' But she went straight into battle and secured [a respite carer] . . . It gave me a breathing space.

The mother felt her situation had been understood and had received a sympathetic response. The help offered by social services was seen as appropriate, and was most appreciated.

Disputed admissions

Other parents were less happy with the response they received from social services. Admission had occurred only after a series of disputes between parents and social services, and was not achieved with a mutual appreciation of the situation. In Chapter 11 we discussed the 'last resort' response, where social services avoid admission to accommodation until all other options have been tried. Some parents also had a similar attitude: a 'last straw' view. They had already tried every alternative, and now accommodation was the only option. These parents found social services' response frustrating and undermining (see Fisher et al. 1986, p.43):

> *Mother:* We'd been offered no help whatsoever. When he ran away to [step-mother] we'd had enough, that was it. We asked for him to be taken into care.
>
> *Interviewer:* Had you thought about it for some time?
>
> *Mother:* Yeah, oh yeah, this had been a long-running thing. I didn't want him to go. In the end I couldn't take it no more 'cos it wasn't us that were suffering, the other children were suffering more. But they wouldn't let us. They offered us respite care, which was a weekend in foster care . . . One day makes no difference. He might as well be here all the time. We wanted a longer period.

Eventually, some parents felt they were forced into underhand ways of obtaining acccommodation. For some, this entailed refusing to let the child return home after s/he had run away or been picked up for an offence:

> *Mother:* They eventually found her, she gave herself up to the police. The police phoned to say, 'We're bringing her back home.' I said, 'Don't bother. I'm not going through this again.'

Some families felt that social services' earlier refusal to offer accommodation pushed them to extreme action, including threats of violence. For some, a request for help was re-interpreted as child abuse (see Farmer and Owen 1995, p.50), and events moved quicker:

> *Mother:* I said to [duty officer], 'Things are so bad I want to kill her. I really do want to kill her.' And he said, 'Have you hit her?' Well, before I went over there [daughter] had punched me and I had a great big swollen lip. Well, I pushed her and she fell into the wall, so I told [duty officer] this. He said, 'Has she marked herself?' I said, 'Well, she's got a bump on her head.' And he said, 'Well, I'll have to come over and see her.' I didn't know what he meant by this, y'know? So he came over and he talked to [daughter], and I'd left the room exactly as it was, as she's smashed it up

and everything. But it seemed all he was interested in was that I'd actually marked her. And he said to me, 'Because you've actually admitted to marking her, we could hold a case conference against you to see if you are all right to keep the other children.'

It would be wrong to interpret parents' 'manipulative' behaviour as deliberate or well thought out. When family crises are erupting, social services' response is not necessarily uppermost in parents' minds. Fisher et al. (1986, p.46) suggest that such manipulation exists by showing that crises occurred when the social worker allocated to the case was on holiday, or at night. However, as the comments above suggest, it is more likely that the 'last straw' determines the families' reaction. There were others who were more immediately involved in the crisis – friends, family, neighbours, teachers, and so on – and often social services was only one of several actors in such situations. As we saw in Chapter 5, the police were involved in many of these circumstances, and were sometimes seen as more sympathetic:

> *Mother:* [Social services] were always pushing it back to us: 'It's your problem.' A woman police constable was very helpful to us. She told us that we could get rid of him, we could get him accommodated: 'It's your right.'

Sometimes these differences were resolved as social services were persuaded to come round to the parents' way of thinking, but in other cases difficult relations remained. Requests for respite care or temporary care were received more sympathetically, as were short-term admissions for younger children. However, some of the parents of teenagers found the refusal of their appeals for admission to accommodation difficult to understand.

Social workers and social services procedures

In this section we consider parents' views of social workers as they became more embroiled in negotiating working relations with social services. The parents' reaction to social workers often depended on whether their views agreed with their own. If the parents felt that social workers thought differently about issues like punishing children or child rearing, their approach was more guarded.

Social workers and social work intervention as supportive

Some parents were satisfied that the social workers had gone along with their version of the problem and how it should be handled, and consequently were more satisfied. As the mother of a teenage girl said:

> *Mother:* The social workers were brilliant, even from the beginning. I don't
> think that they were biased in any way . . . They couldn't have done any
> more . . . At first the social workers are for the child . . . you've got to
> understand that, but as you get to know each other, the situation relaxes.

Other parents felt they reached agreement with social services when it became clear that social services were no more successful at handling their children than they had been, thereby endorsing their view of the problem:

> *Father:* Then they discovered, 'Oh shit, he really is a little bastard,' y'know?

Social workers were also appreciated in difficult situations. One mother who was highly critical of the child protection investigation still found her social worker supportive:

> *Mother:* I have received support from the social services, especially from [pre-
> sent social worker]. I like her. I have no complaints about her: She has
> helped me a lot, actually.

It is not easy to delineate specific aspects of social workers and social work intervention that were automatically appreciated. We have already seen how families reacted differently to the offer of preventive services such as family therapy. There was a suggestion that help with practical problems – financial or housing – was particularly appreciated, but such an approach had to be managed carefully. If you presented too many problems, a request for practical help could be interpreted as 'not coping'; if too few, social services would not accept that the situation was serious enough. One mother had been in long-term contact with the social services department, and received a lot of financial help:

> *Mother:* When you ask for help, you think, 'Oh God,' y'know, 'should I ask for
> that or shan't I?' And you've got this in the back of your mind all the
> time: 'Well, shall I ask for help? I don't know what's going to happen. Are

they going to take my children off me 'cos I've asked for help?' You just don't know. So I'm a bit wary of asking. I only ask when I've got to.

You had to be careful to present as a deserving mother, but not a non-coping one.

One mother expected social workers to help with practical problems, even when she was reminded that some aspects were not within the social workers' remit:

> *Mother:* I think they should have helped find better accommodation.
> *Interviewer:* Social services don't always have a say in the allocation of houses, that's the housing department.
> *Mother:* Yes, but there are hostels and places like that, which would have been better than one room [in a bed and breakfast].

There were particular attributes of social workers and ways of working which parents appreciated (see also Brown 1984, p.97):

> *Mother:* You can actually talk to them now. When [social worker] comes round and sits down, I tell him what I like and basically what I want help with, this sort of thing. Whereas in the past if you said, 'I'm having trouble coping,' I mean, their answer was at that time they'd send someone round, and 'cos the housework was done, that meant I was coping. Whereas now they'll actually listen, y'know: why you aren't coping, this sort of thing.

One mother remembered her first social worker fondly, in contrast to her present one:

> *Mother:* [First social worker] came round regular. She was more for us, as well. With [present social worker], he's not for us. He's not even for [child], because he doesn't have a lot to do with him. I can't understand why he's a social worker, because he doesn't exist as far as we are concerned; [first social worker] did. We'd have a meeting and she'd write it all down, she'd go away and have it all typed. She was brilliant. We could talk to her ourselves, she'd sit there for ages. She'd explain, we'd listen. We don't have that any more with [present social worker].

'Sitting down' seemed to be an indicator of someone who was prepared to take time to listen.

Being supported in bringing up difficult children or in difficult circumstances was also appreciated. Other parents looked to smaller displays of support:

> *Mother:* . . . I used to say [to previous social worker], 'I'm frightened with what [daughter] is going to do.' 'OK, yes, all right', and she used to sit down and have a word with [daughter]. Now [present social worker] is different. I said they couldn't have a sandwich until I did it myself. Now she'd watch them go into the kitchen, she stood in the kitchen while they made themselves a sandwich. Now that's a social worker for you. [Previous social worker] wouldn't have done that.

Contact, or lack of it, was also seen as an indicator of interest:

> *Mother:* [Social worker] is useless. He says he'll visit, then we never see him. Then he drops a card in the minute you are out.

> *Mother:* I've never really been involved with [present social worker]. He hasn't been in touch with me at all, only to say that there is a meeting on such and such a day. I don't see him often since [son] has been accommodated.

Most of the parents were appreciative of at least one social worker with whom they had been in contact, even in cases where they were at odds with social services over the decisions made.

Interference in family matters

A number of parents felt that social services' involvement had been interfering, undermining or controlling. This was particularly the case where there were child protection concerns, and where parents were seen as not coping adequately with bringing up their children. One mother described the sense of shock and intrusion at the scale of a child protection investigation, and the loss of control:

> *Mother:* I don't know, they just came . . . to tell you the truth, this is going to sound really crude and horrible against them, they *barged* in here, which made me even more worked up than what I was. They barged through the door, and I thought to myself, 'I asked for a bit of help', and they knocked on the door and I looked at them, and I thought, 'Well, who are you?' And they came in, and they were watching me. Obviously, they thought I couldn't cope with [baby], which I know I couldn't anyway,

because that is why I asked for help in the first place. And all they were concerned about was what I was up to, what I was doing, had I had anything to eat and things like that. They said that I couldn't, and I admitted it, that I couldn't put [baby] to bed properly, which I couldn't. I didn't ask for the type of help that they gave me.

This mother conveyed the sense of shock and invasion with the emphasised 'barged in' (see also Farmer and Owen 1995, p.54). She was aware of having problems, but the social workers' intervention took away her ability to recognise her problems. Any sense of being in control of the request for help was cast aside. The resentment also produced a justifiable sense of paranoia: 'they were watching me'.

Many of the processes appeared to confirm the parents' marginal status (this was also reflected in their sense of being excluded at meetings, which we explore later in this chapter). Social services appeared to take control, and normal family decision-making was suspended. One mother described how the social worker had said her child '*had*' to go to play school, because he was 'getting out of her control' at home. Another mother ironically noted her marginal status:

Mother: I was told that I was going to be given a plan thing for him, which I didn't get. So I thought, 'Well, they know what they are doing. They are the high-ups. I'm just me, just the baby's mother.'

Another mother described her sense of powerlessness when faced with the scrutiny of social services:

Mother: They want to take over your kids, social services. All right, they're your kids, but they seem to be in charge of them. You're not in charge of them now, *they* are sort of thing, and it's nice, sort of like, when they help you, but they go too far . . . Like, I smacked [son], he was playing up one day, and I smacked him and I forgot [social worker] was actually here. Well, 'You shouldn't do that, you can do it another way,' and they seem to be taking over. They seemed as if they're in charge of your kids. 'You do what we want you to do, you're only looking after them,' sort of thing, 'They're only on loan to you,' sort of thing, and 'We're in charge of the kids.' Or, like, another thing is the kids, ehm, you complain, say, 'It's not fair, I'm trying my best with my kids,' and it's people up the road, they get away with blue murder and leave their kids on their own, and I gets told that I've left my kids on their own when I've never. Whatever you do, it doesn't seem fair, y'know? Social services have got all their priorities wrong at the moment. People that need help, it's too late for them to do anything about, and the people that are trying, they are down their necks 24 hours a day once they've got their clutches on you.

This was part of a long monologue in which the mother gradually upgraded her depiction of social services' control of her family life. She did not merely repeat the same phrase, but extended and elaborated the experience of interference: 'they're in charge of your kids' is extended to 'they're only on loan to you', and in 'their clutches'.

Distrust of social services for interfering and not dealing with the right families was a common theme. One mother told of her suspicions about social services as a result of contacts unrelated to her son being accommodated:

> *Mother:* I'll give you an example. My daughter fell on a nail and damaged her knee. Someone reported me and said I'd kicked her. Well, I never even hit my children, never mind kick them. Another example of it, they went to a play scheme, and my son, the younger one, he'd been on a slide, he'd taken the skin off his back, and they asked him what had happened to him. He's a little bit slow, he goes to a special school, and he said he didn't know, and without me knowing, they involved social services, and one of the social services went down there and they inspected him, and they called an urgent meeting because they thought he'd been beaten or something. I just look at social services this way: the places they should be and the children they should be dealing with, they never get it right.

Some of these descriptions by parents were complex and evocative. There were some common themes. The wrong sort of help had been offered, contrasts were drawn between those parents who were trying their best and those who were 'the real villains', and social services' intervention was depicted as heavy-handed. The sophisticated use of figurative expressions enriched their descriptions, and effectively portrayed the sense of injustice and intrusion they felt.

Conflicting views of punishment and control

One theme which frequently distinguished social workers' views from those of parents was the appropriate use of punishment. There were several aspects to this apparent gulf – the parents' punishment was seen as inappropriate by social workers, but not their friends and family;

by having their control questioned, parents felt their authority was being undermined, and once accommodated, the rules were not in accord with parents' wishes. This further illustrates the parents' loss of control of their children.

One family was persuaded to place their son in respite care, though they had asked for a longer stay:

> *Mother:* He's a swine when he is at home. He puts the rest of the children through hell, and we've been told we are not allowed to hit him. We are not allowed to do this and that. So, really, they have taken over our child and our home. So he knows they've told him that we are not allowed to do this or that. Every time we say, 'Right, you're going to get a smack' – 'I'll call the police.' They've not helped us at all. He's no better, they've made him worse.

Later, this mother described how he was causing similar problems at the foster home, but the foster carer was also not allowed to control him:

> *Mother:* I asked the foster parent to punish him. He is getting away with it. The [foster carer's daughter] shouldn't have to go through that. I also asked social services for him to be punished because that's the only way to deal with him. He will behave if you punish him. They turned round and said no. She is not allowed to smack him, she isn't allowed to take away his possessions, she isn't allowed to keep him in. The only thing she can do is send him to his room, where he has got all his toys, so it's no punishment. He's sitting up there laughing his head off. We are very strict parents, and when he goes to the foster parents he has got all this freedom.

This mother's attitude to punishment was apparently supported by family and friends:

> *Mother:* When I talk to other women down the school, and every time it comes up, 'Oh, you can't hit them because social services will do this or that. You can't even tell them off now.' That's what a lot of the women say. Half of them have the same attitude as me. They don't have to bring them up, they don't have them 24 hours a day. They only see them for two seconds.

In localities where a number of families were involved with social services, a picture was painted of whole communities at odds with the values and methods of social services. Another mother complained at the different standards in the foster home, which meant her daughter could not readjust to her rules when she returned home:

> *Mother:* I eventually said I'd have her back. My husband said, 'If she comes back it's under our terms, our rules.' But the social worker was trying to say that she's got certain rules that she's learnt outside. I said, 'When she comes back under my roof, it's got to be my rules.' And on top of that she was getting £10 – no, £7 – from them. So there's no way I could afford £7 per week . . . She was allowed to go out when she wanted, and when she was home, it was sort of four nights a week she was allowed out. She'd been to the night clubs. I don't blame the foster parent for that, perhaps they didn't know . . . Obviously, some things I approved of and some I didn't, like how the hell did she manage to get pregnant in care?

Concepts of punishment and rules were important to families. Social services' apparently different standards were seen as reflecting both the middle-class attitudes of the social workers and, sometimes, their lack of experience of bringing up children. However, it was not merely perceived as a difference in preference, but as further unfair condemnation and control of family relations.

Much of the above has focused on the parents' conflicts with and animosity towards social services, so it should be re-emphasised that most parents made *some* complimentary comments regarding social workers and the help they were offered. It was harder for the parents to spend time explaining how helpful social workers had been: 'I've got no complaints' does not lead to a long, detailed description. However, it was also the case that a large proportion of parents had criticisms of social services, and for some, their experiences had given rise to strong feelings of being controlled and undermined. It should also be noted that parents' attempts to portray themselves to the interviewer as morally upright, doing the best for their children and not one of 'those' families that should be the focus of social services scrutiny necessarily entailed a strong attack on their supposed accusers.

What was surprising about some of these descriptions were the sophisticated arguments and justifications some parents used to illustrate their strong sense of being undermined and controlled. Parents who were often seen by professionals as hostile or inarticulate were able to convey their sense of injustice in a convincing manner, and to present their own efforts as the best they could do in the circumstances. Perhaps for some professionals such alternative versions of the situation were construed as the parents failing to face up to their 'real' problems, so were dismissed as 'denial'. However, unless such views are given an adequate hearing, partnership with parents will be difficult to sustain.

Meetings

We discussed the process and content of meetings in Chapter 12. Both local authorities included parents and, where appropriate, children in all meetings. We will see in Chapter 14 that the young people had a fairly consistent dislike of meetings; their parents were more ambivalent, although the majority also found them difficult occasions. The parents were aware of the different types of meetings, and could compare planning meetings with case conferences, and meetings at early stages of contact with later ones. Invariably, the first meeting and the child protection conference were much more distressing than later planning meetings.

The initial meeting

For many of the families, the first meeting the parents remembered was a child protection conference, although the first planning meeting was experienced in a similar way. There were many strangers discussing the family's most intimate matters. The experience was humiliating:

> *Mother:* I felt angry all the way through. There you are, thinking, 'Oh my God, I've failed as a parent,' and there are all these people sitting round – head, deputy head – professional people. I just thought it was an awful set-up, y'know . . . I wasn't overwhelmed, I get bolshie in those sorts of situations. But at one point I stormed out in tears 'cos I felt so humiliated. I felt it was bad enough to have to play into their hands by, y'know, the only way to get help was to hit your daughter. And then to have to sit there . . .

> *Mother:* I walked into the room, and I was nervous as it was, because obviously you're going into something that is like judge and jury on you. And you walk in, and I looked at the people and I thought to myself, 'I've got to sit here in front of all these people, being judged and . . . Well, everyone introduced themselves, like they do, they all go round the table. You don't take it all in, because there's so many people, all going, 'Hello, my name is so and so.' You have to acknowledge them, but you don't take it in . . .

These descriptions are similar to those in Farmer and Owen (1995, p.109–14). A law court metaphor appeared to sum up the experiences of these parents – entering a large room with unfamiliar people and rules, where their behaviour was the main subject for discussion and judgement. They described a double degradation: first, accepting that their care of their children had been identified as deficient, but second, that this was now the subject of an occasion for debate and cross-examination by powerful figures, some known to them, others not. This feeling of being out of place was echoed in descriptions of planning meetings:

> *Mother:* The first time you go, you feel as though . . .
> *Father:* . . . you're an alien.
> *Mother:* Yeah. You don't feel right. You don't say a lot. Whatever they say, you agree with to start with, even if it's not quite what you want.

This mother was now happy with the service offered by social services, but remembered how the first planning meeting had felt. (This was the only comment by the father during the whole interview.) Not surprisingly in such an atmosphere, parents only felt able to contribute either by saying very little or by being hostile. This accords with the authors' observations of meetings described in Chapter 12. Similar reactions of anxiety and anger were described by parents to Farmer and Owen (1995, p.116) in relation to child protection conferences.

Meetings were also experienced as a collective group of people who held a joint view of where the family was going wrong:

> *Father:* Everybody told us we were wrong at that planning meeting . . .
> *Interviewer:* Usually each person has a talk . . .
> *Mother:* Yeah, and they all had a jolly good go at me . . .

The parents appeared to feel alienated from the professionals at meetings, some of whom might have been sympathetic or helpful. One mother described the professionals as 'clucky' and 'like mother hens' – all knowledgeable and condemnatory of her inappropriate child care. The formality and ritual of discussion and expressing opinions were experienced as humiliating. Yet dramatic and strong expressions of emotions were ever-present. The anxiety provoked by meetings was also related to discussing family crises in front of teenage children:

> *Mother:* To sit there in the room with your child and have to discuss that sort of thing, it's just unbearable. Maybe, sort of, you could discuss it with

your social worker, and maybe then they could say at the meeting: 'Well, [mother] thinks this or that.'

This mother felt she would prefer not to attend a meeting where the feelings were too intense, as long as her point of view was represented. Another parent was embarrassed that *her* parents, with whom she rarely talked openly, were invited to the meeting. It did seem that at some meetings the family members were expected to act out the family disputes. The parents reported incidents including tears, storming out, attempted assaults on family members and turning over the coffee table.

Decision-making

Some meetings were organised as an occasion for debate and discussion, whereas others were more concerned with making decisions. Farmer and Owen (1995, p.116) comment that at child protection meetings, parents feared that their children would be placed in care, even if it was not being actively considered. In some of these planning meetings, decisions about accommodation or rehabilitation were very much to the fore. This sense of the power to impose decisions on the families exacerbated the impersonal and collective nature of the meeting.

Some of the procedures were seen as manipulative: it was felt that some meetings were organised in such a way that only certain topics were acceptable for discussion and consideration, whilst others were discouraged. One mother was aware that social services wanted her child to return home, and she was reluctant to go along with this. However, she felt that the meetings did not allow open discussion of the matter:

> *Mother:* Well, I don't know how to say this. They only ask the questions when they know the answer. When they ask me about how he is doing at home, they only want to hear the good points. They don't want to know about his bad behaviour. They cover it up. They want him back home. They aren't going to do him any good.

Other parents felt that the nature of the questioning at meetings pressurised them to make decisions:

> *Mother:* They put pressure on you, sort of, like: 'Do you think it's best for this, or do you think it's best if we do that?'

The meetings encouraged (perhaps required) a style of questioning –
'What is happening?' 'Why?' 'What should happen next?' – which moved
the discussion in directions which were inevitable, yet for which the
parents were not ready. One mother had placed her children in accommodation because she was in a bed and breakfast and suffering some
distress. She needed a break, but was reluctant for the children to
return to the bed and breakfast. However, the tenor of the meeting was
that because of her living arrangements and the children's need for a
home, they should go to live with their father:

> *Mother:* I told them [my situation], so they said, 'Well, you've got to decide
> what you want to do with them at the meeting.' So I said, 'Well, let
> them stay with their dad,' and I signed some papers for the social services
> to let them stay with their dad and their nan . . . They said, 'Are you
> happy with that?' I said, 'Yeah.' But I wasn't really. I just wasn't thinking
> properly.

Another family was faced with the revelation that their oldest son had
been abusing his sister. He was immediately admitted to accommodation, but the mother felt that the subseqent meeting was too eager to
make decisions and plan for the future:

> *Mother:* They shouldn't have chucked everything at me. I was in too much of a
> state to really make any decent decision . . . Everything was too raw and
> the questions were too personal, you know what I mean? Everything
> about that first meeting wasn't right. I mean, for that first meeting, it
> maybe should have been a case of, 'Well, we are going to be looking into
> those allegations. In the mean time he'll be staying here. Are you happy
> with that?' And I could have bit back my tears and said, 'Yes, I'm quite
> happy with that.' 'Then we'll arrange a planning meeting for so and so,
> when we've got more idea about what's going on.' Now, that I could
> have probably coped with. There was too much thrust at you, it was too
> much to cope with.

Although the mother calls this 'that first meeting', it was only the first
in this episode. The family had been the subject of several previous
meetings, demonstrating that familiarity did not compensate for the
emotional content of meetings. The meeting appeared to be an entity
separate from its participants, the professionals were depicted as speaking with a single voice, and decisions were received as a uniform
opinion, and thus imposed a transcendent sense of judgement on those
present. (Lewis (1994, p.110) describes uniformity of opinion in child

protection conferences which operates against disagreement as 'group-think'.) In a number of these quotations, the use of 'they' represents the professionals, and is contrasted with 'us', the family. The extensive use of reported speech dramatically emphasises how the meeting is perceived as speaking with a single voice in conversation with the parent. Farmer and Owen (1995, p.114) describe the isolation experienced by parents at child protection conferences, highlighting the need to be accompanied by friends or advocates. (See also Corby (1987).)

Later meetings

As they became more familiar with social services' procedures, some parents understood what was happening, and could make a contribution. Others, however, remained reserved:

> *Interviewer:* How do you find those sorts of meetings?
> *Mother:* Some were all right, some wasn't. She was with some [foster parents], I didn't like them at all. But it was a home for [daughter]. At that type of meeting I used to clam up. I didn't say anything. They used to say 'Oh, you are not saying anything.' I used to say, 'No. It's all right, I'm just taking it all in.'

The mother quoted earlier who described the first meeting as 'too raw and . . . personal' now found it fairly easy to talk in meetings, especially with her present social worker:

> *Interviewer:* Do you find you can get your point of view over at meetings now?
> *Mother:* Yeah, definitely . . . I will tell [social worker] exactly what I think, and if I think something is not brought up, I will actually put over my point of view. You don't feel intimidated that you can't turn round and say, 'I want this and that.' But then again, [social worker] is quite happy to turn round and say, 'No, we can't do that.'

Another mother felt that the meetings were helpful in order to keep a check on promises that had been made:

> *Interviewer:* Where do you find them the most helpful?
> *Mother:* Yeah, in the meetings. When they've said they are going to do this and that and nothing's done.
> *Interviewer:* Is that better than just talking to your social worker?
> *Mother:* Yes. It makes me laugh, what's said in the meeting and it never gets done.

Some later meetings were merely to monitor the placement, and the parents were happier with the lower emotional content. They accepted that they should attend such meetings, even if they were less involved in the child's care:

> *Mother:* It is very different [when you are planning the next step]. They are quite easy and comfortable to go to. Generally speaking, the planning meetings are all right, and you get your minutes, and if something hasn't been done, you can go back to [social worker].

Other later meetings were still stressful if difficult decisions were being made:

> *Mother:* At the last meeting, it was very difficult. I didn't agree with what they were doing [advertising for foster carers]. I also decided that I don't want any further contact with [son]. No more visits, no contact. It was very hard. I feel hurt by what he did . . .

Almost without exception, parents talked of the meetings as uncomfortable experiences, particularly initial meetings and case conferences, but later meetings could also be stressful if difficult decisions were being made or new crises occurred. (Similarly, a quarter of the parents interviewed in Triseliotis et al. (1995, p.215) felt they had been unable to express their opinions at key meetings, and in a few cases the social workers were completely unaware of the parents' feelings of exclusion.) However, in our own study most parents eventually became more used to the meeting, and felt better able to contribute – as one parent said, 'You learn their ways.'

Summary

Throughout this book we have alluded to the concept of working in partnership with parents. Ryan (1994, p.4) suggests that although it is not mentioned in the Children Act, it is the central theme in the Guidance, and this applies to the provision of accommodation. For example, Volume 2 states:

> ◆ Partnership with parents and consultation with children on the basis of careful joint planning and agreement is the guiding principle for the provision of services within the family home and where children are provided with accommodation under voluntary arrangements. Such arrangements

are intended to assist the parent and enhance, not undermine, the parent's authority and control. (DoH 1991a, para.2.1)

Listening to and understanding parents' views of their family problems, social services' procedures and the services available is a vital first step. Marsh and Fisher (1992, p.7) note that partnership has become the 'dominating principle in welfare provision . . . recasting the relationship between users and services'. But they also note the difficulty faced by workers in developing appropriate working practices, particularly in areas of risk and conflict. Aldgate (1992) suggests that a major change of approach is required, from a pathological model to an ecological model which recognises the environmental stresses on an individual's functioning.

In this chapter we have heard parents describe their experiences of and attitudes to their children being admitted to accommodation. Some were generally satisfied with the extent to which their views directed the provision of services. They felt that social workers listened carefully to their problems, sympathised with their predicament and offered services which were appropriate and supportive. This applied to the offer of accommodation, especially if it was a respite care programme or on the basis of family support. It also applied when parents felt that social services (eventually) came to understand and experience their children's behaviour difficulties. Other parents were resentful about the admission to accommodation, however, particularly when they felt it was undertaken in an atmosphere of criticism and undermined their parental abilities. Whether the pressure to accommodate came from the parents or social workers, their parenting abilities were being questioned, and their parental authority was being undermined, not enhanced. Consequently, they felt excluded from decisions, their commitment to planning was half-hearted, and they avoided subsequent social services contact.

What can we learn from parents' views to enable us to develop accommodation in an atmosphere of family support and partnership? First, it is clear that particular features of the circumstances of the admission determined how accommodation was offered and received. Accommodation offered as respite care for children with disabilities or behaviour difficulties, or where the parents had health problems, was clearly seen by all parties as supporting families. Extending a family support approach to families which are 'not coping' and whose children are at risk or out of control has been the subject of recent research and comment (Audit Commission 1994; DoH 1995).

A family support approach acknowledges parents' desire to establish that they are caring, and recognises their efforts to bring up their children in difficult circumstances, whether they result from marital problems, lack of income or poor housing. The Guidance recognises parents' needs and problems whilst acknowledging that services under Section 20 of the Children Act are provided primarily to meet the needs of children. However, it also recognises environmental and personal pressures:

♦ Parents are individuals with needs of their own. Even though services may be offered primarily on behalf of children parents are entitled to help and consideration in their own right. Just as some young people are more vulnerable than others, so are some mothers and fathers. Their parenting capacity may be limited temporarily or permanently by poverty, racism, poor housing or unemployment or by personal or marital problems, sensory or physical disability, mental illness or past life experiences. (DoH 1990, p.8)

It concludes: 'Lack of parenting skills or inability to provide adequate care should not be equated with lack of affection or irresponsibility' (DoH 1990, p.8). Aldgate (1992, p.91) considers that parents should be seen as 'valuable resources and therefore should be valued by society'. Such an approach does not fit easily with the 'legacy of child rescue' (Aldgate 1992, p.92). Parents' experiences of being undermined and criticised as social workers gatekeep the provision of accommodation do not support families in caring for their children, and are in stark contrast to the family support associated with respite care or short-term family relief.

Second, we noted at the beginning of this chapter that parents' accounts were complex, describing events in ways that depicted them as caring parents, if not always coping ones. The complexity and subtlety of these accounts was surprising, and resisted simple categorisations of their being 'not coping' or 'rejecting' parents. Their stories appeared more rounded than the social workers' descriptions or the parents' contributions in meetings. They presented long-term views of what had happened to their families, assessments of the many attempts to gain help, as well as plausible explanations of disputed incidents. Whilst clearly this was a one-sided view of the circumstances, our concern is that such views might not be adequately represented in the deliberations and decision-making arenas of social services.

Third, it might be suggested that the way parents present their problems to social services has an important effect on how social services categorises them. If parents present themselves as 'caring but not coping', it seems that social services' response is to offer family support, ranging from a sympathetic ear to accommodation as a break. However, if the parents present themselves as 'caring and competent' and give the impression the child is to blame, their view of the problem is likely to be treated less sympathetically. What our analysis has shown is that parents are careful to present their family problems in a light that is least stigmatising, and such depictions are important features of 'impression management' (Goffman 1959). It is thus likely that responses which confront or undermine these stories are likely to misunderstand the parents' need to protect themselves, and may endanger working in partnership. Social workers need to be aware of parents' need to maintain their view of themselves as caring to avoid the stigma of being blamed for their child's actions.

Fourth, a number of areas of conflict were related to differences between middle-class professionals and working-class families. Differences in perceptions of punishment were a particular source of misunderstanding, with parents reporting that 'normal' control was interpreted as abuse. Such aspects of everyday relations between parents and children displayed the extent to which families felt that social services' scrutiny pervaded their family relations. Reports, meetings and inter-professional discussion may be daily fare for social work professionals, but they are unfamiliar to many working-class families. The experiences of parents supported the discussion in Chapter 12 regarding the appropriateness of meetings.

Fifth, despite parents' descriptions of difficult meetings and unsympathetic responses, some of the dissatisfied parents eventually became familiar with and accepted social services' interpretations and procedures. Some parents felt that it was social services which came to accept their versions of events, not they who had changed. Either way, compromises were made and reasonable working relationships were established. (Cleaver and Freeman (1995, p.69) note that the 'operational perspectives' of parents and professionals in child abuse cases can gradually move closer together, and more satisfactory outcomes can develop.) In particular, they felt better able to contribute at meetings. However, such compromises do not necessarily mean that agreement was freely entered into. Researchers have noted how, once their children are in care, parents are less involved in decision-making (Kufeldt et al.

1989), and in the present study parents described accepting reluctantly that social services could (or would) not help in the way that they wanted.

The provision of accommodation as a supportive service is the aim of the Children Act, and when it was offered in this way, the parents were more satisfied. This was an important message of the *Who Needs Care?* study (Packman et al. 1986). From the interviews in the present study it seems that parents are more in tune with accommodation as a means of supporting their parenting than some social workers are. Listening to parents requires an understanding of their perspectives and sensitivity to family problems, parenting and social services' responses: these are complex issues which require careful negotiation and an acknowledgement of parents' strengths, not simplistic categorisations or rigid gatekeeping. Some writers consider that only by establishing accommodation as a universal provision – open to all and available on demand – can the stigma attached to it be overcome (see Aldgate 1992, p.90).

14 *Young people's views*

In this chapter we discuss the views of young people who were placed in accommodation. (Although some of those interviewed were aged under 13, we will generally use the collective term 'young people' throughout this chapter, since the majority were aged 13 and over.) A number of recent studies on this subject with larger cohorts have elicited similar views to the present study (for example, Fletcher (1993); Willow (1995); Morris and Wheatley (1994); Triseliotis et al. (1995)), but the main difference lies in the aim of our analysis. Half the young people in our cohort had already returned home, and we were more interested in their views of the process of admission and placement than the experience of being in accommodation. Furthermore, we interviewed the young people's parents (or carers) and social workers, which means we can compare their views with those of the young people.

Fewer interviews were conducted with young people than with their parents (18 in all), since some were too young to be interviewed or it was considered inappropriate by the social worker or parent. Not all were 'interviews' in the strictest sense: some of the younger children participated in their parents' or foster parents' interview rather than being interviewed separately. Even so, they made cogent comments about what had happened to them. The more formal interviews lasted as long as their parents' and many young people displayed a similar degree of subtlety and complexity. Others were less forthcoming: those who remained in accommodation were still involved in the experience, and it seemed harder for them to place what had happened to them in perspective. (Other studies have used questionnaires or group interviews, and Willow (1995, p.7) notes that the young people in her sample also found it hard to talk about their emotional needs.) Unlike their parents, where in some ways the admission to accommodation marked the end of an episode, for the young people it was the beginning of a situation which had yet to be resolved. However, they did reflect on earlier admissions and placements, life at home before the admission and the circumstances of the latest admission, but less on their present placement. Those who were now back at home were able to describe the accommodation experience from beginning to end, but some recounted it as a distant experience, better forgotten and not really understood. Others had thought about it at some length, however, and felt able to put it into perspective now.

The events leading to admission to accommodation

In Chapter 13, parents described the admission to accommodation as the culmination of developments over a long period. It was not the result of an isolated incident, rather the last straw in a deteriorating pattern of difficult behaviour and family relations. The young people were less clear about the existence of such a pattern and a history of deterioration. For some, the breakdown at home was unexpected:

> *Young man aged 17:* I actually thought it was quite OK at home. I didn't think there was really anything wrong.

This young person admitted that he had been in trouble with the police and at school, but had felt he was getting on well with his parents. Over 60% of the young people in the study by Triseliotis et al. (1995, p.56) thought they got on well with their parents. Others felt there had been arguments at home, but within the bounds of normality for teenager–parent relations:

> *Girl aged 15:* It was mainly teenager arguments and that. I don't know. The arguments got more and more bad, and I suppose Mum thought she couldn't cope any more.
> *Interviewer:* What was your view of it?
> *Girl:* I knew we was having arguments, but I didn't think it was that bad to have sent me away, if you know what I mean.

Unlike their parents, the young people did not discuss their own behaviour, but described 'lots of rows'. They put these down to personality conflicts with their parents, although the presence of stepparents was highlighted as a factor. They often accepted that they were equally to blame:

> *Young man aged 16:* It wasn't all their fault at all. I used to irritate my mum. Start an argument. I got it down to a fine art. Six of one and half a dozen of the other. I'd annoy her and she'd go mad and start whacking me.

> *Girl aged 15:* We'd argue about anything, really. Me and my mum are totally different, and we just don't get on. We'd row about the stupidest things.

These young people appeared to be normalising or playing down the problems which led up to the admission, unlike their parents. They did not share the 'last straw' view. There were problems, but they were not seen as serious enough to warrant what happened. Whereas the parents saw themselves as normal, concerned parents whose children were out of control, the young people depicted themselves as normal but misunderstood and misrepresented teenagers. None of them thought they had been admitted because they were at risk of abuse or neglect from their parents, even though some of the rows had led to assaults.

Most of these families had a history of contact with social services and had been the subject of a series of preventive interventions. However, the young people described being on the margins of the family's contact with the social worker: the social worker had come to see their parents, and they had seen little of them until the admission to accommodation was imminent. They described participating in a range of interventions, but not often with the family social worker.

> *Interviewer:* Can you remember why you had a social worker?
> *Girl aged 10:* Because I had problems. My brother kept crying and puking.
> *Interviewer:* Did the social worker come to speak to you about it?
> *Girl:* No, she used to talk to my mum.

> *Girl aged 15:* We had a social worker, but I didn't have much contact. They just talked to Mum and Dad.

This girl was involved in a number of social services projects – camping trips, a group at the family centre and counselling sessions with a different social worker:

> *Interviewer:* What did you think of the counselling sessions?
> *Girl:* I just thought it was brilliant to be out of home.
> *Interviewer:* Did they help things at home?
> *Girl:* No, not really. When it came to it, I didn't know what to say, what to talk about. Things would happen, but when it came to seeing her, everything was fine. There weren't much to talk about.

A 15-year-old boy had been admitted to accommodation on three occasions at the request of his mother. However, he did not remember the social worker offering counselling between himself and his mother:

> *Interviewer:* Did you see your social worker regularly?
> *Boy:* Yes.

> *Interviewer:* Did you have sessions with you and your mum to talk things out?
>
> *Boy:* Not really. A couple of meetings, that's all . . . I talked to the social worker, but I don't know why I didn't get on [at home].

One 16-year-old young woman had been in regular contact with the family social worker when her father's mental illness had been acute, two years earlier:

> *Interviewer:* Did you see the social worker regularly?
>
> *Young woman:* Yeah. He used to come round and see us every week and that, and ask us about what we felt about my dad's behaviour and that, try and counsel us and that . . . the social worker just decided that we needed to talk and that, get things out.
>
> *Interviewer:* And was it helpful?
>
> *Young woman:* Yeah, it was helpful to get it off our chest.

Social services also organised a holiday, which she really enjoyed. However, she next saw a social worker the day before she was admitted to accommodation.

In general, the young people enjoyed the holidays and recreational activities offered by social services, but were less clear about the helpfulness of counselling or family therapy, rather like their parents. This rather limited contact with social workers was an important feature which was raised again at the time of admission to accommodation.

The admission to accommodation

Many of these young people had been placed in accommodation on previous occasions. For some, this had happened when they were young children, and they remembered little about it. Others had experienced a series of admissions as teenagers, with the most recent admission being a continuation of the circumstances of the previous ones. The admission they describe is the one which began the present series.

The young person's contact with social services was usually a result of their parents' actions, rarely their own. Some had run away from home, but this was played down: it was seen as staying with friends until things cooled down following an argument, rather than a bid to leave home permanently. A girl aged 15 agreed that things were difficult at home, but she thought she had developed her own solution by staying temporarily with friends:

> *Girl:* I thought it was unfair, like, and I had really close friends and they said I could stay there for a little while until my mum had calmed down and that, and Mum wouldn't agree to it. I thought it was really out of order.

A 14-year-old boy had been staying with friends after problems at home:

> *Boy:* They came with a warrant to get me out. They tried before, and I wouldn't go . . . My mum told them I was there, and they come round.

For some, their first contact with a social worker was when they were about to be placed:

> *Young woman aged 16:* [When it blew up] I first went to stay with a friend for a couple of nights, and it was the duty social worker, that man, he come round and said, 'Come on, I'll take you to a place,' and that was it.
>
> *Interviewer:* So when did you first see a social worker?
> *Young woman aged 16:* I ran away before anything happened . . . My mum told me to go to social services, but I wouldn't go as I knew they'd put me in a children's home.

A few wanted to be accommodated. Rather like their parents, they described the circumstances as serious and requiring long-term separation but, also like their parents, they found that social services would not accept their assessment:

> *Boy aged 15:* I felt mostly they were trying to push you back to your parents too much. They wouldn't leave it alone – wanting to work on it and mend it, no matter what the consequences. Even if [stepfather] was trying to kill me off . . . It doesn't bother me now, but at the time when I first came in, they were trying to push me back. I wanted to get out. I think they've accepted it now.

Most of those who were happy to be away from home described their involvement in a passive way, and did not appear to play an active part in the decision-making process:

> *Interviewer:* What were the circumstances that prompted the admission?
> *Young woman aged 16:* You mean what led up to it? We were arguing all the time. We didn't get along.
> *Interviewer:* What was your reaction?
> *Young woman:* Great to be away from home.

This young woman did not remember (or was too embarrassed to recount) the 'last straw' incident described by her mother. The admission 'just happened', although she was happy about it.

A 15-year-old girl also agreed with the decision, but saw it as her mother's:

> *Girl:* Mum suggested it, and I was quite happy to go along with it.

Despite one mother's attempt to explain stays for respite care as a 'holiday', a 10-year-old girl recognised the motivation behind it, although her view was initially somewhat jaundiced:

> *Interviewer:* Why are you going to this lady for weekends?
> *Girl:* For beating up my brothers.
> *Interviewer:* When it was first suggested, what did you think?
> *Girl:* Oh my God. I thought they was going to put me in care.
> *Interviewer:* What did you think being put in care would be like?
> *Girl:* Crap. They give you bread and water, and you're permanently in care. They give you bread and water.
> *Interviewer:* Oh, I see. Who told you that?
> *Girl:* My granddad.

Willow (1995, p.13) notes the extensive use of prison language by the young people in her study, as in this example.

Even when young people were happy to be away from home, they were not sure where they were going or how it would be better – they just wanted to be away. For a number of them the admission took place in an emergency, and they had no opportunity to consider where they were going or what it would be like. Willow (1995, p.6) notes that almost half the respondents were asked their views about being accommodated, but far fewer were asked how it should take place or what they wanted from it. Few admissions were planned in advance, and particular fears were expressed about residential care. Fewer than 10% of the young people in Triseliotis et al. (1995, p.204) considered that they alone had made the decision to be admitted to care or accommodation. Those with no previous experience of care of accommodation were very apprehensive:

> *Girl aged 15:* I was just scared [about going into a children's home]. You hear about the bad things that happen in children's homes and that. And I thought, well . . . I was really angry, scared, hurt.

This girl described not only the shock at the admission to accommodation, but the uncertainty of what would happen next and how long she would stay. After the planning meeting which authorised the admission she was placed in a children's home in the next town, but was not informed about another meeting or when she could contact her family or friends. She ran away after three days. Another girl of the same age had no conception of the plans:

> *Girl:* At first, I thought I would stay there for ever, do you know what I mean?

One boy aged 12 met the foster parents before the placement, but commented that no one asked him whether he wanted to go there, and another young man aged 17, who had had a lot of social services contact, was nevertheless unsure about the process of accommodation and children's homes:

> *Interviewer:* Did you know how long it was going to be for?
> *Young man:* No, I didn't know anything.
> *Interviewer:* Did you know anything about children's homes?
> *Young man:* No, only what people said.

Others knew that the placement was a short-term break and they would be returning home:

> *Interviewer:* Did you know how long it would last?
> *Boy aged 15:* No, I didn't know. I expected I'd go back home, the social worker said. But we still didn't get on.

We are not suggesting that there is widespread bad practice in informing young people about being placed in accommodation; perhaps, given the stress of the admission, they had forgotten what they had been told.

However, the evidence suggests that young people require more explicit procedures or documentation about what is involved in admission to accommodation. Once they became familiar with social services' processes, they became clearer about what might happen to them, and felt able to express themselves. However, the first hours and days were very confusing.

Placement

These young people had experienced fostering or residential placements for a wide variety of reasons, some for a few days, several months or at the beginning of permanent separation. It is therefore inappropriate to expect them to describe similar reactions or recount common experiences. However, there are some similarities in their likes and dislikes, and clearly, the everyday details of life in family placements or residential homes had a great impact on their whole experience of being accommodated.

Residential placements

Less than a quarter of the young people had been in children's homes at some stage. For some, the initial impact was 'scary', but those who stayed more than a few days soon became accustomed to the residential experience. Relationships with the other young people there were seen as particularly important:

> *Boy aged 14:* It was all right. It was a laugh and that.

> *Girl aged 15:* It was a really nice place, but I didn't know anybody, and there were only two other girls there.

One 17-year-old young man, now in a bed and breakfast hotel, remembered one children's home fondly:

> *Young man:* I thought it was a really good children's home. I'd like to be back there. There were really good facilities – a computer, go-kart, it had its own grounds . . .

Although he had revisited the children's home to see the staff, he was no longer in touch with friends he met there.

A 15-year-old girl was in a short-term residential placement, and was clearly reluctant to move on to a family placement:

Interviewer: What would you say to other young people who may be about to be accommodated?

Girl: Ask for [this children's home].

Interviewer: Oh, you like it that much.

Girl: Yeah. The only problem is that the staff aren't allowed to hit the children, just shout at them. Kids take advantage of it. I think they should be allowed to hold on to them.

This was the only adverse comment about life in a children's home – most appeared to fit in easily. There were a few comments regarding how they had talked things through with their key worker and how they remained in contact with the worker either through visiting or outreach programmes. Whilst only a small proportion of the cohort had such an experience, it did appear that residential placements offered valued, if short-term, relationships at critical stages. Willow (1995), Triseliotis et al. (1995) and Fletcher (1994) offer more detailed analyses of young people's views of life in children's homes, although the short stay of the young people in our study suggests a different type of experience. The regime in foster homes was considered more problematic.

Family placements

Whereas the interviews involved little discussion of personalities or rules in children's homes, the reflections on family placements were dominated by assessments of the personalities and idiosyncrasies of foster carers. Some foster carers and their homes were clearly much appreciated:

Young man aged 17: The place I was at, they were all right. They treated me like their son, they were all right.

Boy aged 12: I can go out more here – to play, to the park. At home I was nearly always grounded.

Girl aged 10, in respite care: I thought it was good . . . There was lots of toys in my bedroom . . . In the evening I had some tea, and for supper we had apple and drink . . . I've got my own room, and I've got a dressing table and hot water bottle . . . [My friends] say, 'Ugh, going to a lady's house, it must be scary.' But I say, 'No, it isn't, 'cos she's nice.'

A young man aged 16 had been through four family placements, and described one family as:

> The only foster home I got on with [because] they let me be. They took me as I am.

A 6-year-old teased her foster mother during the interview, saying she wouldn't recommend her to other girls, and said she'd spent the summer being fed 'snacks and sandwiches rather than proper meals'. She was one of the few children from an ethnic minority in the cohort, and there was much animated discussion in the interview about her father teaching the foster mother how to cook African food.

The scarcity of children from ethnic minorities in the cohort and in the localities from which it was drawn means we can offer only a few glimpses of how far these children had their cultural needs met by carers. The 6-year-old girl mentioned above was lucky: she was placed with a foster mother who came from a mixed-race family and who was familiar with the appropriate care of her skin and hair. She also encouraged the resumption of contact with the girl's father. There were a few other black children in the neighbourhood, to whom her foster mother was trying to introduce her, but ironically, efforts to help her remain in her old school were hampering this: there were more ethnic minority families in the area in which she was placed than in her home area, so in this instance pursuit of one goal of the Children Act conflicted with another.

In contrast, the middle-class lifestyle of some foster carers was clearly alien to a number of white, working-class children. Two brothers, aged 9 and 7, talked animatedly of a foster carer who was a 'vegetarian, ugh!' Home-made lentil soup was not popular, but there were other aspects of the care that puzzled and alienated them:

> *Boy aged 9:* I wouldn't recommend her – there were loads of things – just her attitude.
> *Boy aged 7:* When we were there [in summer] she even had her Christmas cake already made!

Despite such unaccustomed foresight, and – in their own words – to be fair, she had some good points too! But the next foster parent was apparently more a 'Gran' figure who fed them sausages and chips and cans of Coke, and was much more popular as a result. Furthermore, there were also dogs to take for walks, which added to their enthusiasm.

A 13-year-old boy was also shocked by the middle-class lifestyle:

> *Boy:* They were like quite posh. Like, 'Wash your hands', 'Have a bath every night', and God knows whatever. [Social worker] said they were nice carers, but I didn't like them . . . So I run away and I didn't want to go back, and they give the place to someone else . . . It was posh, like. They didn't get cheap things. They gets really dear curtains, really thick carpets, like you can put your feet in and it would go up to there [*pointing to his shoe*] and, well, I didn't like it, it was so posh. Their garden, they said, 'Don't walk on the grass.'

Serious complaints were made by some young people about the rules, personalities and behaviour of some foster carers. One 15-year-old girl had spent several periods with a respite carer during the summer holidays, and was unhappy about what she saw as agreements being broken and confidences not kept:

> *Girl:* It was a bit horrible, to be honest. When I was there, I was told, we had agreed that as long as I said what time I'd be in, I could go round my friend's house. But when I was actually staying with her, she wouldn't let me go out at all, unless it was to go round her daughter's . . . [Later] I spoke to the social worker, and he got out the papers and it actually did say I could go out as long as I come back when agreed.

She thought it was a nice house, and there was a dog there, 'which was nice'. However:

> *Girl:* One girl came to stay for the last week of the holiday, 'cos her foster parents were going on holidays, and she comes up to me and said, 'I knows why you're here,' and I goes, 'How do you know?' And she goes, '[Foster carer] told me.' And she knew when I was born, and most of my past, which [foster carer] had told her. So I wasn't happy about that.

A 16-year-old young woman had a more basic dislike of the foster carer, her regime and her lifestyle:

> *Young woman:* It was one of those houses, like, you know what I mean, you walk in and it's all like immaculate. And I was thinking, 'Oh no, you can't step out of line.' I remember thinking to myself, oh it's hard to say it . . .

it's like somebody who's middle-class, trying to dress up the house as upper-class, you know what I mean? It all looked false and horrible, not authentic. Everything had its place, oh I don't know how to explain it . . .

Although she had been aged 15 at admission, this was more of a lodgings placement. She appreciated the independence, but she found the regime strict and the 'carer' unfriendly:

> *Young woman:* Mealtimes, if you weren't there by six you had no dinner at all. You had to take your shoes off before you went in the house. My room was always freezing. I wasn't really allowed out of my room. I couldn't sit in the living room unless there was somebody else in the house. Like, if I was the only one in I had to sit in my room. And I wasn't allowed to help myself to food from the kitchen, it was like breakfast before nine . . . She wrote it all down . . . Most of the time I sat in my room and watched TV. Because I was so far away [from home] I couldn't go out in an evening because there was only one bus once a hour, so I had to rely on friends who had cars to come and pick me up . . . I didn't really get on with them. I remember it being my sixteenth birthday and they didn't even get me a card, and I'd been there, what, three months . . . I just thought, 'Well, you're meant to be a carer,' and they didn't bother.

This young person spent nearly five months in this unhappy placement, but felt unable to relate her isolation to the social worker, and eventually drifted home, also without contact with the social worker. Triseliotis et al. (1995, p.190) also note the resentment of some young people over the rules and restrictions in foster care.

There are a number of features about young people's uncertainty about foster care. We have described the alien, middle-class lifestyle and routines, and how they were treated by the foster carers. It was in the detailed descriptions of life in foster care that they were able to depict the accommodation experience as either socially enriching or uncomfortable and alien. More fundamentally, Willow (1995, p.11) notes young people's feeling of not really fitting in to a foster family, and being disloyal to their own family. Fletcher (1993, p.105) concludes that young people did not feel represented by their social workers regarding issues in foster care.

School

Most young people remained at the same school during their stay in accommodation (or remained without a school place). For those accommodated for shorter periods, their school life appeared to have been little affected, and this was seen as crucial in continuing normal contacts. This sometimes involved long taxi rides, but two children described this as an exciting feature of the placement. However, a number reported that they were wary about telling school friends that they were in accommodation:

> *Interviewer:* Did your school friends know you were [in accommodation]?
> *Girl aged 10:* No, but one of them heard 'cos another girl told her, and she spread it around school, I think.
> *Interviewer:* Were you unhappy about that?
> *Girl:* Yeah. I beat her up.

Willow (1995) and Fletcher (1993) offer more comments on the stigmatising and supportive roles of school while young people were in accommodation.

A 12-year-old boy talked about the reaction of others in school:

> *Boy:* [One of the bad things about being accommodated] is getting the mickey taken out of you at school . . . other kids say, 'Where's your mum?'

In the case of those who were in accommodation and had no school place for longer periods, efforts were made to return them to education, with differing degrees of success. One 15-year-old boy was in a tuition unit after several years of truancy and exclusions:

> *Interviewer:* Do you feel you have caught up what you have missed?
> *Boy:* Yeah. I've done pretty well. I thought I wouldn't be able to do it, but I've done all right.
> *Interviewer:* Will you be doing GCSEs?
> *Boy:* Yes, I think so. English, English Language, Art, Maths.

However, a 17-year-old young man reported having been in a children's home some distance from his home area, with no school place for most of his last school year:

> *Young man:* They couldn't get me into a school round there.

Interviewer: So what did you do all day?

Young man: Be bored. There was only certain times you had the TV room open. You weren't allowed to go out in school time either. If the staff weren't busy they'd sometimes sit down and play cards with you . . . Eventually, they got me into a tuition centre. She was giving English and Maths that I'd done in middle school.

Concern has been expressed about the education received by young people while they are looked after (Jackson 1987; Fletcher-Campbell and Hall 1990). Our interviews give the impression that school circumstances changed little as a result of admission. For those well established in school, great efforts were made to avoid interrupting a stable situation. However, for some, without proper schooling it was often difficult to re-establish adequate school provision once in accommodation. For those who stay in care for longer periods, the disruption to education caused by changes of placement, painful experiences and stigma appears to exacerbate these problems (Fletcher 1993, p.106).

Contact with family

The young people in our sample had widely differing relations with their family once they were in accommodation: some had very little subsequent contact, whereas others visited home regularly, and soon returned there. Our impression is that great efforts were made by social workers to maintain contact, at least initially, although, as mentioned earlier in this chapter, for one young person this appeared to be a failure to accept the inevitable. In the interviews with the parents and foster carers of the younger children there were descriptions of great efforts to support regular contact with and visits to parents – for example, in hospital. The older teenagers also reported visits home for the weekends or for the evening, involving considerable work by all concerned. However, for some it was not clear how such 'contact' linked with the plan for rehabilitation. In a discussion with a young woman aged 16, who had gone home, and her mother, the visits home appeared to bear little relation to future plans:

Interviewer: At the meetings, did you discuss how long the placement would go on, whether you'd come back home or move on to something else?

Daughter: It just said 'not known' on the thing, didn't it?

Interviewer: That seems surprising.

Daughter: 'Cos . . . me and my mum. No one knew when you [mother] were prepared to accept me back, really. Me and my mum, really.

Interviewer: They were waiting for a signal from you.

Mother: They were waiting for a miracle. Honestly. They seemed to think just separating us would solve things, there was nothing happening in between. It didn't seem to make sense.

This young woman eventually returned home herself, without family counselling or social worker mediation.

We mentioned earlier that there appeared to be little family work before admission, and it was not apparent that such a service formed a part of family contact once a young person was admitted to accommodation. Meetings played an important role in maintaining contact. Even if relations between parents and their children remained strained, the parents could be persuaded to come to meetings, as this was where their child's future was being discussed:

Young man aged 16: At first I saw [parents] hardly at all, only when they came to meetings.

Those who were in accommodation on a long-term basis did not envisage returning home, but most maintained contact with their parents. They now seemed to take these arrangements in their stride, and saw these more fragmented relations as preferable:

Boy aged 15: I stay weekends now. It's better now I'm not living at home permanently.

Girl aged 15: When I'm not living at home and I go back for weekends, me and my mum get on really well.

Despite being away from home for over eighteen months, one young man found his mother to be the most helpful when he came to move into a bed-sit:

Interviewer: How are things now with your family?

Young man aged 17: I go round now and again, and we seem to be getting on fine, just go round there, have a cup of tea. If she's busy, go again.

Interviewer: And you say that she has helped you with finding this place?

Young man: Yes. Look through the papers. Now I'm seeing Mum quite a bit, and when I was at the other place, I was at college, she came in to help tidy the place up, and when I moved into here, she helped me out with a lot of stuff, all the bedding, Mum got me that.

However, for others, who were more clearly separated from their parents, there were regrets:

> *Girl aged 15:* Sometimes when I go on visits I think I wish I could to come back home to live, because of my little brothers and sister and my kitten, but I know that if I go back we'll just start arguing and that.

> *Boy aged 15:* [Mother] wrote me a letter the other day, saying she doesn't want to talk to me on the phone any more . . . It takes a long time for wounds to heal. I phone and talk to [my sister] and she tells me how they are.

Obviously, relationships between children and parents vary, and it did appear that great efforts were made to keep up contact, even when relations were strained. However, it was not always clear how far contact was linked to a planned return home. For those who now accepted that a permanent return home was unlikely there were some encouraging signs that contact could lead to supportive relationships later on (Bullock et al. 1993).

Change of placement or return home

Whereas the early decisions concerning admission to accommodation appeared beyond their control, the young people reported having a greater influence over later developments (Triseliotis et al. 1995, p.206). For younger children, the return home was more dependent on the circumstances of their parents, but in the case of teenagers it often depended on relations with their parents, and they considered that they had greater control over subsequent placements or the return home. Even so, for three young people it was the act of running away from the placement which prompted the return home. (Willow (1995, p.10) notes that nearly three-quarters of her respondents had lived in placements they did not want, and had resorted to running away, aggression or self-harm to express this.):

> *Interviewer:* Did you decide you were coming back home?
> *Young woman aged 16:* I ran away and went to stay with a friend for a couple of nights and didn't turn up at one of the meetings. Mum just said, 'Come home.'

> *Girl aged 15:* I ran away from the children's home on the third night. They still wouldn't let me out, and I felt I'd had enough.

There was pressure on one young man aged 17 to move to a children's home nearer his home, but he did not want 'another move':

> *Interviewer:* Did they say to you, 'Do you want to move to [children's home]?'
> *Young man:* No, they said I was moving. Every time they said that, though, I went out on the run. So they didn't move me. I told them lots of times I didn't want to move.

Others were offered a choice of children's home, or supported the plans to look for a more appropriate family placement or lodgings:

> *Girl aged 15:* I had the choice of here or [another children's home].

> *Boy aged 15:* I want to move to my own place. I've been to see [supported lodgings].

> *Young man aged 16:* They are now looking for a family. I realise it will be difficult to find one.

In general, these young people felt that eventually the social services had listened to their views, and later moves were generally in accord with their wishes:

> *Young man aged 16:* It's got better, much easier to talk now. Now, perhaps because I'm older, they ask my opinion. It's not just the first placement they find, but the one that suits you best. Maybe it's just my social worker, but if things annoy or upset me, the social worker will discuss it out in the open.

Whether social services were listening to them or the young people were now listening to social services is not clear, but in any case they felt more in control, even if it might involve running away on occasion to make their feelings known.

Meetings

Almost without exception, these young people expressed strong dislike of the meetings they attended:

> *Young man aged 16:* They were horrible.

> *Young woman aged 16:* I didn't like it at all.

> *Young woman aged 16:* I've never been able to talk in front of strangers.

Those with more experience were slightly more relaxed about them, but even they remembered embarrassing meetings, and still found expressing their point of view very difficult:

> *Young man aged 16:* When I was younger I used to sit there and people used to sit and talk about me. Now they ask my opinion.

Meetings were uncomfortable, sometimes degrading experiences, and even the more 'laid-back' respondents summoned up strong reactions when meetings were mentioned. The younger children did not generally attend the meetings, but one 10-year-old boy was aware of their importance. One of the authors was present when his mother returned home from a child protection conference, and the boy was eager to find out the outcome:

> *Boy:* Mummy, are we going into care?

The young people saw two purposes to meetings: to make decisions and plan the future, but also to examine present behaviour and tell them off:

> *Young man aged 17:* They were reasonable, apart from the one at [children's home]. They were saying I was giving out drugs and that. That wasn't reasonable.

The general approach of meetings did not excite much criticism. There were few complaints about who was present, although some felt teachers should not be there. There was little criticism of *what* was said – that was generally felt to be fair – it was the *way* matters were discussed and the right of the meetings to make decisions they questioned:

> *Young woman aged 16:* I think they listened to my side of the story, but I've always thought they listened to my mum more than they listened to me, because she's an adult, she should know more than a child knows. I think they did understand, but they didn't do much . . .

> *Young woman aged 16:* It was like other people deciding what to do with my life for me, and I don't like that.

> *Boy aged 15:* All these people sitting round and saying I need this and I need that. What do they know?

These young people questioned the legitimacy of meetings by criticising the approach of 'experts' and their right to decide what was best: how did they know, on the basis of such short contact, what should happen? They were also critical of the way only certain viewpoints were taken seriously – those of the adults. The young people's views were heard but ignored, because they were not adults (Triseliotis et al. 1995, p.214). Another factor underlying such comments might be concern about the extent to which their private family conflict had become a subject for public scrutiny and control. Unlike their parents, who had requested professional involvement, they had been less aware of the potential power of professionals' interference, and the first meetings in particular appeared to come as something of a shock.

Few of these young people remembered being given any preparation for the meetings, either from their key worker or social worker, and they all clearly found them a difficult arena in which to make a contribution:

> *Interviewer:* Did you feel you had the opportunity to say what you felt?
> *Young man aged 16:* If I'd wanted to, yes.
> *Interviewer:* Did you?
> *Young man:* Not always. If I went to a meeting I usually just sat there, just waited until I could go again. When I was at the meeting, they asked me if there was anything I wanted to say. I said 'No'.

> *Boy aged 15:* I just used to draw on the table, or something like that. They just used to bore me.

> *Young woman aged 16:* I just felt silly, sitting there, everyone discussing me. I hated it. So I just sat there and . . . I feel totally uncomfortable in those sorts of situations. I hated it.

> *Girl aged 15:* I can think of a million things I want to say, and when I'm in the meeting I can't remember them.

Some young people clearly wished they were not present:

> *Boy aged 15:* They are a bore. You sit there and they talk about you and you say 'yes' and 'no'. Not much use really. They should just come and see you and tell you, and you say what you want then.

Comments about being bored, feeling silly or wanting to leave convey uncomfortable situations where young people did not feel able to contribute and which they would have preferred to avoid. Although they knew they could say what they wanted, and sometimes thought in advance what to say, none of the young people saw them as forums in which they felt able to express themselves. They could have talked, they were asked to contribute, but generally they chose not to. This suggests that they felt there was not much point in talking – perhaps they would not be taken seriously, perhaps what they said would be further criticised, perhaps talking would open up their inner thoughts to listeners who might not be welcome. Fletcher (1993, p.109) found that 60% of his sample felt that their views were listened to at meetings, but many considered that they were not involved in the decisions. They felt 'ignored, patronised and their opinions are of little value'. Willow (1995, p.27) reports similar findings, and notes in particular the professionals' use of language and the concentration on the youngsters' perceived failures. Whatever the reason, the young people in our sample strongly believed that meetings were uncomfortable occasions, and for some they were the worst part of being placed in accommodation:

> *Interviewer:* Is there any advice you would give to others in your situation?
>
> *Boy aged 12:* Dunno, but those big meetings are a bit hard. I could warn them about that.

The importance of friends

In discussing admission to accommodation with these young people, we concentrated on their relations with their families and social services. However, in most interviews the importance of their friends became apparent, although such relationships never formed an explicit part of the negotiations between their families and social services. Friends were important in a number of ways and at different stages of the accommodation process.

For many young people, friends were the first place to seek help when there were problems at home. They were a principal reference group and opinion-former, where they could discuss what was happening at home and work out whether their problems were normal or not. One young woman aged 16 had wanted her friends to be allowed to attend the planning meeting to help her put her point of view:

> *Young woman:* I know it sounds silly, but all the people [at the meeting] were grown-up. I was the only child. It would have been nice to have someone on my side.

A number of the young people stayed with friends before being admitted to accommodation. For some this had been a temporary stay for a few days until they could return home or were admitted to accommodation; for others the stay lasted weeks, even months. Some friends were 'stable' families whom social services might (and sometimes did) consider as potential (private) foster parents. Others were almost local 'Fagins', who would welcome and harbour runaways. Such friends had sometimes become the focus of the dispute between the parents and young people, and social services was caught between the parents, the young people and the friends' families. In one case they supported a mother in admitting to accommodation a young person who had been living with an 'unsuitable' family; in another case they refused to help a mother remove a young person from an 'unsuitable' family. The main difference between these circumstances appeared to be that in the first case the mother was easier to work with than in the second. However, the position social services took was important in subsequent developments, since siding with either party legitimised the chosen arrangement and undermined the other. Friends' families could then become the focus for the young person's future, or be easily cast aside.

Few of these arrangements lasted very long, with or without social services' legitimisation, and few became official placements. Often the young persons realised that they had outstayed their welcome, especially if there was no financial assistance:

> **Young woman aged 16:** I thought, 'Something's really got to be done. I can't live off my friends.'

One young man took his mother's Family Allowance to give to the family with whom he was staying, but asked to be admitted to accommodation when there were problems in the friend's family.

Access to friends was also a key feature of the initial experience of accommodation. One young woman aged 16 was very upset that she could not see her friends after being admitted:

> **Young woman:** I didn't have no one to talk to after the meeting. I didn't know no one in the home. I really needed to speak to someone about what I had been through, but they wouldn't let me out to see, like, my friends. So I was really angry, upset, mixed up.

One girl was placed in a children's home some distance from her family, but was able to rely on her friends with cars to keep in contact, and another girl aged 15 complained to her social worker about being unable to see her friends in respite care.

Overall, friends were more important than social workers (and we, the authors) had realised, and they were largely excluded from the decision-making process (and from our research interview schedule). It is important to recognise the importance of friends to young people who are in accommodation. Just as the opinions of other professionals and family members are sought and continuity at school has been recognised, so the importance of the opinions of friends and continuity of relationships with them should be acknowledged. Such involvement is likely to reinforce the young people's position at the expense of the parents', but even so, this chapter has demonstrated the lack of support which young people experience in the accommodation process, and sometimes their friends may help rather than hinder a resolution. (Triseliotis et al. (1995, pp.53, 253) report that although young people confided in friends and found them a source of support, over time their help was not always consistent.)

Summary

This research is based on a small sample and cannot be considered representative, but it does display similarities and contrasts with the larger studies. The young people's accounts are complex and sometimes confused, but in general, they did not feel they were included in all stages of the decision-making process – before the admission, the choice of placement, the admission itself and at meetings. But the situation sometimes improved when they understood the system better. We asked them to summarise their overall reactions to being placed in accommodation:

> *Young man aged 17, in bed and breakfast:* By then I decided I didn't want to be with social services any more. I just didn't want social workers with me all the time . . . They don't know where I am now. I very much doubt they will come down to see me.

> *Young woman aged 16:* I wouldn't advise it to anyone. I hated it . . . It was a nightmare.

Young man aged 16: I'd advise [other young people] to go [into accommodation] as a last resort. It's all right moving out and going to a different family, but your family's still your family, no matter what they do. There's always a little bit of love and loyalty inside you.

Young man aged 16: I wouldn't recommend it to anyone. It's not your home. It's nothing like home.

Young woman aged 16: I'd say just stay and carry on [putting your point of view]. Social workers aren't as bad as they first seem.

Girl aged 15: The social worker was on my parents' side, not accepting my view. They took the same line as my parents – suggested I could have the baby aborted. No way!

Boy aged 15: Yeah. They have listened to my point of view.

Girl aged 15: Most of what has happened I have been happy about . . . Yeah, they have listened to my point of view.

Interviewer: Did you like it [at respite carers']?
Boy aged 13: No. That's why I am going to try and stay at school now.

Interviewer: What would you say to anyone else going [to respite carer]?
Girl aged 10: It's nice. She's kind.

In general, a sense of powerlessness is apparent in these accounts, whether the young people consider they have been listened to or not, whether they like their carers or not. Some were more explicit about their lack of voice, but none appeared to make their position clear, except by running away. They seemed more isolated from their social workers than their parents were, and resentful of social services' intrusion. It was noted in Chapter 6 that the social workers felt that the young people were less involved in the decision to admit them to accommodation, and Willow (1995) concludes:

♦ A very sad feature of the majority of the young people we interviewed was their low self-esteem and the overwhelming sense of rejection they felt.

Meetings, in particular, were a forum that they found puzzling, with strange ways of discussing issues, and a site for further embarrassment and criticism. The very public discussion of their behaviour and that of their families appeared to have been especially painful and humiliating. None appeared to have felt adequately prepared for such occasions, or supported in their position, and most found themselves unable to express their opinions properly.

Given the requirement to 'listen to children', and complaints by some parents that children were listened to too much, there is clearly a need to reconsider what 'listening to children' means to the children themselves. Fletcher (1993, p.102) concludes:

♦ There is evidence, particularly from the responses on family links, decision-making and when things go wrong, that the provisions in the Children Act 1989 on taking account of the wishes of young people are not working.

She suggests ways of making meetings more informal, increasing young people's participation, and recommends a charter setting out enforceable standards. Willow (1995, p.27) also notes the importance of consulting young people more and, unless compromises are reached, there are potentially major dangers in attempting to enforce decisions. However, we have spoken to parents who feel equally powerless, so listening more to the young people may only decrease parents' participation. Fletcher's suggestion (1993, p.105) that young people should be regarded as 'clients in their own right, as distinct from their families and carers' may further undermine the parents' position, and furthermore, this is not straightforward when children are accommodated under Section 20. However, the marginal position of young people, especially in the negotiations leading up to the admission to accommodation, suggests that much could be gained by including them at an earlier stage, by giving them an equal opportunity to their parents to outline problems and suggest possible solutions. Our data suggests that young people may be more prepared than their parents to make compromises, once they are included.

Once accommodated, it is clear that the purpose, experience and length of placement must be discussed, negotiated and seen as 'in their best interests'. There is a danger of a double rejection for children and young people, since they may leave their home against their will, but must also enter accommodation which is alien and scary. This study has not concentrated on the experience and outcome of accommodation, and there is considerable work in progress to improve that experience, for example the 'Looking After Children' (Ward 1995) project. However, whilst we have promoted accommodation as a service to parents, it must also be developed as a service from which children and young people benefit, and which they see as furthering their best interests.

We have suggested that the everyday features of placements were more important in the young people's experiences than is usually recognised. There have been many debates within social work about the relative merits of residential or foster care, but such considerations have usually focused on the long-term placement needs of children. Given that these young people were largely happy about their residential placements but many were critical of family placements, does there need to be a re-examination of short-term stays? In particular, do the everyday aspects of foster carers' routines and regimes need to be considered more care-fully? Are we aware of the impact of certain middle-class conventions on these young people? This does not take into account any impact of being exposed to living conditions which might be more lavish than those at home. This is not to suggest that family placements should attempt to mirror what might be impoverished home conditions, but perhaps greater attention should be paid to young people's comments on middle-class idiosyncrasies and perceived unfairness. Also, perhaps residential placements might (initially) be more acceptable to young people, since they have been likened to short-term residential holiday accommodation – as some described them, 'a laugh'.

Of particular interest is a group which is clearly important and com-pletely excluded from the current processes – *friends*. We have heard how for teenagers, friends were the people to run to and the place to gain support, respect and recognition. Yet not only were friends exclud-ed from proceedings, often they were seen as part of the problem. Friends were a mixed group, however: some were peers, others were adults (usually friends' parents). The importance of these relationships, however 'unsuitable', was that the young people had formed them themselves. For the social services to either overthrow or legitimise such arrangements was seen as unnecessary interference – 'out of order'. This is not to suggest that friends should automatically contribute to the formal discussions about family disputes, but at least their influence should be recognised, and they might be seen as one of the few supporters of the young people on such occasions.

15 *Conclusions*

In this chapter we will try to draw together some of the themes which have run through the discussion and analysis of the substantive chapters. This is a complex study, given that child care policies, practices and attitudes are in a state of flux, and we have considered these in relation to only one aspect of the Children Act. Nevertheless, it encapsulates and illustrates many of the principles of the legislation as a whole.

The impact of the 'no order principle'

We begin with the impact of the 'no order principle', from which we believe many of our other findings flow. We have seen that in contrast to past practice, children considered to be at risk of harm and those (particularly teenagers) whose behaviour is disruptive and troublesome are now entering local authority accommodation in large numbers – indeed, these two groups formed the majority of the admissions we studied. Comparison with the cohort in the *Who Needs Care?* study (Packman et al. 1986) shows that although they are not identical, they bear a strong resemblance to the children removed from home by means of court orders in the past.

The shift away from court orders to voluntary arrangements was noted in the first Department of Health report on the Children Act, which found evidence that 'the diminishing number of episodes under court orders has been balanced by an increase in voluntary provision' (DoH 1993, p.22). Subsequent figures (DoH 1996) suggest that a modest increase in court orders has occurred since the earliest days of implementation of the Children Act. Nevertheless, we can say with some confidence that the 'no order principle' is having considerable impact on practice.

This change in emphasis also relates to much recent discussion about the balance in social services work between child protection and family support, and the perceived neglect of the latter (Baldwin and Spenser 1993; Audit Commission 1994; DoH 1995). The present study suggests a considerable degree of overlap between these two functions, yet some of the recent debate implies they have been treated as separate and mutually exclusive strands of activity. Accommodation – itself a support service – was provided for substantial numbers of children who had been placed on the Child Protection Register, and for as many again where child protection concerns were current. Few were accommodated as the direct result of an investigation, but for most, risk was an element in the assessment of need.

It was also evident that the families of children at risk had received other types of support services in the past, and continued to receive them during and after the child's period in accommodation. Indeed, the priority given to allocating such services to child protection cases suggested they were first in line for family support.

Within the parameters of our study, the problem appeared to be not that child protection cases received no support, but rather that support was concentrated on such families, perhaps to the exclusion of many others in need of help. However, an alternative conclusion might also be reached: since protection concerns were voiced about so many children in the cohort, had notions of risk come to dominate the professional discourse, and were these concerns being exaggerated in order to gain access to scarce resources? If so, perhaps child protection cases were not being overlooked in the provision of support services, nor were they receiving the lion's share; rather, it may be that risk arising from need was being emphasised, when need on its own might not have been enough to qualify for help.

The prominence of difficult teenagers among those placed in accommodation is also a consequence of legal change. Yet the full implications of the 'no order principle' seem not to have been anticipated in the volumes of Guidance that accompanied the legislation. For instance, there is an absence of discussion of disruptive adolescents as candidates for Section 20 admission in the volume on family support (DoH 1991a), yet we have seen how powerfully their inclusion affects the planning process and the accommodation experience itself. Difficult young people strain the coping and caring capacities of parents and professionals alike.

It is perhaps for these reasons that, despite new legislative provision, so few 16-year-olds were admitted during the study period (six in all) and, on the other hand, so many left accommodation at the same age. There appeared to be an uneasy acceptance on the part of professionals that reaching school-leaving age warranted a degree of independence that the vulnerability of the young people belied – a worrying feature of practice that is vividly illustrated in a recent study of young people leaving care (Biehal et al. 1995). Inevitably, the voluntary nature of accommodation makes it difficult to resist the wishes of insistent teenagers and/or their parents, but we believe that greater efforts to put the case for preparation for independence and continued protection could and should be made. The sorry state of some of the teenagers at follow-up suggests that a lengthier period of support and more rigorous after-care were sometimes badly needed.

We have also seen that the inclusion of 'difficult' cases within Section 20 affects how and when accommodation is planned. Planning, in the sense of a careful sequence of inquiry, assessment, preparation and eventual placement of the child, was evidently difficult to achieve with any consistency. A major reason for this was the high rate of emergency admissions, which were often associated with a crisis of care involving risk or behaviour. Where relationships were fraught, or where families which had not previously been in contact with social services 'erupted', most planning had to take place after admission.

Given that such cases are now much more likely to involve accommodation, a substantial proportion of emergency admissions may be inevitable, and should perhaps be regarded as a fact of life for social services departments, rather as accident and emergency departments are an integral aspect of hospital care. It follows that the skills of crisis management, as well as crisis avoidance, may be more necessary now than ever before. Whilst we accept that some emergencies are inevitable, would earlier intervention and more positive, continuing family support have reduced their number? Could accommodation be preventive? The striking differences between the emergency admission rates in our two sample authorities suggest that attitudes to accommodation play a major part, and choices are available to practitioners and policy-makers. The benefits of planned admissions were clear both in the social workers' views of positive working relations and in the parents' (if not necessarily the children's) satisfaction with the service offered. The consequences of 'last resort' responses were increased numbers of admissions, and greater, and possibly long-term, acrimony and distrust.

The impact of the 'no order principle' also has consequences for the status of accommodation as a voluntary service of family support. In law, the voluntary nature of Section 20 has certain limitations. Although parents have the right to remove a child from accommodation when they choose, the provision of accommodation is not available on demand. Families cannot simply ask for their children to be accommodated without justification. In other words, it is not consumerist, in the sense of being available to all, but must be subject to negotiation, and should depend on a shared assessment of need.

We have seen that the modern 'volunteered' and the new 'respite' cases fit well into this model. For these important minorities, needs are mutually agreed and services are offered on terms that give great satisfaction to both the providers and receivers of support. But we have also seen that where risk or the extremes of adolescent acting-out behaviour are concerned, both the voluntariness and the supportiveness of accommodation can be undermined. Parents, children, or both, are sometimes pressured into an admission or dissuaded from a withdrawal under implicit or explicit threat of compulsion.

Partnership

What can be said about *partnership*, which underpins the Children Act as a whole and brings together so many of the elements that have been considered throughout this study? To what extent do enduring parental responsibility, family participation and the voluntariness and positive support of the service offered combine to create the partnership approach that is advocated? Concepts like 'participation', 'partnership' and 'empowerment' cover a wide variety of circumstances and relations concerning families and social services which cannot be easily implemented through a unitary set of prescriptions (Buchanan 1994; DoH/ Social Services Inspectorate 1995).

In the child protection arena, for example, it is acknowledged that 'different models of partnership and participatory practice . . . may be appropriate at different times' (DoH/Social Services Inspectorate 1995). However, providing essential information to family members, involving them in the planning and decision-making process and encouraging their active participation are all seen as vital ingredients in moving towards partnership. At the very least, openness and honesty should be displayed.

In practice, as our study and those of other researchers show (for example, Farmer and Owen 1995; Thoburn et al. 1995; Thoburn et al. 1996), the road to partnership is not easy to negotiate. We have seen, for example, that the participation of parents and children in the planning process did not invariably occur, and when it did, it was not always an easy or comfortable matter. Participation did not necessarily mean co-operation or consensus. Drawing from our quantitative data, the participation of a significant minority of parents and a rather smaller proportion of children was said to be 'difficult'. Our family interviews and the meetings we attended shed further light on this, as we heard about or witnessed parents being challenged, humiliated or silenced in some encounters, and learned how uncomfortable and alienated some children felt in meetings. Participation by all parties is therefore neither guaranteed nor necessarily positive, and the resulting 'partnership' may be unbalanced, and sometimes openly antagonistic.

Similarly, our study shows that the voluntariness of some Section 20 accommodations is somewhat suspect. Who did or didn't want the admission was one of the questions we asked, and in most cases at least one of the parties to the negotiation was seen as reluctant or resistant. In only a quarter of admissions were parents, children and social services personnel all said to be in favour of accommodation at the point of entry, and the positive aspects of this service for families were not wholeheartedly endorsed, either by family members or by the social workers themselves.

Why are the necessary ingredients for a constructive partnership apparently lacking? One reason must be that partnership is a *process*, but admission to accommodation is an *event*. Partnerships are to be aimed at, worked on and developed over time. It is no accident that parental participation and agreement were least likely to occur where admissions were undertaken in an emergency, or where parents were previously unknown to social services and had no prior experience of accommodation. Over time, however, some more constructive partnerships can be developed, and at the time of the two-year follow-up a substantial minority of parents had participated in varying degrees of 'shared care'. Some had even become more comfortable and confident in participating in planning meetings: 'You learn their ways.'

A further complication is the number of potential partners whose wishes and feelings have to be reconciled. The parents themselves do not always agree, and it is obvious that children and their parents do not necessarily see accommodation, or the situations that give rise to a need for it, in the same light. Our quantitative data showed that children tended to be wary of admission if they had experienced it before and if the admission was carefully planned or perceived as 'respite' for parents –

the exact opposite of parental views. Furthermore, for the children, emergencies were sometimes of their own making, and in a few cases led to a request or demand that they be admitted, against the will of their parents. In contrast, some of our interviews revealed youngsters who were shocked and surprised that their parents saw their behaviour as warranting such a drastic step.

If we add the views of the professionals to the equation, the problems for partnership multiply. For example, the Children Act ideal of accommodation offered as a positive support service to families is clearly having difficulty in taking root in social services departments that have a long-established 'last resort' stance. Shortage of adequate and appropriate resources, a powerful commitment to other forms of support, and experience of the harms that local authority care can sometimes inflict lead to a deep-rooted resistance to admissions. Indeed, resistance was rather more in evidence among social workers than among parents, whose appreciation of the benefits of accommodation was often expressed in this as in other studies (for example, Williams 1996). Such resistance was also much more in evidence in Shire than in County, and the consequent reluctance to offer accommodation was likely to be met with resentment and antagonism from the families seeking help.

Other aspects of the Children Act also pose obstacles to establishing good working partnerships. The challenge of respecting parental rights whilst safeguarding the best interests of children is not new, since these were the twin concerns of previous child care legislation, but the 1989 Act gives added emphasis to both, thus sharpening the dilemma. Parental responsibilities are to be emphasised and encouraged, but the duty to safeguard and promote the best interests of the child is paramount. Furthermore, balancing these two potentially conflicting goods has to be set in the context of other legal changes. (For example, we discussed the effects of the 'no order principle' in encouraging the use of accommodation as an alternative to Emergency Protection Orders and Care Orders in Chapter 1.)

Where risk is the predominant issue, we have seen that social services tend to favour – and press hard for – an admission, whilst some (but by no means all) parents are reluctant. More precisely, it is the parents of children where risk of harm is an immediate concern, and who are newly caught up in the machinery of child protection, who are most likely to be suspicious and resentful of the service offered.

In contrast, where a youngster's acting-out behaviour is the issue causing most concern, the parents – and sometimes the young people themselves – are more likely to press for admission to accommodation, and it is the social services departments who are the reluctant partners.

Models of partnership

Although the situation in practice is extremely complex, we can simplify it by deriving three models of partnership that may apply to admission to accommodation.

The first approaches the ideals embodied in the legislation and Guidance, where parents and social services arrive at a mutual assessment of need, and all see accommodation as the service of choice to meet that need. It is most evident in (but not exclusive to) the subgroup we have called the 'volunteered', where accommodation meets the needs of a family in crisis, often as a result of parental ill health or absence, or where the strains of parenting a difficult or disabled child suggest the provision of relief through providing a placement. Ironically, the promotion of voluntary care was a theme which developed, in part, out of *Who Needs Care?* (Packman et al. 1986). Does the fact that this group continues to represent only about a third of all admissions mean that intentions to increase genuine voluntariness will always be restricted by the prevalence of conflict and concern? Yet, as we have seen, some respite care programmes and 16+ schemes were not included under the Section 20 umbrella. If these clearly voluntary arrangements were incorporated, the proportion of truly voluntary cases would increase dramatically, and some of the stigma that still attaches to some of the other cases might also be removed.

The second model has been identified by researchers in the child protection field (for example, Thoburn et al. 1995; Thoburn et al. 1996) as 'enforced partnership', or in the words of several of the social workers we interviewed, a 'sham partnership'. Here, the parents (though less often the children) either fear or dispute assessments and allegations of harm, and are reluctant partners in the negotiation. It is social services staff – and sometimes those of other agencies – who are pressing for admission, to assess and protect the child. Accommodation is urged in preference to court proceedings because of the 'no order principle' and because it is judged that the parents will probably co-operate. Sometimes the threat of legal proceedings is made explicit, to induce co-operation: 'It's Section 20 or we go to court', 'If she attempts to remove him, we'll take out an Emergency Protection Order.'

Parental co-operation in these circumstances is often reluctant or unreliable, and suspicions and resentment may be expressed: 'Participation is deteriorating – they know the department doesn't want him to come home.' Social workers can be equally uncomfortable: 'It's not really voluntary. It's a sham partnership, and control is really what's wanted.' For them, there are two main issues. If openness is lacking and the parents are unaware of the consequences of non-co-operation, then the dishonesty of the arrangement causes concern. Yet, where the consequences of non-co-operation *are* made clear to the parents there is still unease about its doubtful legality. How can continuing parental responsibility and the right to remove a child from accommodation at will exist alongside threats to punish and prevent parents should they choose to exercise those rights?

A third model, and one that has received less attention in other studies, is that of the insistent family and the reluctant social services department. Parents may reach the end of their tether and demand that social services take on responsibility for a difficult child. There are also young people who want to be removed from their families and who sometimes view the higher living standards and companionship of residential care as an attractive option. We have seen that the agencies are often reluctant to oblige – because of a shortage of appropriate placements, for fear they will do no better in attempting to control acting-out behaviour or from a conviction that family relationships may be permanently fractured if they collude with the separation. In such situations, other strategies may be attempted to avert admission, but the parents, the young people, or both, can force the professionals' hand by creating a crisis in which they have no choice: the young person is homeless and at risk, or violence is threatened, and the ubiquitous emergency admission occurs. Here, the enforcement stems not from powerful agencies pressurising families, but from frustrated families pressurising agencies – albeit agencies which may have contributed to the families' frustrations by failing to offer accommodation as a positive service.

Thus, partnership in the context of admission of children to Section 20 accommodation presents challenges to all parties, and full agreement and co-operation are unlikely to be achieved from the outset in all but a minority of cases. Conflicts of interest between parents and children, shame at parental 'failure' and the lingering stigma of 'putting a child into care', differing perspectives on the effectiveness of the accommodation service and inequalities of knowledge and power between 'us' and 'them' all conspire to make the process a difficult one.

Voluntariness

The problem of maintaining genuine voluntariness in situations where risk to the child is feared is a further complication. Threatening court action if parents try to exercise their rights by withdrawing their child from accommodation may be experienced as little different from requiring notice or assuming parental rights, in which case, what has changed? Even if the practice is legal (which some question), can it be said to be in the spirit of the Children Act? However, if such warnings or contingency plans are never to be contemplated, can voluntary accommodation continue to be used for children who are at risk of significant harm, or must all such cases go to court? If so, the implications for courts, families and for accommodation as a broad-based service are huge.

This is a dilemma that our study cannot fully resolve. From the child's point of view, the modest proportion of cases which proceeded to Care Orders in the space of two years suggests that adequate protection *can* be provided by means of accommodation and other support services for the majority of children at risk. From the parents' perspective, there was evidence that the perceived deceits of 'sham partnerships' certainly rankled with some, but these were generally cases which were already moving into the court arena and were destined to result in Care Orders. This accords with the parental perspectives on care proceedings revealed in a parallel study (Hunt et al. forthcoming), where parents of previously accommodated children were bitter at the perceived manipulation and coercion that led to 'voluntary' care in the first place, and to the 'betrayal' when court proceedings followed. Our data does not reveal how the majority of 'at risk' families felt when no such action was taken, but a related study (Thoburn et al. 1996) suggests that accommodation in such cases – however limited its voluntariness – is generally preferred to the daunting experience of being taken to court.

Nevertheless, we would agree with Owen (1992) that in the interests of social justice, openness and honesty are required of the professionals, even if this antagonises parents and children at first. Negotiating and mediating skills of a high order are also necessary in order to overcome the conflicts inherent in so many situations in a constuctive way.

Further, agencies should be aware that their negative attitudes towards accommodation, which construe it as a service of 'last resort', not only contribute to high levels of unplanned emergency admissions, but also to hostility and disaffection among families seeking a support service that is being withheld.

The children's welfare

How was the welfare of the children safeguarded or enhanced through the medium of accommodation? Inevitably, our conclusions are tentative because our focus has been mainly on decision-making and events close to the admission, and detailed measures of the children's well-being were not part of our original design. Nevertheless, there are some broad indications of what the experiences entailed.

Listening to the child was clearly high on the agenda of the social services departments, and we were aware of some imaginative practice developments in communicating with very young children. Listening to children has been developed in child protection, where the central concern is to take children's disclosures seriously, and once taken into care, the child's involvement in planning and decision-making has rightly been enhanced. From our study we can see that most children were said to be involved in the planning process, though our interviews suggested that they did not necessarily see it that way. The majority attended the various kinds of meetings that were the formal setting for making decisions and plans, but such settings were neither comfortable nor usually effective places for many youngsters to make their voices heard, and we question their value for all but a few bold individuals in this respect. However, it is in the admission to accommodation itself where the centrality of the voice of the child was least clear. Promoting Section 20 as a support to the family can be equated with providing support to parents. Not only were the children sometimes inadequately consulted and their version of events not heard, it was often difficult for them to see what the benefits for them might be.

Once in accommodation, however, there were some encouraging signs that old lessons had been well learned. Much attention was given to preserving family integrity by maintaining contact between children and family members and friends, and by placing nearly all siblings together. Heroic attempts to preserve continuity of schooling were also made, though returning excluded youngsters to education was less successful. The need for committed joint work between social services departments, education departments and individual schools, and the difficulties involved, were very evident.

'Shared care'

Varying degrees of 'shared care', where parents continued to play an active role, were also apparent. The extension of regular respite beyond disabled children to other youngsters whose parents needed regular support was beginning to develop, though the numbers were very small. Further experiments of this kind, through specialist foster carers, adaptable daily child-minders and a flexible use of family centres, residential homes and boarding schools, might enhance support, not only for families of young children but also for some parents and teenagers at loggerheads (Triseliotis et al. 1995, p.281). Indeed, other research suggests this is a fruitful area for development, with measurable benefits for children and parents (for example, Aldgate, forthcoming).

The effects of accommodation on children

The impact and quality of the accommodation experience for the children concerned also emerges in our follow-up material. Inevitably, given the broad range of family situations in which accommodation is now being used, that experience is immensely variable. We have seen that for some, a single, brief episode apparently meets a need, whilst other children remain in accommodation for months or even years, and yet others again move in and out of care. However, although this has always been the case, two fundamental changes have occurred in the overall pattern of admissions.

One is the steep rise in *repeat* admissions, such that the rate of readmission has doubled within a decade. More than half the youngsters in our study had been admitted more than once within the space of two years, and a substantial minority had experienced several episodes. Since very few of the latter were enjoying regular respite care, for many readmission meant further disruption through changing placements.

Responding creatively to this new pattern presents a formidable challenge. Can repeat admissions be foreseen and managed, so that places are reserved for them? Should fostering regulations be relaxed to allow tried and tested homes to take in an extra child already known to them? Is there a case for turning the clock back and developing more flexible group care facilities for older children to return to? One favoured solution that tends to be counter-productive is to allow admissions only as a last resort. Paradoxically, this appears to lead in the opposite direction: more readmissions of a difficult, long-term nature.

A second more subtle change lies in the arena of planning for children once they are admitted to accommodation. A besetting sin of the past was 'drift' – the failure to be decisive or to move quickly enough to determine whether or when a young child should return home or be subject to alternative plans for 'permanence' in another family setting. There are hints in our data that this may be less of a problem now. Planning for accommodated children is more systematic, and meetings to review the child's needs and his/her family's circumstances are an established feature of practice. Nevertheless, in a few cases, delays in establishing 'permanence' for very young children still occur – not often because of inactivity on the part of social services, but because a range of different options are considered and tried, one by one.

The Children Act's emphasis on the vital role of the family, in its widest sense, sometimes means that initially, strenuous efforts are made to support and improve parental caring, to be followed in the event of failure by involving partners, grandparents and other relatives in alternative care plans. The whole process can become protracted as several options are tried and tested, and delays in the court process add to uncertainties. In the mean time, the young child's eventual future remains uncertain. Thus, for some children, 'drift', in the sense of a lack of planning and action, is being replaced by a long drawn-out sequence of different plans and actions that are potentially no less damaging and disruptive. Balancing the Act's twin concerns – the child's welfare and the responsibility and integrity of the family – is no easy matter.

Organisational influences

Lastly, comparison of the two local authorities in our study has highlighted the influence of organisational features on services, attitudes and outcomes. Two local authorities with similar socio-economic characteristics displayed important differences in organisational structure and tradition which directly affected the implementation of Section 20. Shire maintained centralised and specialist traditions which were reflected in a central direction to its child care policy and, in particular, an unambiguous 'last resort' stance to the use of accommodation. County, on the other hand, with generic and decentralised traditions, was less uniform in its attitudes towards and use of accommodation. Such traditions were also reflected in the different emphasis on alternatives to accommodation, and the different approaches to gatekeeping strategies. The effect on outcomes was less clear, except that in Shire there was a gloomier view of the extent to which the children's needs had been met, and a higher rate of long-term readmission, whereas County had a higher proportion of children in long-term care.

The link between organisational features, services offered and outcomes is complex. The changes in the organisational structure of the two social services departments did not appear in themselves to be the critical feature, although change in both departments was highly disruptive. It appeared to be in the departmental traditions, and their culture, that established ways of working had become fixed. Traditions about the autonomy of social workers to make decisions, and attitudes concerning when accommodation was appropriate and what the balance of family and residential placements should be, appeared to persist, despite changes to organisational structure. What this suggests is that structural changes are unlikely to be enough to alter established working practices. Nor does the reframing of accommodation in the Children Act and the unprecedented amount of detailed Guidance guarantee uniformity, since we have seen how different interpretations and emphases are still possible in practice. Both authorities thought they had decentralised their services; both felt they had implemented the Children Act; both considered they were working in partnership with parents. However, 'decentralisation', 'implementation' and 'partnership' mean diffent things in different contexts.

Summary

What is our overall verdict on the implementation of Section 20 of the Children Act? It is necessarily tentative, because we have looked at practice in only two local authorities, and our study began only a year after the legislation came into force. Nevertheless, there have been many positive developments. Families and children who might previously have faced lengthy and expensive court proceedings are being offered support and protection without apparent detriment to their welfare. Promising respite arrangements for stressed parents and their children are beginning to develop, and should be encouraged and expanded. Great efforts are being made to involve parents and children in planning and decision-making, and other professions and agencies are being included in the process. Maintaining the accommodated child's links with family, neighbourhood and school is a priority. Offering a range of support services from within and outside social services departments, as a complement to accommodation, is current practice. Among the longer-term cases there is little evidence of 'drift', or a failure to plan and be purposive.

Nevertheless, there is also a debit side, and the Act itself poses fresh problems for policy-makers and practitioners. Principles of voluntarism, participation and partnership with families are challenged by the 'no order principle' and the inclusion of so many children who need protection, as well as those who are difficult and disruptive. Holding on to these principles, or adapting them in open and honest ways to meet the most difficult circumstances, requires wide discussion and further development (DoH, 1995; Thoburn et al. 1995). Planning meetings also need to be much more user-friendly. Too often, parents and children are overwhelmed, humiliated or alienated in a forum that is all too familiar to the professionals, but alien and alarming to them, and the inclusion of a family friend or supporter could be beneficial. The marked increase in repeat admissions also means that social services departments must devise new ways of ensuring continuity of placements if repetition is not to compound the trauma of leaving home.

Finally, old attitudes die hard, and a 'last resort' stance is alive and well, despite the positive intentions of the Children Act. There are parents, and even some children, who value accommodation much more highly than the social services departments themselves do, and are frustrated by their gatekeeping policies. 'Last-resortism' can also prove to be self-defeating – social services' resistance can lead to family disaffection, more emergency admissions, hurried placements and belated planning. Improving the situation requires more than an attitude change: far more resources need to be made available. This, perhaps, is the greatest challenge to implementation of the Children Act in the future

Appendix:
Schedule of children
accommodated

Authority
_____

Family name   Dept code
_____

Child's name
_____

District/area
_____

Social worker/care manager
_____

Section A   *Referral/request/trigger*

1   (a)   New or old case? Live or dormant?

_____

     (b)   Who referred/requested help? (Please note *all*.)

_____

_____

2   Reasons for referral/request/trigger

_____

_____

_____

Section B   *Family background*

3   Carers in household (identity and relationship)

_____

_____

4 Carers' ethnic origin and first language

_____

5 If parent(s) live *outside* household:
   In contact with child?

_____

   In contact with social services department?

_____

6 Significant others/relatives (in or out of household) important to
   child/family

_____

7 Number of children in household (admitted and not admitted)

_____

8 Step- or half-siblings among them?

_____

Section C   Household circumstances

9 Carer(s) employed? Type of work?

_____

   Is this a significant issue?

_____

10 Income source

_____

   Is finance a significant issue?

_____

11 Housing – type and standards

_____

   Is accommodation a significant issue?

_____

12 Neighbourhood (e.g., isolated, close-knit, run-down, delinquent,
   drugs, prostitution, etc.)

_____

   Is this a significant issue?

_____

Section D   The carer(s)

13 Health:
   (a)   Physical   Significant issue?

   (b)   Mental   Significant issue?

14 Parenting – assessed strengths/weaknesses

Physical and emotional care

Is this a significant issue?

15 Is neglect or abuse alleged/suspected?

16 Any other aspects of carer(s) behaviour of significance (strengths or weaknesses)?

17 Family relationships and their significance:
   (a)   'Marital'

   (b)   Carer(s)–child

   (c)   Between siblings

   (d)   With wider family

   (e)   With others

18 Carer's childhood: abused, in care, other relevant separations (e.g., hospitalised, institutionalised, etc.)?

Section E   The child

19 Date of birth

20 Gender

21 Ethnic origin and first language

22 Health:
   (a) Physical   Significant issue?

   (b) Mental   Significant issue?

   (c) Special needs (quasi-medical, e.g., poor sight, hearing, speech, etc.)

23 Education:
   Subject of statement/in process of full assessment?

   Significant issues re. attendance, exclusion, attainments, etc.?

   Whose concern – parents and/or social worker?

   School type

24 Young persons of 16+ education/employment

25 Behaviour (good or bad).   Significant issue?

   Who complains?

26 Has child ever been on Child Protection Register?

   What category?

27 Has child been in care/looked after before?

   Give details/dates

Section F   Admission to accommodation

28 Assessment of child 'in need' according to Children Act criteria (achieving reasonable standard of health and development; impairment of health and development or disabled) or significant harm

_____

_____

29 Reason(s) for the decision to accommodate

_____

_____

30 Other services (Part III and other)

_____

_____

The planning process

31 Was parent/child participation easy/difficult in this case?

_____

32 Was planning formalised through meeting, review or child protection conference?

_____

Before or after admission?

_____

33 If formalised, which family members participated?

_____

Were they prepared/briefed?

_____

34 Wishes/feelings of parents/child re. admission

_____

Who was asking/initiating?

_____

Who persuaded whom?

_____

The plan

35 How does the plan address the following:
   (a)   Purpose(s) of accommodation?

_____

   (b)   Proposed time-scale?

_____

(c)   Child's needs and how to meet them?

_____

(d)   Tasks/responsibilities of all parties?

_____

Placement

36 (a)   Type of placement

_____

(b)   Close to home/school?

_____

(c)   If *not*, can child still go to old school?

_____

(d)   Sharing with siblings?

_____

(e)   Was finding a placement a problem?

_____

Was there any choice?

_____

Was it appropriate or not? – Why?

_____

(f)   Arrangements for family contact: with whom, how often, how?

_____

37 Social worker's comments on issues of:
(a) **Partnership/parental responsibility** (E.g., did they attend
    planning and placement agreement meetings, accompany child
    to placement, undertake caring tasks?)

_____

(b) **Child's wishes/needs** (E.g., how were child's wishes ascer-
    tained? Were they in line with/at odds with perceived needs?)

_____

_____

*Copies of the follow-up schedules are available, on request, from
    Jean Packman, c/o Dartington Social Research Unit, Warren House,
    Warren Lane, Dartington, Totnes, Devon TQ9 6EG.

References

Adler, M. and Asquith, S. (1982) *Discretion and Welfare*, London: Heinemann

Aldgate, J. (1992) 'Respite care for children – an old remedy in a new package', in Marsh, P. and Triseliotis, J. (eds) *Prevention and Reunification in Child Care*, London: Batsford

Aldgate, J. (forthcoming) *The Use of Short-term Accommodation Under the Children Act 1989*

Audit Commission (1994) *Seen But Not Heard: Co-ordinating Community Child Health and Social Services for Children in Need*, London: HMSO

Baldwin, N. and Spenser, N. (1993) 'Deprivation and child abuse: Implications for strategic planning in children's services', *Children and Society*, Vol.7, No.4

Barclay, P. (1982) *Social Workers: Their Role and Tasks*, London: Bedford Square Press

Bebbington, A. and Miles, J. (1989) 'The background of children who enter local authority care', *British Journal of Social Work*, Vol.19, No.5

Biehal, N., Clayden, J., Stein, M. and Wade, J. (1995) *Moving On: Young People and Leaving Care Schemes*, London: HMSO

Brown, C. (1984) *Child Abuse Parents Speaking: Parents' Impressions of Social Workers and the Social Work Process*, Bristol: Bristol University, School of Advanced Urban Studies

Buchanan, A. (ed.) (1994) *Partnership in Practice: The Children Act 1989*, Adlershot: Avebury

Bullock, R., Little, M. and Millham, S. (1993) *Going Home: The Return of Children Separated from their Families*, Adlershot: Dartmouth

Bullock, R., Little, M. and Millham, S. (1994) *The Characteristics of Young People in Youth Treatment Centres*, Dartington: Dartington Social Research Unit

Challis, L. (1990) *Organising Public Social Services*, Harlow: Longman

Clarke, J., Cochrane, A. and McLaughlin, E. (eds) (1994) *Managing Social Policy*, London: Sage

Cleaver, H. and Freeman, P. (1995) *Parental Perspectives in Cases of Suspected Child Abuse*, London: HMSO

Corby, B. (1987) *Working with Child Abuse: Social Work Practice and the Child Abuse System*, Milton Keynes: Open University Press

Craig, J. (1985) *A 1981 Socio-economic Classification of Local and Health Authorities of Great Britain*, London: Office of Population Censuses and Surveys

DHSS (1985) *Social Work Decisions in Child Care: Recent Research Findings and their Implications*, London: HMSO

DHSS, Home Office, Lord Chancellor's Department, Welsh Office and Scottish Office (1987) *The Law on Child Care and Family Services*, Cm 62, London: HMSO

Dingwall, R., Eekelaar, J. and Murray, T. (1983) *The Protection of Children: State Intervention and Family Life*, Oxford: Basil Blackwell

DoH (1980, 1984, 1988, 1991) *Children Looked After by Local Authorities, England*, London: Government Statistical Service

DoH (1988) *Report of the Inquiry into Child Abuse in Cleveland, 1987*, Cm 412, London: HMSO

DoH (1989) *An Introduction to the Children Act, 1989*, London: HMSO

DoH (1990) *The Care of Children: Principles and Practice in Regulations and Guidance*, London: HMSO

DoH (1991a) *The Children Act 1989. Guidance and Regulations, Volume 2: Family Support, Day Care and Educational Provision for Young Children*, London: HMSO

DoH (1991b) *The Children Act 1989. Guidance and Regulations, Volume 3: Family Placements*, London: HMSO

DoH (1993) *Children Act Report 1992*, Cm 2144, London: HMSO

DoH (1994) *Children Act Report 1993*, Cm 2584, London: HMSO

DoH (1995) *Child Protection: Messages from Research*, London: HMSO

DoH (1996) *Children Looked After by Local Authorities: Year Ending 31 March 1994, England*, London: Government Statistical Service

DoH/Social Services Inspectorate (1995) *The Challenge of Partnership in Child Protection: Practice Guide*, London: HMSO

Farmer, E. and Owen, M. (1993) *Decision-making, Intervention and Outcome in Child Protection Work*, Bristol: University of Bristol, Department of Social Policy

Farmer, E. and Owen, M. (1995) *Child Protection Practice: Private Risks and Public Remedies*, London: HMSO

Fisher, M., Marsh, P. and Phillips, D. (1986) *In and Out of Care: The Experience of Children, Parents and Social Workers*, London: Batsford/ British Agencies for Adoption and Fostering

Fletcher, B. (1993) *Not Just a Name: The Views of Young People in Foster and Residential Care*, London: National Consumer Council

Fletcher-Campbell, F. and Hall, C. (1990) *Changing Schools, Changing People: The Education of Children in Care*, Slough: NFER

Flynn, N. (1990) *Public Sector Management*, London: Harvester Wheatsheaf

Forrest, R. and Gordon, D. (1993) *People and Places: A 1991 Census Atlas of England*, Bristol: Bristol University, School of Advanced Urban Studies

Fox, L. (1982) 'Two value positions in recent child care law and practice', *British Journal of Social Work*, Vol.12, No.3, pp.265–90

Gardner, R. (1985) *Child Care Reviews*, London: National Children's Bureau

Giller, H. and Morris, A. (1981) *Care and Discretion: Social Workers' Decisions with Delinquents*, London: Burnet Books

Goffman, E. (1959) *The Presentation of Self in Everyday Life*, Garden City, New York: Doomsday Anchor Books

Hadley, R. and McGrath, M. (1981) *Going Local: Neighbourhood Social Services*, London: Bedford Square Press

Hardiker, P. (1977) 'Social work ideology in the Probation Service', *British Journal of Social Work*, Vol.7, No.2

Hargreaves, R.G. and Hadlow, J. (1995) 'Preventive intervention as a working concept in child care practice', *British Journal of Social Work*, Vol.25, No.3

Holman, R. (1988) *Putting Families First: Prevention and Child Care*, London: Macmillan

Home Department, Ministry of Health and Ministry of Education (1946) *Report of the Care of Children Committee* (The Curtis Report), Cmnd 6922, London: HMSO

House of Commons Social Services Committee (1984) *Children in Care* (The Short Report), London: HMSO

Hunt, J., Macleod, A., Freeman, P. and Thomas, C. (forthcoming) 'The Last Resort: Child Protection, the Courts and the 1989 Children Act', report to the Department of Health

Jackson, S. (1987) *The Education of Children in Care*, Bristol: University of Bristol, School of Applied Social Studies

James, A. (1994) *Managing to Care*, Harlow: Longman

Jones, A. and Bilton, K. (1994) *The Future Shape of Children's Services*, London: National Children's Bureau

Jones, A. and May, J. (1992) *Working in Human Services Organisations: A Critical Introduction*, Melbourne: Longman Cheshire

Knapp, M. (1987) *The Economics of Care*, Oxford: Basil Blackwell

Kufeldt, K., Armstrong, J. and Dorosh, M. (1989) 'In care, in contact?', in Hudson, J. and Galoway, B. (eds) *The State as Parent*, Dordrecht: Kluwer

Lewis, A. (1992) 'An overview of research into participation in child protection work', in Shemmings, D. and Thoburn, J. *Participation in Practice: A Reader*, Norwich: University of East Anglia

Lewis, A. (1994) *Chairing Child Protection Conferences: An Exploration of Attitudes and Roles*, Adlershot: Avebury

Lipsky, M. (1980) *Street Level Bureaucracy: Dilemmas of the Individual in Public Services*, New York: Russell Sage Foundation

Lupton, C., Barnard, S. and Swall-Yarrington, M. (1995) *Family Planning? An Evaluation of the Family Group Conference Model*, Portsmouth: University of Portsmouth

Marks, D. (1992) *Decision-making in Education Case Conferences: A Summary of a Three Year Research Project*, Manchester: Manchester Polytechnic

Marsh, P. and Fisher, M. (1992) *Good Intentions: Developing Partnership in Social Services*, York: Joseph Rowntree Foundation

McDonnell, P. and Aldgate, J. (1984) *Reviews of Children in Care*, Oxford: Oxford University, Department of Social and Administrative Studies

Millham, S., Bullock, R., Hosie, K. and Haak, M. (1986) *Lost in Care: The Problems of Maintaining Links between Children in Care and their Families*, London: Gower

Morris, S. and Wheatley, H. (1994) *Time to Listen: The Experiences of Children in Residential and Foster Care*, London: Childline

Owen, M. (1992) *Social Justice and Children in Care*, Adlershot: Avebury

Packman, J. (1968) *Child Care: Needs and Numbers*, London: George Allen and Unwin

Packman, J. and Jordan, B. (1991) 'The Children Act: Looking forward, looking back', *British Journal of Social Work*, Vol.21, No.4

Packman, J., Randall, J. and Jacques, N. (1986) *Who Needs Care?: Social Work Decisions about Children*, Oxford: Basil Blackwell

Parton, N. (1985) *The Politics of Child Abuse*, London: Macmillan

Parton, N. (1991) *Governing the Family: Child Care, Child Protection and the State*, London: Macmillan

Petch, A. (1988) 'Answering back: Parental perspectives on the children's hearings system', *British Journal of Social Work*, Vol.18, No.1

Rowe, J., Hundleby, M. and Garnett, L. (1989) *Child Care Now: A Survey of Placement Patterns*, London: British Agencies for Adoption and Fostering

Ryan, M. (1994) *The Children Act 1989: Putting it into Practice*, Adlershot: Arena

Scott, R.D. (1974) 'Cultural frontiers in the mental health services', *Schizophrenia Bulletin*, Vol.10

Sinclair, R. (1984) *Decision-making in Statutory Reviews on Children in Care*, Adlershot: Gower

Stein, M. and Carey, K. (1986) *Leaving Care*, Oxford: Basil Blackwell

Thoburn, J., Brandon, M., Lewis, A. and Way, A. (1996) *Safeguarding Children with the Children Act, 1989*, draft report to the Department of Health, Norwich: University of East Anglia

Thoburn, J., Lewis, A. and Shemmings, D. (1993) *Family Participation in Child Protection: Report to the Department of Health*, Norwich: University of East Anglia

Thoburn, J., Lewis, A. and Shemmings, D. (1995) *Paternalism or Partnership?: Family Involvement in the Child Protection Process*, London: HMSO

Triseliotis, J., Borland, M., Hill, M. and Lambert, L. (1995) *Teenagers and the Social Work Services*, London: HMSO

Wallace, M. and Denham, C. (1996) *The ONS Classification of Local and Health Authorities of Great Britain*, London: HMSO

Ward, H. (ed.) (1995) *Looking After Children: Research into Practice*, London: HMSO

Webb, A. and Wistow, G. (1987) *Social Work, Social Casework and Social Planning: The Personal Social Services since Seebohm*, Harlow: Longman

White, R., Carr, P. and Lowe, N. (1990) *A Guide to the Children Act, 1989*, London: Butterworths

Whitmore, R. (1984) 'Modelling the policy–implementation distinction: the case of child abuse', *Policy and Politics*, Vol.12, No.3, pp.241–67

Williams, M. (1996) *Parents, Children and Social Workers: Working in Partnership under the Children Act, 1989*, Adlershot: Avebury

Willow, C. (1995) 'A word in edgeways', unpublished report cited in Willow, C. (1996) *Children's Rights and Participation in Residential Care*, London: National Children's Bureau

Willow, C. (1996) *Children's Rights and Participation in Residential Care*, London: National Children's Bureau

Index

Guardian ad Litem
service 40
Guidance 3, 4, 39–40,
129, 132, 205
on parents 5, 229
on partnership 205,
227–8, 263
on placements 66, 122
on planning 59–60,
61, 154

Hadlow, J. 169
Hardiker, P. 166
Hargreaves, R.G. 169
harm
likelihood of 88
significant 72, 175
Headquarters 15
child care policy and
24–5, 26
role of 14, 17–18, 19, 21
health
of children 54–5, 100,
104, 118, 134
of parents 51, 90–1,
102, 104–5, 107,
134
see also mental
health
health visitors 196–7
holiday schemes 77, 119,
135, 145, 235
home-based services 4
home helps 62, 119, 135,
145
home tuition 56
homelessness 51
household composition
50, 101, 110, 116
housing 51, 114, 116, 216
humiliation 84, 203, 204,
222, 261, 270
Hunt, J. 265

illness of parents, as
reason for admission
78, 102, 104–5
impression management
230
inconsistency of
parenting 52, 102
independence 258–9

preparation for 144,
157
information about
admission
for family 260
for young people
238–9
interference, social
services involvement
seen as 217–19
intra-familial placements
48, 66–7, 77, 98, 122

James, A. 13

last-resortism 124–7, 129,
131, 266, 270
centralised
management and
133, 152–3, 268
emergency admissions
and 129, 133,
152–3, 266
parental responsibility
and 125, 133
from parents'
perspective 213
learning difficulties 55
leaving accommodation
147, 152, 157, 247–8
legal status, change to
148–50
Lewis, A. 176, 199, 225
listening to children 211,
251, 255, 266
listening to parents 216,
228, 231
local authority *see* social
services departments
local government 14–15
reorganisation of
15–19, 44
Local Government
Review 39
lone-parent households
50, 53, 90, 101, 104,
132, 134

McDonnell, P. 65
management teams 42

see also area level
management;
divisional level
management
manipulation by parents
214, 264
marginal status
of children 250, 251,
255
of parents 218, 226
marital problems 51, 92,
102
Marsh, P. 228
material help 144, 157
meetings (*see also* child
protection
conferences; planning
meetings) 63–5,
176–204
children at 122, 266
parents at 179–95
parents' views of 222–7
young people's views
of 248–51, 254–5
mental health of parents
51, 90–1, 92, 95, 102,
110
monitoring data 62–3
moral danger 72, 73, 87, 89
mothers
care histories of 53,
92, 103, 110, 117
mental health of 90–1,
95
vulnerability of 51,
53–4, 93
multi-agency involvement
60, 61, 269

need 4, 54, 88
assessment of 49, 88
needs of the child 3,
150–2, 153, 154, 157
neglect 88, 206
and admission for
protection 69
concern about 52, 58,
74, 98, 102
emotional 92
negotiation 5, 6, 59, 173,
265
within social services
126–7

Index by Mary Norris